Over as Far as America is Concerned: Gerald R. Ford and the
Latter Years of the Vietnam War

by

Christopher S. Yelonek

Revised Edition

Cover photo: Courtesy of the Gerald R. Ford Presidential Library.

Photo taken by David Hume Kennerly.

Over as Far as America is Concerned: Gerald R. Ford and the

Latter Years of the Vietnam War

To my mother, the staff of the Gerald R. Ford Presidential Library,

the faculty of Eastern Michigan University, Dr. Ramold, and

Ronald Nessen.

Abstract

Over as Far as America is Concerned focuses on the decision President Gerald R. Ford faced in the latter years of the Vietnam War. On whether or not to launch a bombing campaign. A decision could have reintroduced American combat forces into the Vietnam War. By analyzing the American political landscape of the mid-1970s, the situation of the Vietnam War in the post-1968 Tet Offensive period, and the Cold War politics of the 1970s to understand why President Ford chose not to launch a bombing campaign. Instead, President Ford made the choice of evacuating as many people as possible in April 1975. Because of the political realities his presidency faced, President Ford chose to garner support for his top priorities of his Administration.

Table of Contents

Acronyms

ABC – American Broadcasting Company

ACTOV - Accelerated Turnover of Assets

ACTOVLOG - Accelerated Turnover of Logistics

ARVN - Army of the Republic of Vietnam

CBS – Columbia Broadcasting System

CCP – Chinese Communist Party

CIA – Central Intelligence Agency

CPSU - Communist Party of the Soviet Union

CRIMP - Consolidated RVNAF Improvement and Modernization Plan

DAO - Defense Attaché Office

DMZ - Demilitarized Zone

DRV – Democratic Republic of Vietnam

FANK - Force Armee' Nationale Khmer

GDP – Gross Domestic Product

GNP – Gross National Product

HES - Hamlet Evaluation Surveys

ICCS - International Commission of Control and Supervision

JGS - Joint General Staff

KGB - Committee for State Security also known as Komitet Gosudarstvinnoi Bezopasnosti

KIA – Killed in Action

KL – Kingdom of Laos

KM - Kilometer

KR - Khmer Republic

MIA – Missing in Action

MR – Military Region

MRs – Military Regions

NATO – North Atlantic Treaty Organization

NBC – National Broadcasting Company

NCNRC - National Council of National Reconciliation and Concord

NLF – National Liberation Front

NPF - National Police Force

NSC – National Security Council

OPEC - Organization of Petroleum Exporting Countries

PAVN - People's Army of Vietnam

PF – Popular Forces

PLAF - People's Liberation Armed Forces

POW – Prisoner of War

PPA – Paris Peace Agreement

PRC – People's Republic of China

PRG - Provisionary Revolutionary Government

PRP - People's Revolutionary Party

RF – Regional Forces

RVN – Republic of Vietnam

RVNAF - Republic of Vietnam Armed Forces

SAA - Second Appropriations Act

SALT - Strategic Arms and Limitations Treaty

SEATO - South East Asian Treaty Organization

U.S. – United States

USAF – United States Air Force

USN – United States Navy

USSR – Union of Soviet Socialist Republics also known as the Soviet Union

VFW - Veterans of Foreign Wars

VNAF - Vietnamese Air Force

VNMC - Vietnamese Marine Corps

VNN - Vietnamese Navy

VPAF - Vietnamese People's Air Force

WSAG - Washington Special Actions Group

Introduction

"From the beginning of our involvement in the area (Southeast Asia), I had always thought that we (the U.S.) were doing the right thing" wrote President Gerald Ford as he reflected back on the Vietnam War in his book, *A Time to Heal: The Autobiography of Gerald R. Ford.*[1] President Ford felt that American and Republican Vietnamese victory in the Vietnam War could have been achieved.[2] Based upon this evidence President Ford provided in his autobiography, he had a hawkish stance. A hawk is someone who has or had a stance that supported an armed conflict.[3] However, at his April 23, 1975 address at Tulane University in New Orleans, President Ford stated "today America can again regain the sense of pride that existed before Vietnam but, it cannot be achieved by refighting a war that is finished, as far as America is concerned."[4] President Ford took the stance of a hawk on the Vietnam War. Although later in 1975, President Ford uttered the words at Tulane University that nearly every dove[5] wanted to hear since the presidency of Lyndon Johnson that their president would not continue to use military force in Southeast Asia.

In the period between the signing of the Paris Peace Accords in 1973 to the end of April 1975, the Democratic Republic of Vietnam (DRV) and their ally the National

---

[1] Gerald R. Ford, *A Time to Heal: The Autobiography of Gerald R. Ford* (New York: Harper and Row, 1979), 248.

[2] Ibid., 249.

[3] "Definition of Hawk," Merriam-Webster, Incorporated, last modified 2015, accessed July 25, 2015, http://www.merriam-webster.com/dictionary/hawk.

[4] Gerald R. Ford, Excerpt Related to Vietnam from President Ford's address at Tulane University (Reading Copy of Entire Speech), April 23, 1975, Under "Selected Document on the Vietnam War," Gerald R. Ford Presidential Library, Ann Arbor, Michigan, 12, accessed February 27, 2014, http://www.fordlibrarymuseum.gov/library/document/0122/1252291.pdf.

[5] A dove is someone who has a political stance against armed conflict. From "Definition of Dove," Merriam-Webster, Incorporated, last modified 2015, accessed July 25, 2015, http://www.merriam-webster.com/dictionary/dove.

Liberation Front (NLF aka the Viet Cong) steadily escalated their efforts against the

Republic of Vietnam (RVN) that led to a massive offensive in 1975.[6] Generally, the U.S.

Federal Government had been very supportive of the RVN's efforts to resist a communist

takeover through the estimated expenditure at "over $112 billion there since 1950."[7]

President Richard Millhouse Nixon and many American military officers believed that the

Vietnam War could have resulted in American victory through the heavy application of

bombing. In addition, the U.S. was conducting aerial reconnaissance over the DRV, even as

late as 1975.[8] On March 25, 1975, President Nguyen Van Thieu of the RVN requested that

President Ford launch a bombing campaign against communist forces in Vietnam during the

DRV's 1975 offensive.[9] In a report compiled by General Frederick C. Weyand for President

Ford dated April 4, 1975, Weyand states that the most effective option available to the U.S.

in Vietnam is at the very least a brief bombing campaign.[10]

---

[6] F. Charles Parker, "Vietnam and Soviet Asian Strategy," *Asian Affairs*, Volume 4, Number 2 (November – December, 1976): 106-107, accessed January 30, 2014, stable URL: http://www.jstor.org/stable/30171458.

[7] John C. Donnell, "South Vietnam in 1975: The Year of Communist Victory," *Asian Survey*, Volume 16, Number 1 (January, 1976): 11, accessed January 30, 2014, stable URL: http://www.jstor.org/stable/2643276.

[8] Letter, Legal Advisor George H. Aldrich, Acting to Ambassador McClosky, Memorandum for Ambassador McClosky, January 13, 1975, National Security Advisor Presidential Country Files for East Asia and the Pacific: Vietnam, box 19, folder 1, document 3, Gerald R. Ford Presidential Library, Ann Arbor, Michigan.

[9] Jerrold L. Schecter, "The Final Days: The Political Struggle to End the Vietnam War," in *Gerald R. Ford and the Politics of Post-Watergate America*, Volume Two, Edited by Bernard J. Firestone and Alexei Uginsky (Westport, Connecticut: Greenwood Press, 1993), 544.

[10] Report to the President of the United States on the Situation in South Vietnam, General Frederick C. Weyand to President Gerald R. Ford, April 4, 1975, "Vietnam Assessment Report by General Frederick C. Weyand" from Selected Documents on the Vietnam War, PDF, 12, Gerald R. Ford Presidential Library, Ann Arbor, Michigan, accessed May 25, 2015, http://www.fordlibrarymuseum.gov/library/exhibits/vietnam/032400081-001.pdf.

President Thieu stated the U.S. had abandoned the RVN due to the lack of military action within Southeast Asia and the decrease in aid during the period of 1973 through 1975.[11] Essentially, there was no major U.S. military action outside of the evacuation of the RVN during the latter years of the war. President Ford, who was a hawk, supported American efforts in Vietnam, allowed American forces to conduct aerial reconnaissance over the DRV, and was encouraged to launch a bombing campaign against DRV forces, never sent a bombing campaign into the conflict. During the Mayaguez Incident, a U.S. Navy hostage rescue mission of an American merchant ship off the coast of the then recently established Democratic Kampuchea.[12] President Ford ordered the use of military force before he informed congress of his actions.[13]

Concerning the historiography on President Ford's decision on a possible bombing campaign into the Vietnam War in the spring 1975, there has been very little written about the decision-making process of Ford's choice not to launch a campaign. The majority of what has been written on Ford's decision on a bombing campaign is not covered in depth and some of it is simplistic. In addition, the historiography of Ford's presidency on Vietnam seems more concerned about who in the American sphere of the Vietnam War is at fault for the Fall of Saigon. Some historians essentially just reiterate what President Ford had written in his book, *A Time to Heal*, where White House photographer David Kennerly was able to persuade President Ford that the RVN was a lost cause.[14] President Ford did request $792

---

[11]Donnell, "South Vietnam in 1975," 3-4.

[12] "Capture and Release of *SS Mayaguez* by Khmer Rouge Forces in May, 1975," American Merchant Marine at War, last modified 2000, accessed October 23, 2015, http://www.usmm.org/mayaguez.html.

[13]Ford, *A Time to Heal*, 280-81.

[14] Ibid., 253.

million as recommended by General Weyand from the U.S. Congress for the RVN as emergency funds.[15] Nowhere in Ford's 442 page autobiography did it state anything about the decision based upon General Weyand's recommendation for bombing. President Ford only devoted ten pages to the final days of the RVN, in his book *A Time to Heal*.[16] The historical problem of President Ford and the debate on a possible bombing campaign into Vietnam is not limited to political history alone.

Even from a military history standpoint, there is a lack of study on President Ford and General Weyand's bombing recommendation. Historian Mark Clodfelter has written one of the best historical monographs on American air campaigns in the Vietnam War, entitled, *The Limits of Air Power: The American Bombing of North Vietnam*. Clodfelter concludes his book with the Linebacker II bombing campaign and the Paris Peace Agreement (PPA). Only very briefly does Clodfelter touch upon President Ford's decision not to launch a bombing campaign in one short paragraph. Where Clodfelter states a bombing campaign after the PPA was never conducted because Nixon was no longer president of the U.S. to push for bombing campaigns in the Vietnam War and congress put forth prohibitions on American military activity in Southeast Asia.[17]

The U.S. Air Force's monograph *The Vietnamese Air Force, 1951-1975: An Analysis of its' Role in Combat and Fourteen Hours at Koh Tang* suggests that it was a piece of legislation known as the Cooper-Church Amendment prohibited American military forces from engaging in another bombing campaign in the Vietnam War.[18] Although President

---

[15]Ford, *A Time to Heal*, 253-54.

[16] See pages 248-57 of *A Time to Heal*.

[17] Mark Clodfelter, *The Limits of Air Power: The American Bombing of North Vietnam* (New York: Free Press, 1989), 201-02.

Ford's decision to not launch a bombing campaign lacks focus in the discussions contained in *The Last Flight from Saigon* by Tomas G. Tobin, Arthur E. Laehr, and John F. Hilgenberg. *The Last Flight from Saigon* authors suggest numerous American aircraft within the region of Southeast Asia were redeployed to other regions for the 1976 fiscal year, which made a bombing campaign unfeasible.[19] Other historians have touched on this historical problem of the Ford Presidency, but they do not discuss in depth the reasons why President Ford declined to re-introduce American bombers into the Vietnam War.

John Robert Greene in his book *The Presidency of Gerald R. Ford* states while General Weyand approved of a bombing campaign, White House photographer David Hume Kennerly was able to persuade Ford to abandon Saigon, thereby supporting a lost cause narrative.[20] To explain the reason why there was not a bombing campaign in Vietnam during 1975, Greene is dependent on President Ford's *A Time to Heal*. James Cannon, does not deviate very much in his brief discussion on the fall of Saigon from what was written in *A Time to Heal*.[21] Cannon does not even bring up in his discussion of the Weyand mission's of the bombing recommendation.[22] Still, there have been other historians who have written

---

[18] United States Air Force, *The Vietnamese Air Force, 1951-1975: An Analysis of its' Role in Combat and Fourteen Hours at Koh Tang*, edited by Major A.J.C. Lavalle (Washington, D.C.: Office of Air Force History, United States Air Force, 1985), 57-58, accessed May 22, 2015, http://www.afhso.af.mil/shared/media/document/AFD-101013-043.pdf.

[19] Tomas G. Tobin, Arthur E. Laehr, and John F. Hilgenberg, *Last Flight from Saigon* (Washington, D.C.: United States Printing Office), 6-7, accessed May 22, 2015, http://www.afhso.af.mil/shared/media/document/AFD-100928-008.pdf.

[20] John Robert Greene, *The Presidency of Gerald R. Ford* (Lawerence: University of Kansas, 1995), 137-38.

[21] James Cannon, *Gerald R. Ford: An Honorable Life* (Ann Arbor: University of Michigan, 2013), 371-72.

[22] Ibid.

about the Ford Administration's debate on a bombing campaign into Vietnam outside of what was written in *A Time to Heal*.

In the chapter titled *The Final Days: The Political Struggle to the End the Vietnam War* from the second volume of *Gerald Ford and the Politics of Post-Watergate America*, Jerrold L. Schecter also utilizes the lost cause narrative. Schecter states that Ford could not have supported the RVN with American military support due to congressional and public opposition as one aspect of why Ford never intervened militarily into Vietnam.[23] A complicated matter brought up by Schecter was the Richard M. Nixon–Nguyen Van Thieu correspondence, interpreted by some individuals who participated in the late years of the Vietnam War as a defense agreement between the U.S. and the RVN.[24] An agreement President Ford had no knowledge at the time he entered office, which had later influenced Ford's decision making process.[25] Schecter also states President Ford did not want to become a hypocrite because he negotiated to end American bombing campaigns in Southeast Asia during 1973 when he was the House minority leader for the Republican Party.[26]

Douglas Brinkley writes in *Gerald R. Ford*, while President Ford felt it was necessary for the U.S. to aid the RVN's defense. President Ford was limited in his Presidential powers on security through the War Powers Act of 1973, forcing him to stipulate decisions concerning military deployments with the 93 Congress, who was opposed to sending further aid in any form to RVN.[27] Brinkley briefly states that President Ford did not want to make

---

[23] Schecter, "The Final Days," 550.

[24] Ibid., 543-44.

[25] Ibid.

[26] Ibid., 550.

the Vietnam War his war, as Ford's predecessors have done.[28] Causing President Ford

endorse the secret letters President Nixon had sent to RVN President Thieu promising

American intervention into Vietnam if the DRV violated the PPA.[29]

In *The Flawed Architect: Henry Kissinger and American Foreign Policy,* Jussi

Hankimaki employs the lost-cause narrative as well; he states that it was Secretary of State

Dr. Henry Kissinger and Central Intelligence Agency (CIA) Director William Colby who

urged President Ford nothing could be done for the RVN.[30] Dr. Kissinger was a key figure in

both the Nixon and Ford Administrations due to his knowledge of diplomacy, hence why he

remains the only individual of holding the position of National Security Advisor while as

Sectary of State.[31] On the other hand, T. Christopher Jespersen wrote in *Dr. Kissinger, Ford,*

and Congress: The Very Bitter End in Vietnam that President Nixon, President Ford, and Dr.

Kissinger were too incompetent to make solid decisions that were practical in being utilized

in Southeast Asia.[32] With the historiography on the subject of the Ford Administration's

debate to send a bombing campaign into Vietnam, it leaves plenty of room for more in depth

and objective analysis of history on the subject.

---

[27] Douglas Brinkley, *Gerald R. Ford (The American Presidents Series: The 38th President, 1974-1977),* General Editor Arthur M. Schlesinger Jr. (New York: Henry Holt and Company, 2007), 87-88.

[28] Ibid., 89-90.

[29] Ibid.

[30] Jussi Hanhimaki, *The Flawed Architect: Henry Kissinger and American Foreign Policy* (Auckland: Oxford University, 2004), 390-91.

[31] "Biographies of the Sectaries of State: Henry Alfred Kissinger," United States Department of State: Bureau of Public Affairs – Office of the Historian, accessed August 2, 2015, https://history.state.gov/departmenthistory/people/Kissinger-henry-a.

[32] T. Christopher Jespersen, "Kissinger, Ford, and Congress: The Very Bitter End in Vietnam," *Pacific Historical Review,* Volume 71, Number 3 (August 2002): 441-42, accessed January 10, 2014, stable URL: http://www.jstor.org/stable/10.1525/phr.2002.71.3.439.

While the lost-cause narrative is valid, it does not fully explain why President Ford accepted the possible American re-escalation in the Vietnam War would not have a positive outcome on the conflict. Quite often when authors utilize the lost-cause narrative, they study President Ford in a vacuum on the issue of Vietnam. While some authors discuss Ford's beliefs before he was sworn in as President of the United States.

One of the best works on the topic of President Ford's bombing campaign decision in the Vietnam War is David L. Anderson's *Gerald R. Ford and the Presidents' War in Vietnam*. Anderson claims that while President Ford was a major supporter of the American war effort in Southeast Asia, he was also a major critic of the strategies utilized in the region.[33] Where President Ford felt the American commitment to the RVN needed to be limited to proxy endeavors, and he was fully aware of the negative American public opinion towards the use of U.S. military forces in the Vietnam War when he entered his presidency.[34] The problem with Anderson's article on President Ford is that he does not discuss in depth of the issues Ford inherited from Nixon's presidency, a common historiographical error on Ford's decision for a bombing campaign in general. Despite his errors, Anderson does touch on President Ford's decision-making process.

In his article, Anderson points out that before he entered the White House, Ford was a Congressional member of the House of Representatives for twenty-five years.[35] President Ford's decision-making style and the relationships with his staff are often downplayed by some authors. Robert Hartmann writes in his memoirs *Palace Politics: An Inside Account of*

---

[33] David L. Anderson, "Gerald R. Ford and the Presidents' War in Vietnam," from *Shadow on the White House: Presidents and the Vietnam War, 1945-1975*, edited by David L. Anderson (Lawrence, Kansas: University Press of Kansas, 1993), 186-87.

[34] Ibid.

[35] Ibid., 185.

the Ford Years, that President Ford preferred to deliberate and research the issues faced

before him before making a decision.[36] Since there is a lack of in-depth, far-reaching

discussion on President Ford's decision to not to launch a bombing campaign against the

DRV. There needs to be an expansion of the conversation and not the acceptance of short

answers.

Quite often on the subject of President Ford's decision on a possible bombing

campaign, many authors study the topic in a vacuum. What is missing from many works on

President Ford's decision in the latter days of the Vietnam War is an in-depth description of

the events leading up to the Paris Peace Accords, President Ford's relationship with

Kennerly, American public opinion, and the major events that occurred outside of Southeast

Asia while the Vietnam War was taking place. Building upon the previous historiography of

President Ford's choice in the matter of declining to launch a bombing campaign into the

Vietnam War, Ford was severely conflicted. On one hand, Ford was very supportive of

American efforts to stop the flow of communism in Southeast Asia. On the other hand,

President Ford felt that American strategy in the region needed to be based on proxy

endeavors.

In his autobiography, President Ford stated that he trusted Kennerly's opinion on the

Vietnam War and cites Kennerly's professionalism while never discussing his relationship

with the photographer.[37] Delving into the relationship between President Ford and Kennerly

is excluded in several works on Ford's decisions in the latter days of the Vietnam War.

---

[36] Robert T. Hartmann, *Palace Politics An Inside Account to the Ford Years* (New York: McGraw-Hill 1980), 178.

[37] Ford, *A Time to Heal*, 251.

9

What is quite often ignored by many authors is American public opinion around the time of Ford's presidency. By the end of the Vietnam War, Americans had such strong negative emotions toward the RVN that over three quarters of Americans opposed sending military aid in the form of equipment.[38] Due to Ford's Congressional career, it was in his professional nature to observe public opinion in order to understand the political environment.[39] Other significant historical events, including but not limited to the 1973 oil crisis, Nixon's Presidency, the pardon of Nixon, influenced President Ford's later decision making.

When he entered the Oval Office, President Ford understood the state of affairs of the U.S. well enough to make his top objective of his presidency to restore the American nation's trust in their government in his transition file.[40] Above all, in his inaugural address, President Ford hoped to convince Americans who had been deeply hurt in the past to put aside their differences come together to resolve the issues the U.S. was facing during his presidency.[41] His objective of bringing the American nation together to work on other important issues was a goal President Ford refused to waver from. Even when certain options threatened to isolate President Ford politically from contributing towards his all together now goal. Because President Ford had chosen the objective of American reconciliation to have the upmost importance during his presidency. President Ford had decided it would be unwise to conduct

---

[38] William L. Lunch and Peter W. Sperlich, "American Public Opinion and the War in Vietnam," *The Western Political Quarterly* Volume 32, Number 1 (March, 1979): 32, accessed September 27, 2014, Stable URL: http://www.jstor.org/stable/447561.

[39] Anderson, "Gerald R. Ford and the Presidents' War in Vietnam," 185.

[40] Hartmann, *Palace Politics*, 165.

[41] Gerald R. Ford, "1 – Remarks on Taking the Oath of Office, August 9, 1974," from *the American Presidency Project*, last modified 2014 by Gerhard Peters and John T. Woolly, accessed May 11, 2015, http://www.presidency.ucsb.edu/ws/index.php?pid=4409.

military air campaigns in the Vietnam War since Ford could have potentially isolated himself politically during the mid-1970s.

Chapter One: We've Got to Get Out of This Place

"To say that we are mired in stalemate seems the only realistic, yet unsatisfactory, conclusion (to the Vietnam War)" was the statement made by news reporter Walter Cronkite in his televised editorial from *Columbia Broadcasting System (CBS) News.*[1] Cronkite's editorial was broadcasted on February 27, 1968 while the Tet Offensive was under way.[2] The Tet Offensive was a large scale campaign launched by the National Liberation Front (NLF (aka the Viet Cong)) and the Democratic Republic of Vietnam's (DRV) People's Army of Vietnam (PAVN) against the Republic of Vietnam (RVN) during the holiday of Tet in the early months of 1968.[3] American armed forces and Republic of Vietnam Armed Forces (RVNAF) units were able to eliminate the communist gains, while communist forces had suffered heavy casualties, particularly amongst the NLF during the offensive.[4] While in hindsight Cronkite was incorrect in his prediction of the outcome of the Vietnam War during the Tet Offensive, his comments did reflect a major break in the direction of the war. That public and law makers' opinions, would later create developments that greatly contributed to the outcome of the war.

The overall opinions of Americans led to the development of a policy that would alter the course and the American strategy of the Vietnam War. The new policy would allow the

---

[1] Walter Cronkite, 'We are Mired in a Stalemate' Broadcast, CBS News, February 27, 1968," Walter Cronkite, from The Pacifica Radio/ UC Berkeley's Social Activism Sound Recording Project, last modified March 25, 2008, accessed September 23, 2014, http://www.lib.berkeley.edu/MRC/pacificaviet/cronkitevietnam.html.

[2] Ibid.

[3] James H. Willbanks, *Abandoning Vietnam: How America Left and South Vietnam Lost its War* (Lawrence, Kansas: University Press of Kansas, 2004), 5.

[4] Willbanks, *Abandoning Vietnam,* 5.

U.S. to withdraw its combat forces from Southeast Asia while expanding RVNAF. During the time the U.S. was building up the RVN's military, the U.S. pursued a peace agreement with the DRV in response to the change of American public opinion. During the implementation of new American policies in Southeast Asia with the goal to end the American combat role in the Vietnam War, a political scandal emerged which eroded the political support of the president from the American public.

From August 1965 to May 1971, the public opinion researcher, Gallup Incorporated asked Americans the question "in view of the developments since we entered the fighting in Vietnam, do you think the U.S. made a mistake sending troops to fight in Vietnam?"[5] When Gallup first asked this question in August 1965, 61 percent of respondents reported negatively.[6] However, three years later in February 1968, during the Tet Offensive, Gallup found that only 42 percent of respondents replied negatively to the mistake question.[7] In August 1968, the percentage of negative respondents dropped down to 35 percent.[8] In 1968, the U.S. armed forces lost 16,899 individuals in the Vietnam War, the highest causality rate for a single year.[9] There was a brief resurgence of the negative opinion holders to Gallup's

---

[5] William L. Lunch and Peter W. Sperlich, "American Public Opinion and the War in Vietnam," *The Western Political Quarterly* Volume 32, Number 1 (March, 1979): 24, accessed September 27, 2014, Stable URL: http://www.jstor.org/stable/447561.

[6] Ibid., 25.

[7] Ibid.

[8] Ibid.

[9] "Statistical Information about Fatal Casualties of the Vietnam War: DCAS Vietnam Conflict Extract Files Record Counts by Incident or Death Date (Year) (As of April 29, 2008)," National Archives and Record Administration, last modified August 2013, accessed July 26, 2015, http://www.archives.gov/research/military/vietnam-war/casualty-statistics.html#date.

mistake question at 39 percent in February 1969, before bottoming out to 28 percent negative

responses in May 1971, prior to Gallup's removal of the question from their survey.[10]

Between 1965 and 1971, 56,907 Americans were killed in the Vietnam War.[11]

Despite Cronkite's televised editorial, American public opinion became less supportive as the

Vietnam War continued on and as the causalities of American servicemen increased over

time.[12] After General William Childs Westmoreland's 1967 address to congress, where he

appealed to lawmakers that American efforts under the direction of President Lyndon Baines

Johnson were succeeding in Vietnam, the press had become more skeptical and more

investigative towards the subject of the Vietnam War.[13] At the same time, when American

public opinion was growing increasingly negative, government officials in numerous

positions had become more pessimistic, particularly after President Johnson announced his

departure from the 1968 Presidential campaign to focus on a diplomatic solution to the

Vietnam War.[14] Rather than the President Johnson's military resolution to the conflict, which

he originally favored.[15] Since negative attitudes towards the Vietnam War had become more

common within the American public and the Federal Government during the post-Tet

Offensive era of the War, a hawkish anti-communist presidential candidate whose comments

---

[10] Lunch and Sperlich, "American Public Opinion and the War in Vietnam," 25.

[11] "Statistical Information about Fatal Casualties of the Vietnam War: DCAS Vietnam Conflict Extract Files Record Counts by Incident or Death Date (Year) (As of April 29, 2008)," National Archives and Record Administration.

[12] William M. Hammond, "The Press in Vietnam as Agent of Defeat: A Critical Examination," *Reviews in American History*, Volume 17, Number 2 (June, 1989): 318, accessed September 9, 2014, Stable URL: http://www.jstor.org/stable/2702936.

[13] Ibid.

[14] Ibid., 318-19.

[15] Ibid.

as well as political beliefs promised a solution to the conflict that would be favorable to both hawks and doves.

In his 1968 Presidential campaign, Richard Millhouse Nixon made a pledge to voters through his leadership, he would bring the Vietnam War to an agreeable conclusion for Americans and the Nationalist Vietnamese.[16] From the early days of his political career, Nixon articulated a strong anticommunist attitude; however, he did have a functional approach towards foreign policy.[17] While at Guam on July 25, 1969, President Nixon held a news conference where he announced his policies toward Asian allies of the U.S. which became labeled as the Guam or "Nixon Doctrine."[18] The concept of the "Nixon Doctrine" was where the U.S. would support its allies through effective means outside of deployment of American military combat forces against communist threats.[19] In theory, American servicemen would be less likely to be employed in combat roles to support states allied with the U.S. who were facing potential communist conquest. In practice, the Nixon Doctrine within the Vietnam conflict developed into Vietnamization.

The process of Vietnamization was to fortify RVNAF while withdrawing American military forces from Vietnam at appropriate periods.[20] The role of the U.S. was to be

---

[16] New York Times News Service, "Nixon Vows He Will End War," *The Milwaukee Journal*, March 6, 1968, accessed September 28, 2014, 14, http://news.google.com/newspapers?nid=1499&dat=19680305&id=XlgaAAAAIBAJ&sjid=FygEAAAAIBAJ&pg=5069,2870566.

[17] David Reynolds, *Summits: Six Meetings that Shaped the Twentieth Century* (New York: Basic Books, 2007), 228-29.

[18] Jeffrey Kimball, "The Nixon Doctrine: A Saga of Misunderstanding," *Presidential Studies Quarterly*, Volume 36, Number 1 (March, 2006): 59-60, accessed April, 24, 2014, Stable URL: http://www.jstor.org/stable/27552747.

[19] Ibid.

[20] Henry Kissinger, *Ending the Vietnam War: A History of America's Involvement in and Extrication from the Vietnam War* (New York: Simon and Schuster, 2003), 81-82.

downgraded to a support role while RVNAF fought the DRV and the NLF.[21] Essentially, the

combat role of the Vietnam War against communist forces was to be fulfilled by RVNAF,

thereby reducing American casualties, which eroded public support in the U.S.[22] The Nixon

Administration did not implement Vietnamization for the benefit of the RVN so much as it

was for the U.S., whose citizens were becoming more disillusioned with the Vietnam War as

time passed. Vietnamization was carried out despite the fact that statistically, for every

American soldier killed in action (KIA) there were more than three Army of the Republic of

Vietnam (ARVN) soldier KIAs, during the period of 1966 through 1971.[23] National Security

Advisor Henry Dr. Kissinger recalled that Vietnamization would remove the U.S. from the

Vietnam War with or without the DRV participating in a peace agreement.[24] While the best

expectations from the Nixon Administration for RVNAF were to create an ongoing deadlock

in the War.[25] Although the Nixon Administration had a negative rationale to implement

Vietnamization, the process had tremendous impact on RVNAF from the Administration's

viewpoint.

Through Vietnamization, RVNAF expanded in manpower, materials, and

technological sophistication to higher levels than it had previously accomplished for the

majority of the 1960s. To the Nixon Administration, the RVN had a population of 18 million,

who could fill the role left by American troop withdraws and, in theory, had greater incentive

---

[21] Scott Sigmund Gartner, "Differing Evaluations of Vietnamization," *The Journal of Interdisciplinary History*, Volume 29, Number 2 (Autumn, 1998): 250-51, accessed April, 24, 2014, Stable URL: http://www.jstor.org/stable/207045.

[22] Gartner, "Differing Evaluations of Vietnamization," 243-44.

[23] Ibid., 252.

[24] Kissinger, *Ending the Vietnam War*, 81-82.

[25] Ibid.

to fight against communist aggression in the Vietnam War.[26] Regardless of RVN's

manpower available for the defense of the state, it still needed defense equipment. By 1969,

the U.S. finally chose to sell more modern military technology to the RVN for its defense

e.g., the M-16 assault rifle to replace the semi-automatic M-1 Garand within the RVNAF

arsenal.[27] The Consolidated RVNAF Improvement and Modernization Plan (CRIMP)

developed, while it equipped RVNAF into growing force through the 1970 and 1971 fiscal

years.[28] In 1969 alone, ARVN received modern American armor, transportation, small arms,

artillery, and radios, instead of outdated stockpiles from pre-1960.[29] Due to Vietnamzation

and CRIMP, the precedent of the policies led to further growth of RVNAF to a sizable

fighting force in all of its services.

By 1972, the amount of military equipment accepted by ARVN allowed the branch to

form a total of "171 infantry battalions, 58 artillery battalions" and "22 armored cavalry and

tank squadrons."[30] The total assigned strength of ARVN as of May 30, 1973, under the fiscal

year of 1974, reached 461,403.[31] Comparatively, the final strength assigned to ARVN in the

fiscal year of 1968 had been 321,056 men.[32] Through Vietnamization, ARVN became fully

---

[26] Phan Quang Dan, "The Vietnam Experience," *Asian Affairs*, Volume 4, Number 4 (March – April, 1977): 260, accessed January 16, 2014, Stable URL: http://www.jstor.org/stable/30171484.

[27] Hammond, "The Press in Vietnam as Agent of Defeat: A Critical Examination," 317.

[28] Willbanks, *Abandoning Vietnam,* 29.

[29] Ibid., 29 and 31.

[30] Ibid., 31.

[31] RVNAF Quarterly Assessment: Fourth Quarter, Fiscal Year, 1973, Defense Attaché, Saigon, Major General John Murray, 4-1, Folder One 228-07/ RVNAF Quarterly Assessment/ Fourth Quarter, Fiscal Year 1973, Entry #A1 1727: RVNAF Quarterly Assessment Reports; 1973-1975, 228-07 Fourth Quarter 1973 Through 228-07 Second Quarter 1974, Box 1, DAO, Operations and Plans Division/ Readiness Section, Record Group 472, U.S. Forces in Southeast Asia, 1950-1975, National Archives, College Park, Maryland.

[32] Willbanks, *Abandoning Vietnam*, 30.

self-reliant in its recruitment and training of solders by 1973.[33] During the same year, ARVN was in the process of attempting to phase out its older M-41A3 tanks with modern M-48A Patton tanks.[34] While ARVN received vast expansion through Vietnamization, it was not the only service to receive the benefits of the policy. Even the Vietnamese equivalent of the American National Guard experienced positive aspects of Vietnamization.

The Regional (RF) and Popular Forces (PF) of RVNAF were also upgraded with modern small arms and artillery.[35] The purposes of the RF/PF was to maintain security and conduct pacification missions in their respective jurisdictions through light armed units.[36] PF solely focused hamlets or villages, while RF focused on district to provincial security in order to relieve ARVN combat units from security details.[37] Together, RF/PF had a total assigned strength of 518,479 men by May 30, 1973.[38] Despite the attention paid towards the Vietnamese land forces, RVN's other branch grew as well.

The extent of the modernization and expansion of the Vietnamese Air Force (VNAF) was so far-reaching that by 1973, the service branch was unrecognizable to its descriptions from the mid-1960s. In 1968, VNAF began to phase out its turboprop fighter aircraft with jet fighter-bomber aircraft such as the F-5A as well as the A-37.[39] VNAF also upgraded its fleet

---

[33] RVNAF Quarterly Assessment: Fourth Quarter, Fiscal Year, 1973, Defense Attaché, Saigon, MG John Murray, 5-52.

[34] Ibid., 4-5.

[35] Willbanks, *Abandoning Vietnam*, 31.

[36] RVNAF Quarterly Assessment: Fourth Quarter, Fiscal Year, 1973, Defense Attaché, Saigon, MG John Murray, 9-1.

[37] Ibid.

[38] Ibid., 4-1.

[39] Willbanks, *Abandoning Vietnam*, 31.

of C-47 transport aircraft to the C-7s and C-123s.[40] In 1973, VNAF had become one the strongest air services within the region, organized into six divisions, and equipped with 1,700 aircraft.[41] Additional, VNAF was staffed by 60,679 men, in 1973.[42] Although limited in air to air combat through the F-5A, VNAF had a specialty in a ground support role.[43] In January 1974, VNAF would begin its plan to phase out the F-5A for the more advanced F-5E, which was scheduled to have been completed by September 1975 at the latest.[44] VNAF wanted to introduce the F-5E into its arsenal because it could compete with the MIG-21 employed by the Vietnamese People's Air Force (VPAF) in air to air combat.[45]

Like VNAF, the Vietnamese Navy (VNN) also went through massive expansion. For the VNN, two sub-policies had been developed for the implementation of Vietnamization, which were the Accelerated Turnover of Assets (ACTOV) and the Accelerated Turnover of Logistics (ACTOVLOG). ACTOV enhanced recruitment, training (including on-the-job instruction), and the transfer of ownership of American naval vessels to the VNN.[46] Although similar to ACTOV, the policy ACTOVLOG was designed for the VNN to support the other branches of service within RVNAF and to take responsibility over its logistics.[47]

---

[40] Willbanks, *Abandoning Vietnam*, 31.

[41] Ibid., 32.

[42] RVNAF Quarterly Assessment: Fourth Quarter, Fiscal Year, 1973, Defense Attaché, Saigon, MG John Murray, 4-1.

[43] Ibid., 4-3 and 4-4.

[44] Ibid., 4-5.

[45] Ibid., 4-7.

[46] Willbanks, *Abandoning Vietnam*, 32.

[47] Ibid., 32.

The VNN had expanded rapidly. In the 1968 fiscal year, the VNN had the strength of 17,178 men.[48] Conversely, as of May 30, 1973, the VNN had strength of 41,256 men.[49] As the U.S. Navy was dismantling its brown water navy,[50] it was transferring its vessels over to the VNN.[51] Which the VNN owned "over five-hundred" former American brown water navy vessels halfway through 1970.[52] Brown water navy vessels were not the only ships the VNN obtained through Vietnamization; the service gained cargo ships, amphibious ships, and patrol craft for a blue sea navy.[53] The amount of vessels under the command of the VNN approximated to "over 1,700 surface ships."[54] Under the command of the VNN, the Vietnamese Marine Corps (VNMC) grew in correlation with the VNN expansion. The total strength of the VNMC was only 8,271 men in the 1968 fiscal year.[55] By May 30, 1973, the VNMC had a total strength of 15,484 men.[56] According to John G. Murray of the Defense Attaché of the U.S. embassy in Saigon, the VNMC was one of the best trained and the best

---

[48] Willbanks, *Abandoning Vietnam*, 30.

[49] RVNAF Quarterly Assessment: Fourth Quarter, Fiscal Year, 1973, Defense Attaché, Saigon, MG John Murray, 4-1.

[50] Inland and coastal water navy from Institute of Medicine (U.S.) Committee on Blue Water Navy Vietnam Veterans and Agent Orange Exposure, *Blue Water Navy Vietnam Veterans and Agent Orange Exposure: Historical Background* (Washington, D.C.: National Academies Press, 2011), accessed July 26, 2015, http://www.ncbi.nlm.nih.gov/books/NBK209598/.

[51] Willbanks, *Abandoning Vietnam,* 32.

[52] Ibid.

[53] Ibid.

[54] Ibid.

[55] Ibid.

[56] RVNAF Quarterly Assessment: Fourth Quarter, Fiscal Year, 1973, Defense Attaché, Saigon, MG John Murray, 4-1.

coordinated units within RVNAF.[57] However, the expansion of the VNN through Vietnamization was only one aspect of the total growth of RVNAF.

The modernization and growth of each service of RVNAF through Vietnamization was staggering. RVNAF was no longer receiving dusty stockpiles of military surplus; it was purchasing modern weaponry through the U.S. Government, from manufacture's shipping warehouses. Collectively, all the branches of RVNAF had a total strength of 1,097,301 men by May 30, 1973.[58] By comparison, the 1968 fiscal year, RVNAF only had a total strength of 717,214.[59] By the mid-1970s, ARVN and VNAF became the fourth largest army and air force respectively in the world.[60] While the VNN had been transformed into the fifth largest navy in the world.[61] Even though RVNAF had numerous improvements through Vietnamization, RVNAF's abilities to defend the RVN from communist forces would be put to the test in 1972.

During Vietnamization, RVNAF faced the challenge to push back the DRV's 1972 Easter Offensive with the U.S. in a support role.[62] PAVN under the command of General Vo Nguyen Giap, invaded the RVN in a four pong attack.[63] General Giap launched one prong of

---

[57] RVNAF Quarterly Assessment: Fourth Quarter, Fiscal Year, 1973, Defense Attaché, Saigon, MG John Murray, 8-6 and 8-7.

[58] Ibid., 4-1.

[59] Willbanks, *Abandoning Vietnam*, 30.

[60] T. Christopher Jespersen, "Kissinger, Ford, and Congress: The Very Bitter End in Vietnam," *Pacific Historical Review* Volume 71, Number 3 (August, 2002): 443, accessed January 10, 2014, Stable URL: http://www.jstor.org/stable/10.1525/phr.2002.71.3.439.

[61] Ibid.

[62] Phan Quang Dan, "The Vietnam Experience," *Asian Affairs* Volume 4, Number 4 (March - April, 1977): 264, accessed January 16, 2014, Stable URL: http://www.jstor.org/stable/30171484.

[63] Willbanks, *Abandoning Vietnam*, 127.

attack across the Demilitarized Zone (DMZ) into Military Region (MR) I to capture Quang

Tri the eponym provincial capital.[64] While another line of attack in MR II, worked to confine

Kontum within the Central highlands for its strategic roadways, with a third assault on An

Loc to serve as a foothold to launch an assault on the RVN capital of Saigon in MR III.[65] All

the while within MR IV, communist forces were to bog down RVNAF.[66]

On March 30, General Giap ordered PAVN to commence the Easter Offensive

(March 30, 1972, was the Thursday before Easter, hence the name Easter Offensive).[67] While

General Giap's 1972 Offensive was set in motion, President Nixon was in Beijing, in the

People's Republic of China (PRC) on a diplomatic visit.[68] President Nixon would not stand

for a communist takeover of the RVN; thus, he ordered numerous bombing strikes against

the DRV, including B-52 squadrons carrying bomb loads of thirty tons per aircraft.[69] B-52

bomber strikes were also used to support ARVN combat operations in within the RVN.[70]

After months of heavy combat, RVNAF was able to blunt the PAVN's Easter Offensive but

with a high number of causalities.[71] PAVN was able to seize Nationalist territory within the

RVN; however, the small gains that PAVN made were at a far greater cost in men and

---

[64] Willbanks, *Abandoning Vietnam*, 127.

[65] Ibid.

[66] Ibid.

[67] Clodfelter, *The Limits of Air Power*, 152.

[68] Parker, "Vietnam and Soviet Asian Strategy," 105.

[69] Clodfelter, *The Limits of Air Power*, 153-54.

[70] Lam Quang Thi, *The Twenty-Five Year Century: A South Vietnamese General Remembers the Indochina War to the Fall of Saigon* (Denton, Texas: University of North Texas, 2001), 278 and 285-86.

[71] Willbanks, *Abandoning Vietnam*, 151-52.

materials than RVNAF had paid in their defense.[72] The costly outcome of the 1972 Easter

Offensive had caused a great deal of speculation about American and Nationalist Vietnamese

political policy.

Since RVNAF did not capitulate during the 1972 Easter Offensive, many participants

and observers of the Vietnam War hypothesize on the value of Vietnamization. Central

Intelligence Agency (CIA) Director, William Colby, stated that RVNAF had proved itself

during the 1972 offensive; therefore, Vietnamization was a success and would continue to be

a success as long as the U.S. maintained its support role.[73] In an attitudinal survey of U.S.

Army generals who served in the Vietnam War that was conducted in 1974, it was found that

the majority of respondents believed that ARVN could defend the RVN with the odds in the

Nationalists favor.[74] ARVN General Lam Quang Thi stated that during the immediate

aftermath of the 1972 offensive, ARVN forces could defeat the elite units of PAVN.[75] Many

the Nationalist Vietnamese believed PAVN were more highly trained soldier compared to

ARVN.[76] The populace of the RVN had high morale and was very supportive of ARVN

during the latter half of 1972.[77] However, General Thi agreed with CIA Director Colby that

---

[72] Willbanks, *Abandoning Vietnam*, 151-52.

[73] William Colby with James McCarger, *Lost Victory: A Firsthand Account of America's Sixteen Year Involvement in Vietnam* (Chicago: Contemporary Books, 1989), 343.

[74] Douglas Kinnard, "Vietnam Reconsidered: An Attitudinal Survey of U.S. Army General Officers," *The Public Opinion Quarterly* Volume 39, Number 4 (Winter, 1975-1976): 450, accessed January 16, 2014, Stable URL: http://www.jstor.org/stable/2748499.

[75] Lam Quang Thi, *The Twenty-Five Year Century*, 289-90.

[76] Ibid.

[77] Ibid., 289.

in order for Vietnamization to be successful, the policy needed the U.S. to maintain its support role.[78]

While the Easter Offensive was taking place on April 26, 1972, President Nixon declared to the American public on broadcast television and radio that Vietnamization was a success since RVNAF had been holding ground against the communist invasion.[79] Because of President Nixon's Vietnamization beliefs, American troop withdraws would continue.[80] Like CIA Director Colby and General Thi, President Nixon emphasized the support role the U.S. needed to fulfill in order to for the RVN to maintain its independence.[81] In a Gallup poll conducted in early April 1971, found that 58 percent of respondents stated they would find it upsetting if communist forces conquered the RVN.[82] In the same 1971 Gallup poll, the researchers discovered that 54 percent of respondents preferred to "end the war by accepting the best possible compromise settlement even though it might sooner or later allow the Vietnamese Communists" conquer the RVN.[83] According to the April, 1971 Gallup poll, Vietnamization was an acceptable policy to pursue to the American public because it allowed the U.S. to withdraw from the Vietnam War without a communist victory in the conflict (in theory). Since President Nixon, CIA Director Colby, generals, and the Nationalist

---

[78] Lam Quang Thi, *The Twenty-Five Year Century*, 289-90.

[79] "129-Address to the Nation on Vietnam, April 26, 1972," President Richard Nixon from *the American Presidency Project*, last modified 2014, by Gerhard Peters and John T. Woolley, access October 12, 2014, http://www.presidency.ucsb.edu/ws/index.php?pid=3384.

[80] Ibid.

[81] Ibid.

[82] "Seeing Red: The Cold War and American Public Opinion," John Kenneth White, from *Conference on the Power of Free Inquiry and Cold War International History*, accessed October 12, 2014, http://www.archives.gov/research/foreign-policy/cold-war/conference/white.html.

[83] White, "Seeing Red: The Cold War and American Public Opinion."

Vietnamese populace declared Vietnamization a success, Americans were more willing to accept the policy. Still, unanimity is very rare in politics.

Despite the positive perceptions of Vietnamzation, there were differing opinions. From the beginning of the planning stages for Vietnamization, National Security Advisor Dr. Henry Kissinger pointed out to President Nixon that the policy would not end the Vietnam War.[84] Additionally, Dr. Kissinger commented on the American troop withdraws "would become like 'salted peanuts' to the American public" who were demanding for an acceptable conclusion to the Vietnam War that removed American servicemen from the conflict.[85] Dr. Kissinger even wrote President Nixon a memorandum on October 30, 1969 on his concerns on the viability of Vietnamization, which were ignored by Nixon.[86]

Dr. Kissinger was not the only one to have doubts on Vietnamization. RVN President Nguyen Van Thieu feared that once the U.S. completed its troop withdraws, American support for the RVN would be withdrawn as well.[87] Knowing that the U.S. wanted to conclude the Vietnam War through a negotiated peace with the DRV, President Thieu became apprehensive about the possible peace agreement.[88] President Thieu's lack of faith in the political aspects of Vietnamization would create another issue for the U.S.

By 1972, the U.S. had to not only convince the DRV to accept a peace agreement, but the RVN as well. In order to persuade the Vietnamese, the Nixon Administration would

---

[84] Kissinger, *Ending the Vietnam War*, 92-93.

[85] Ibid.

[86] Ibid., 93-94.

[87] Willbanks, *Abandoning Vietnam*, 165.

[88] Ibid., 165-66.

employ political and military strategies in order to obtain a peace agreement.[89] President

Nixon's attempts to establish a peace agreement for the Vietnam War would differ greatly

from President Johnson's attempts.

During the early months of 1964, the Johnson Administration decided to employ a

bombing campaign that was to eliminate the DRV's and the NLF's ability to fight, that could

escalate the American participation in the conflict if needed.[90] President Johnson's approach

for a military solution to the Vietnam War can be summarized with the concept of gradual

response. Where the U.S. would send more military forces to meet the communist escalation

of the conflict when it occurred.[91] The rationale for gradual response was to maintain

American prestige around the world, to counter communist aggression, and to allow

lawmakers to divert greater attention social reform programs that would later be known as

the Great Society.[92] Gradual response bombing eventually evolved into the campaign Rolling

Thunder due to growing political unrest in the RVN.[93] Rolling Thunder differed from gradual

response since it was an orderly campaign.[94]

When President Johnson sought a diplomatic solution to the Vietnam War, the DRV

made it a condition that, for negotiations to begin, the U.S. needed to cease the Rolling

Thunder campaign.[95] President Johnson agreed to cease Rolling Thunder on March 31, 1968

---

[89] Willbanks, *Abandoning Vietnam*, 182-83.

[90] Clodfelter, *The Limits of Air Power*, 45-46.

[91] Ibid., 44.

[92] Ibid., 44.

[93] Clodfelter, *The Limits of Air Power*, 62-63.

[94] Kissinger, *Ending the Vietnam War*, 38.

[95] Ibid., 51.

in exchange for a possible peace agreement.[96] However, a peace agreement to end the

Vietnam War was never written during the Johnson era of the conflict and Nixon was

determined to fulfill his pledge to end the conflict.[97]

In response to the DRV's 1972 Easter Offensive and their failure to resume

negotiations, President Nixon ordered the U.S. Armed Forces to carry out "Operation

Linebacker I."[98] The campaign Linebacker I called for a large scale the bombing of the war

making capability of the DRV, including the mining of sea ports and the bombing

transportation routes.[99] The air armada to carry out Linebacker I was massive and led to a

considerable deployment of U.S. Air Force (USAF) aircraft in the Pacific area which

included Southeast Asia. As of March 31, 1972, in the Pacific area there were 83 B-52Ds, 10

B-57G Canberra tactical bombers, 30 F-105 Thunderchief tactical bombers, and 315 fighters

made up of F-4 Phantom II, which could function as bombers as well.[100]

Starting on May 10, 1972, the Linebacker I campaign began.[101] By June 30, 1972,

there were 202 B-52Ds, an unreported number of B-57Gs, and 455 fighters in possession

deployed within the Pacific area.[102] Furthermore, the USAF was authorized to have 537

---

[96] Kissinger, *Ending the Vietnam War*, 51.

[97] Ibid., 52.

[98] Clodfelter, *The Limits of Air Power*, 156.

[99] Ibid., 156 and 158.

[100] "United States Air Force Statistical Digest: Fiscal Year 1972, Twenty-Seventh Edition," Management Information Division Directorate of Management Analysis Comptroller of the Air Force Headquarters, United States Air Force, Published September 15, 1973, accessed October 14, 2014, 85-86, http://www.afhso.af.mil/shared/media/document/AFD-110412-052.pdf.

[101] Clodfelter, *The Limits of Air Power*, xi.

[102] "United States Air Force Statistical Digest: Fiscal Year 1972, Twenty-Seventh Edition," 94-95.

fighters in Pacific area.[103] By August 8, 1972, the U.S. Navy (USN) had ordered the

deployment of "three of the six carriers in the Tonkin Gulf to devote all of their softies to

Linebacker."[104] Fighter-bombers were utilized for the majority of the bombing raids with

laser-guided smart bombs.[105] The extensive use of the smart bombs led to a deficiency of

guidance pods available for the bombs since the USAF was planning to launch forty-eight

raids per day into two different bombing routes alone, which began in August.[106]

Negotiations for a peace agreement would resume although President Nixon would not make

the same mistake as predecessor.

While Linebacker I was under way, President Nixon felt wary of negotiations until

after his predicted reelection as opinion polls were displaying in summer 1972.[107] During a

press conference on August 29, 1972, the question was asked that without a peace agreement,

would the Nixon Administration bring an end or a decline to the Linebacker bombing

campaign?[108] President Nixon's response was "absolutely not" until substantive progress was

made during negotiations for a peace settlement to the Vietnam War and that the DRV

needed to allow development to take place in negotiations.[109] Based on Johnson's and the

Nixon Administration's experience in the peace talks with the DRV, President Nixon had

---

[103] "United States Air Force Statistical Digest: Fiscal Year 1972, Twenty-Seventh Edition," 95.

[104] Clodfelter, *The Limits of Air Power*, 161.

[105] Ibid., 159.

[106] Ibid., 161.

[107] Kissinger, *Ending the Vietnam War*, 298-99.

[108] "276 – The President's News Conference, August 29, 1972," President Richard Nixon, from *the American Presidency Project*, last modified 2014, by Gerhard Peters and John T. Woolley, accessed October 20, 2014, http://www.presidency.ucsb.edu/ws/index.php?pid=3548.

[109] Ibid.

developed a hardline stance on the exchange for bombing cessation to allow peace

negotiations to continue.

In 1969, the Nixon Administration had inherited the negotiations for the Vietnam

War peace agreement with Dr. Kissinger being one of the central negotiators.[110] However,

Dr. Kissinger quickly learned that the DRV were really attempting to create the illusion of

parley to the international public, while trying to convince the American negotiators to accept

their terms without compromise.[111] Later, while the Paris Peace Conference was under way

in the public view, Dr. Kissinger had developed secret negotiations with the DRV's high

ranking, ruling Lao Dong Party Politburo member Le Duc Tho.[112] During the public session

of negotiations on August 16, 1971, a deadlock had developed between the U.S. and the

DRV.[113] The Nixon Administration sent a message to resume peace talks with the DRV on

November 19, 1971, but the DRV were not inclined to respond due to their preparations for

the 1972 offensive.[114] Until the latter half 1972, Dr. Kissinger was unable to make progress

in negotiations with Le Duc Tho.

After President Nixon's August 29, 1972, press conference, Dr. Kissinger's

negotiations with Le Duc Tho moved into a new direction. The first breakthrough in

negations came during the September 26 and 27, 1972 meetings from Le Duc Tho who listed

the DRV's "'final' offer.'" In their demands, the DRV agreed to withdraw PAVN from Laos

and Cambodia, where the warring parties would exchange prisoners of war (POWs) after a

---

[110] Kissinger, *Ending the Vietnam War*, 86-87.

[111] Ibid., 87-88.

[112] Quang Dan, "The Vietnam Experience," 264.

[113] Kissinger, *Ending the Vietnam War*, 224-25.

[114] Ibid., 229.

region wide ceasefire would take place. Which marked the first time the communists were in accord with the U.S. about PAVN's deployment within the mentioned states. For the rest of the late September sessions, Le Duc Tho reiterated previous demands that were unacceptable to the U.S., but he did agree to meet with Dr. Kissinger again on October 8, 1972.[115]

When Dr. Kissinger and Le Duc Tho meet again, another breakthrough was made. Le Duc Tho suggested that first a military agreement be made between the U.S. and the DRV to allow a withdraw, an exchange of POWs, and a ceasefire between the two parties. When Le Duc Tho moved on to the political agreement, his offer was that the two Vietnamese states create national accords and hold free elections for the people to determine the future of the Vietnamese nation after a ceasefire. For the first time in negotiations for a peace agreement in Vietnam, the DRV abandoned its demand for a coalition government that would have given the communists the greater political power over the nationalists.[116]

Other breakthroughs included that PAVN would cease its infiltration. Although, the DRV claimed that no PAVN units were deployed in the RVN. Additionally, the U.S. could supply military goods as replacement pieces in the RVNAF arsenal. As opposed to prior stipulations that the U.S. end its military aid to the RVN. After the October negotiation sessions came to a close, Dr. Kissinger felt optimistic that the negotiations would lead to a favorable conclusion to the Vietnam War. Despite the fact some issues remained disputed. The October negotiations concluded on positive terms; however, the U.S. would discover that there were more roadblocks to a peace agreement.[117]

---

[115] Kissinger, *Ending the Vietnam War*, 321-22.

[116] Ibid., 327-28.

[117] Ibid., 327-28, 321-22 and 336-37.

Despite the American efforts to persuade the DRV to accept a peace agreement, the

U.S. needed to convince the RVN to accept the agreement as well. Since the lawmakers of

the RVN did not have the confidence to defend their state alone, according to Dr.

Kissinger.[118] In a meeting between White House Security Advisor General, Alexander Haig

of the U.S. Army and President Thieu along with the Republican Vietnamese National

Security Council (NSC), President Thieu demanded that changes be made to the proposed

peace agreement according to his stipulations word for word in order for the RVN to accept

the agreement.[119] The highly contested terms by the RVN of the proposed peace agreement

were the issues of the lack of a PAVN withdraw from the RVN, which had been removed

from negotiations since 1970.[120] Following the instructions from Dr. Kissinger, Haig

informed President Thieu that due to the outcome of the 1972 Senatorial elections, there was

a risk that Congress would eliminate funding for American aid to the RVN.[121] However,

President Thieu did not feel assured that the U.S. had the best interests of the RVN during

negotiations.[122] Therefore, President Thieu offered to send a representative to meet with

President Nixon personally before negotiations resumed in November 1972.[123]

President Nixon responded to President Thieu's stipulations and concerns in a letter

dated November 18, 1972.[124] In the November 18 letter, President Nixon stated that although

---

[118] Kissinger, *Ending the Vietnam War*, 354.

[119] Ibid., 384-85.

[120] Ibid.

[121] Ibid., 385.

[122] Ibid., 386-87.

[123] Ibid.

[124] Letter, President Richard Nixon to President Nguyen Van Thieu, November 18, 1972, Vietnam –
Correspondence from Richard Nixon to Nguyen Van Thieu, Box 13, Richard B. Cheney Files, Gerard R. Ford

the President Thieu's proposed alterations would be pursued by Dr. Kissinger in the negotiations.[125] It was unrealistic to expect the DRV to accept the alterations and that a complete PAVN withdraw from the RVN would not happen.[126] Additionally, President Nixon made it very clear that the U.S. would not abandon its pursuit for a peace agreement while encouraging President Thieu to support the effort for an agreement before American public opinion turned negative on American support for the RVN.[127] While resistance for a peace agreement was building from the RVN, they would not be alone.

While the RVN was reluctant to accept a peace agreement to conclude the Vietnam War, the DRV would build greater resistance towards the agreement. Before negotiations for a peace accord for the Vietnam War resumed, President Nixon was reelected to the presidency on November 7, 1972.[128] In his remarks of his election victory, President Nixon stated he would continue to support undivided U.S. pursuit for "peace with honor" not only in Southeast Asia but the entire world.[129] During the November 1972 negotiation sessions, Dr. Kissinger presented President Thieu's proposed alterations to the peace agreement to Le Duc Tho, who forbad the vast majority of the alternations.[130] By the end of the November sessions, Le Duc Tho was not inclined to discuss with diplomatic legal experts on the details

---

Presidential Library, 1, PDF page 7, accessed May 24, 2015,
http://www.fordlibrarymuseum.gov/library/document/0005/1561601.pdf.

[125] Letter, President Nixon to President Thieu, November 18, 1972, 1, PDF page 7.

[126] Ibid.

[127] Ibid., 1-2, PDF pages 7-8.

[128] Willbanks, *Abandoning Vietnam*, 173.

[129] "414 – Remarks on Being Reelected to the Presidency, November 7, 1972," President Richard Nixon, from *the American Presidency Project*, last modified 2014 by Gerhard Peters and John T. Woolly, accessed October 26, 2014, http://www.presidency.ucsb.edu/ws/index.php?pid=3702&st=&st1=.

[130] Kissinger, *Ending the Vietnam War*, 389-90.

for the proposed peace agreement's procedures, and the sessions ended with conformity only on minor technical issues.[131] Instead, slow progress the negotiations would reach an impasse.

When negotiations pick back up again in December 4, 1972, the DRV's Politburo had caught on to the emerging small rift between the U.S. and the RVN on the intended peace settlement. Le Duc Tho took full advantage of the rift at the very beginning of the December negotiation sessions by rejecting the previous agreements on issues made in October and November. By December 7, Le Duc Tho finally made a few compromises with Dr. Kissinger involving some of the lost previous agreements. After several days, Le Duc Tho still refused to discuss the protocol and finer details of the proposed peace agreement.[132]

When Le Duc Tho finally wanted to discuss the issue of the DMZ on December 12, 1972 the language he demanded to be used, allowed infiltration into the RVN through the removal of the word "civilian" in the proposed agreement. Finally, the DRV sent their proposals on the protocols. The draft for the International Commission of Control and Supervision (ICCS), limited the entire staff to a total of 250 people, which included support teams for the inspectors to monitor the entire state of the RVN. Under the liaison Joint Military Commission, which was to hold exclusive membership for the Nationalists and the NLF, allowed NLF members into every political district of the RVN. In one of the protocol drafts, it stated that in order for the DRV to accept a ceasefire, the VNAF and the VNN would need to terminate all security operations. On December 13, the last day of the month's negotiation sessions, Le Duc Tho re-introduced several communist requirements through "seventeen brand-new gratuitous phrases," i.e., re-presenting old demands of the DRV in

---

[131] Kissinger, *Ending the Vietnam War*, 394-95.

[132] Ibid., 395, 397-98, and 401-02.

different words. At the end of the day Dr. Kissinger traveled back to Washington, D.C. to personally inform President Nixon the outcome of the negotiations.[133]

While in Washington, the Nixon Administration had to develop a solution for the December negotiations deadlock. With a stalemate in the peace process, the DRV believed that they could obtain a peace agreement that was very favorable towards them or the U.S. Congress would cut funding for the American military effort in Southeast Asia.[134] To President Nixon, allowing the DRV to gain the advantage over the RVN was unacceptable.[135] President Nixon also wanted to persuade President Thieu that the RVN still had the support of the United States.[136] President Nixon believed the only option available to him was to launch another bombing campaign.[137] The campaign would consist generally of B-52s due to weather restrictions and the theory that the massive use of B-52s would destroy the DRV's will to fight.[138] President Nixon ordered the bombing campaign, which became known as Operation Linebacker II, to begin on December 18, 1972.[139] Like previous American bombing campaign in Vietnam, Linebacker II would be a colossal operation.

Operation Linebacker II was a short campaign, only lasting twelve days. However, it was an intensive campaign with concentration on targets in Hanoi and Haiphong.[140] By the

---

[133]Kissinger, *Ending the Vietnam War*, 404-05, 405-06, 406-07, and 407-08.

[134] Ibid., 409.

[135] Willbanks, *Abandoning Vietnam*, 180-81.

[136] Ibid.

[137] Kissinger, *Ending the Vietnam War*, 410-11.

[138] Ibid., 411.

[139] Clodfelter, *The Limits of Air Power*, 183-84.

[140] Willbanks, *Abandoning Vietnam*, 181.

end of Linebacker II, "over 40,000 tons of bombs" were employed in the campaign.[141] For

the 729 B-52 sorties alone, the bombers dropped over 15,000 tons of bombs onto thirty-four

targets throughout the campaign.[142] When the opportunity was present, the USAF and the

USN utilized 1,216 fighter-bomber sorties during Linebacker II.[143]

Haiphong harbor was selected since it was a strategically important route to receive

military supplies from the Union of Soviet Socialist Republics (USSR aka the Soviet

Union).[144] With the naval blockade of the DRV's Haiphong harbor, Linebacker II reduced

the harbor's imports from "160,000 tons per month" to "30,000 tons per month."[145] In the

process of Linebacker II, the air sorties were able to destroy an entire fourth of the DRV

petroleum reserves, inflicted damage to ten airfield runways, damaged at least "372 pieces of

rolling stock," destroyed 500 interdictions in the DRV's rail lines, damaged at least 1,600

PAVN complexes, and cut about 80 percent of electric production through bombing.[146]

Additionally, 191 warehouses were destroyed in the campaign.[147] Before the Linebacker II

began, President Nixon sent had an important issue to discuss with President Thieu.

On December 17, 1972, President Nixon sent a message to President Thieu

concerning the Nationalist Vietnamese President's reluctance towards the proposed peace

---

[141] Willbanks, *Abandoning Vietnam*, 181.

[142] Brigadier General James R. McCarthy and Lieutenant Colonel George B. Allison, *Linebacker II: A View from the Rock, United States Air Force Monograph Series, Volume VI, Monograph Eight* (Washington, D.C.: Office of Air Force History, United States Air Force, 1985), 171, accessed October 27, 2014, http://www.afhso.af.mil/shared/media/document/AFD-101013-045.pdf.

[143] Clodfelter, *The Limits of Air Power*, 194.

[144] Parker, "Vietnam and Soviet Asian Strategy," 105.

[145] McCarthy and Allison, *Linebacker II*, 171.

[146] Ibid., 171.

[147] Clodfelter, *The Limits of Air Power*, 194.

agreement to end the Vietnam War.[148] In the December 17 letter, President Nixon stated the

movement towards a peace agreement along with the Linebacker campaigns was "to convey

to the enemy my determination to bring the conflict to a rapid end–as well as to show what I

am prepared to do in case of violation of the agreement," a line echoing a prior statement.[149]

In a previous letter to President Thieu, dated October 16, 1972, President Nixon had stated

once a ceasefire was implemented, the U.S. would still provide the RVN with economic and

military aid that would be appropriate under the proposed peace agreement.[150] President

Nixon pledged to President Thieu that if the DRV violated the peace agreement, "it would

have the most serious consequences."[151] Essentially, President Nixon created an informal

defense agreement with the RVN through his correspondence with President Thieu. In

another letter dated December 18, 1972, President Nixon informed President Thieu, he

understood President Thieu's reluctance towards the proposed peace agreement.[152] However,

President Nixon declared the U.S. would sign the peace agreement, with or without the

RVN's endorsement of the agreement.[153] While Linebacker II was underway, President

Nixon kept pushing for a peace agreement.

---

[148] Letter, President Richard Nixon to President Nguyen Van Thieu, December 17, 1972, Vietnam – Correspondence from Richard Nixon to Nguyen Van Thieu, Box 13, Richard B. Cheney Files, Gerard R. Ford Presidential Library, 1, PDF page 5, accessed May 24, 2015, http://www.fordlibrarymuseum.gov/library/document/0005/1561601.pdf.

[149] Ibid., 2, PDF page 6.

[150] Letter, President Richard Nixon to President Nguyen Van Thieu, October 16, 1972, Vietnam – Correspondence from Richard Nixon to Nguyen Van Thieu, Box 13, Richard B. Cheney Files, Gerard R. Ford Presidential Library, Ann Arbor, Michigan, 3, PDF page 23, accessed May 24, 2015, http://www.fordlibrarymuseum.gov/library/document/0005/1561601.pdf.

[151] Ibid.

[152] Letter, President Richard Nixon to President Nguyen Van Thieu, December 18, 1972, Vietnam – Correspondence from Richard Nixon to Nguyen Van Thieu, Box 13, Richard B. Cheney Files, Gerard R. Ford Presidential Library, Ann Arbor, Michigan, 1-2, PDF pages 7-8, accessed May 24, 2015, http://www.fordlibrarymuseum.gov/library/document/0005/1561601.pdf.

On December 22, 1972, the Nixon Administration sent a message to the DRV stating, if they did not resume serious negotiations, the U.S. would continue its Linebacker II campaign.[154] Four days later, the DRV responded that it could only resume negotiations if the Linebacker II operation ceased.[155] The Nixon Administration agreed to the bombing halt, thirty-six hours after the DRV agreed to resume negotiations for peace with Le Duc Tho as the only leader of the DRV delegation by January 1973.[156] By December 28, 1972, the DRV agreed to the Nixon Administration's terms.[157] In the last two days of Operation Linebacker II, sixty bomber sorties carried out their raids before bomber commanders were informed to discontinue all Linebacker II missions by December 29, 1972.[158] With the Linebacker II operation concluded, negotiations once again resumed.

Before Dr. Kissinger left for Paris, he expressed his concern that the peace agreement to conclude the Vietnam War could have a disastrous outcome for the RVN. President Nixon however, instructed Dr. Kissinger to settle on the favorable terms of the proposed agreement while looking over the diplomatic approach to the January sessions. As scheduled, negotiations for the peace agreement recommenced on January 8, 1973; but it was not until the next day when a breakthrough occurred. Le Duc Tho told Dr. Kissinger that the DRV would accept the November 23 draft which included, terms on travel through the DMZ favorable to the U.S., the parties concerned would sign on different pages with their

[153] Letter, President Nixon to President Thieu, December 18, 1972, 1-2, PDF pages 7-8.

[154] Kissinger, *Ending the Vietnam War*, 416.

[155] Ibid., 416-17.

[156] Ibid., 417.

[157] Ibid.

[158] Clodfelter, *The Limits of Air Power*, 189.

respective allies, a ceasefire in Laos shortly after a ceasefire in Vietnam, and to enforce in the best of the DRV's abilities, a ceasefire in Cambodia. By January 13, the American and DRV delegations had agreed to a full completed draft of a peace agreement to end the Vietnam War with protocols. For the first time, the American and DRV delegations dined together in celebration after the mutual agreement on the completed draft of the peace agreement. While the DRV had agreed to the proposed peace accord, the RVN still had to agree to the accord.[159]

In order to convince President Theiu to accept the completed proposed peace agreement, President Nixon stated in a letter dated January 16, 1973, that the U.S. would sign the agreement. Additionally, all forms of American aid for the RVN would be eliminated if President Thieu worked to prevent the implementation of the agreement. President Thieu responded to President Nixon's message with a letter, demanding alterations to the proposed peace agreement such as articles that completely removed PAVN units south of the DMZ. President Nixon was furious with President Thieu and sent a few more messages along the same line as the January 16 letter to President Thieu. By January 21, President Thieu agreed to accept the proposed peace agreement and sent RVN Minister of Foreign Affairs, Charles Tran Van Lam, to negotiations in Paris for alterations to some passages. Finally, after years of negotiations, the major parties involved in the Vietnam War agreed to sign a peace accord to end the conflict.[160]

In the evening of January 23, 1973, President Nixon announced on a nationwide broadcast the initialing of the Paris Peace Accord (PPA) between Dr. Kissinger and Le Duc

---

[159] Kissinger, *Ending the Vietnam War*, 420-21, 422-23, and 424.

[160]Ibid., 427-28.

Tho. While a formal signing ceremony would take place on January 27, by "2400 Greenwich Mean Time, January 27, 1973," the ceasefire would begin in Vietnam. Additionally, President Nixon announced that all American POWs would return to the U.S. by the end of sixty days. Within his announcement, President Nixon dignified the sacrifices made and bravery of all the allied participates who fought for Southeast Asia's independence from communism. At the time, it seemed that President Nixon had fulfilled his 1968 presidential campaign promise to end the Vietnam War with honor. Unfortunately, the achievement of the PPA was to be short lived.[161]

While American public and lawmakers' opinion toward the Vietnam War became more negative, Americans were open to a new strategy. In response to the negative attitude Americans had for the Vietnam War, Nixon won the U.S. Presidency with his vow to create an acceptable conclusion to the conflict. While serving as president, Nixon's policy for bring the American combat effort to a close was through Vietnamization. The concept of Vietnamization was to create a balance that was acceptable to the U.S. and the RVN. While the U.S. withdrew combat forces from Southeast Asia. President Nixon implemented the policy of Vietnamization to expand the strength and capability of RVANF, to fill the void left from the exit American armed forces. Through Vietnamization, RVNAF became a strong military that was able to push back PAVN's 1972 offensive with the assistance of American air power.

All the while, the Nixon Administration pursued a peace agreement with the DRV to create a favorable departure for the U.S. in Southeast Asia. For several years the DRV

---

[161] President Richard Nixon, "12 – Address to the Nation Announcing Conclusion of an Agreement on Ending the War and Restoring Peace in Vietnam, January 23, 1973," from *the American Presidency Project*, last modified 2014, by Gerhard Peters and John T. Woolly, accessed October 27, 2014, http://www.presidency.ucsb.edu/ws/?pid=3808.

resisted in reaching a peace agreement. Therefore, the Nixon Administration utilized

bombing campaigns to entice the Communist Vietnamese to conclude the Vietnam War. By

1973, the DRV agreed to sign the PPA. However, the RVN refuse to sign the PPA as well. In

order to persuade the RVN to accept the peace agreement, President Nixon promised full

American support in the form of air power on the condition the DRV violated the agreement.

After long negotiations, the Vietnamese parties and the U.S. signed the PPA.

Chapter Two: Changes

While the Vietnam War was emerging towards the formal signing of the PPA, a

series of events had transpired in Washington, D.C. that would greatly affect the outcome to

the War. The episodes concerning the Nixon presidency led to Gerald Rudolph Ford to the

American Presidency. Ford's rise to the presidency was very unique in the sense that he was

neither elected as president nor vice president. Due to charges of corruption during his

service as governor of Maryland, Vice President Spiro T. Agnew resigned after receiving a

plea deal in 1973, which led to Ford being appointed as the vice president on December 6,

1973. Nearly a year later, Ford became the president after President Nixon resigned due to

charges of criminal corruption. The events of the Nixon White House had caused Ford

deviate from his career plans.[1]

Ford's political ambitions never included the presidency;[2] his goal was to become

Speaker of the House.[3] Ford was willing to become Vice President of the U.S. since he had

offered his services in the 1960 Presidential Campaign to then Vice President Nixon, and

Ford was included on a list of possible running mates in the 1968 election.[4] After Agnew

resigned during his corruption scandals, Robert Hartmann,[5] Congressman Ford's personal

---

[1] Robert T. Hartmann, *Palace Politics: An Inside Account of the Ford Years* (New York: McGraw-Hill, 1980), 5-6.

[2] Gerald R. Ford, *A Time to Heal: The Autobiography of* (New York: Harper & Row and Reader's Digest Association, 1979), 5.

[3] Ford, *A Time to Heal*, 85.

[4] Hartmann, *Palace Politics*, 6-7.

[5] Hartmann was appointed to the position of Counsellor to the President shortly after Ford had entered the presidency from Ibid., 175 and 208.

aide speculated that President Nixon required a vice president who was a "Mr. Clean."[6]

Someone who was widely respected by the two major political parties, a loyal Republican

who had right wing leanings, but a moderate attitude, which made Hartmann believe that his

employer would fit the mold.[7] In 1973, Ford had plans to retire from politics within the next

couple of years; however, he felt he could not turn down President Nixon's offer to become

Vice President.[8] Ford and Nixon had been friends for 25 years by the mid-1970s, and during

their friendship, both had campaigned for one another on several occasions.[9] During the early

to mid-1970s, President Nixon was involved in the Watergate scandal, which increased the

chances of Vice President Ford becoming president one way or another.

Shortly after Ford's appointment to the vice presidency, Gallup discovered that 46

percent of respondents in their poll had a preference for Ford as president over Nixon; while

22 percent of respondents were undecided, and 32 percent stated they Nixon favored as

president.[10] According to Gallup, the American public favored Nixon to be removed from

office amidst the Watergate scandal.

In 1972, the Watergate scandal began with five individuals breaking into the offices

of the Democratic National Committee in order to place listening bugs within the offices;

however, three officers of the Metropolitan Police Department of the District of Columbia

---

[6] Hartmann, *Palace Politics*, 15-16.

[7] Ibid.

[8] Ron Nessen, *It Sure Looks Different from the Inside* (Chicago: Playboy Press, 1978), 3-4.

[9] Ford, *A Time to Heal*, 5.

[10] Nessen, *It Sure Looks Different from the Inside*, 5.

arrested the five men in the act.[1112] Nixon's former counsel, John W. Dean III, had informed

federal prosecutors about the President's participation in the cover-up of the scandal in

1973.[13] While as vice president, Ford was guaranteed by President Nixon in several

conversations that the President was in no way connected to the Watergate scandal.[1415] Ford

believed President Nixon; one aspect was through Ford's philosophy that honesty was out of

respect others.[16] Additionally, Nixon had been a friend and collogue of Ford's for many years

along with the fact that Ford served as Nixon's vice president.[17] Over time, however, the

truth of President Nixon's connections to the Watergate scandal would be revealed to Ford

and the American public.

On July 24, 1974, the U.S. Supreme Court unanimously ruled that President Nixon

was required to follow a trial subpoena to hand over his the tapes of his conversations in the

White House to the Federal prosecutor in the Watergate trails.[18] Some of the tapes ordered by

---

[11] Alfred E. Lewis, "5 Held in Plot to Bug Democrats' Office Here," *Washington Post*, June 18, 1972, from *Washington Post* Politics: The Watergate Story, accessed September 16, 2014, http://www.washingtonpost.com/wp-dyn/content/article/2002/05/31/AR2005111001227.html.

[12] The individuals involved in the Watergate break in, were paid $460,000 dollars to keep their silence, and that President Nixon had no concern about paying an additional total of $1 million to the arrested intruders. From Carl Bernstein and Robert Woodward, "Dean Alleges Nixon Knew of Cover-up Plan," *Washington Post*, June 3, 1973, from *Washington Post* Politics: The Watergate Story, accessed September 16, 2014, http://www.washingtonpost.com/politics/dean-alleges-nixon-knew-of-cover-up-plan/2012/06/04/gJQAgpyCJV_story.html.

[13] Ibid.

[14] Ford, *A Time to Heal*, 5.

[15] "In an hour, long televised question-and-answer session with 400 Associated Press managing editors," President Nixon declared he was not guilty of charges concerning the Watergate scandal, most notably through his "'I'm not a crook' speech." From Carroll Kilpatrick, "Nixon Tells Editors, 'I'm Not a Crook,'" *Washington Post*, November 18, 1973, from *Washington Post* Politics: The Watergate Story, accessed September 19, 2014, http://www.washingtonpost.com/politics/nixon-tells-editors-im-not-a-crook/2012/06/04/gJQA1RK6IV_story.html.

[16] Ford, *A Time to Heal*, 5.

[17] Ibid.

the Supreme Court proved that Nixon lied about his involvement in the Watergate scandal.[19] The information on President Nixon's tapes came to Vice President Ford's knowledge the first of two August 1 meetings with General Haig, who was then serving as the White House chief of staff.[20][21] After learning of the existence of the "smoking gun" tapes from Haig, Ford became shocked, extremely frustrated, and deeply hurt by President Nixon's lies.[22] However, Ford felt he had to publicly support Nixon since he was the vice president and Ford did not want to appear as if he was attempting to undermine the Nixon Presidency for personal gain.[23][24] More troubles were on the way before the sun had set on August 1, 1974.

Haig met with Ford a second time on August 1. This time, however, Haig had been under a great deal of stress since he looked as if he was "beaten and harassed" to Ford.[25] Haig wanted to meet with Ford alone and not include Hartmann as a witness.[26] At the second meeting, Haig went over the opinions discussed at the Nixon White House, which included

[18] John P. MacKenzie, "Court Orders Nixon to Yield Tapes; President Promises to Comply Fully," *Washington Post*, July 25, 1974, from *Washington Post* Politics: The Watergate Story, accessed September 19, 2014, http://www.washingtonpost.com/politics/court-orders-nixon-to-yield-tapes-president-promises-to-comply-fully/2012/06/04/gJQAZSw0IV_story.html.

[19] Ford, *A Time to Heal*, 1-2.

[20] Ibid.

[21] Not even President Nixon's attorney, James St. Clair, had knowledge of the information contained in the requested tapes until shortly before August 1. From Ibid., 2.

[22] Ibid., 6.

[23] Ibid., 5.

[24] Even before Vice President Ford had learned of the "smoking gun" tapes, he had attempted to put as much space between himself and the Watergate controversy as possible, which is one reason Ford took so many trips during his vice presidency as well as to help relieve stress from the political situation at the time. From Hartmann, *Palace Politics*, 122-23.

[25] Ford, *A Time to Heal*, 3.

[26] Ibid.

President Nixon declaring himself temporary disabled under the Twenty-fifth Amendment, pardoning himself before charges are formally made, or being pardoned at a later more appropriate time.[27] Vice President Ford responded with a noncommittal answer, stating "I want some time to think."[28]

Immediately after Haig left Ford's office, Hartmann met with Vice President Ford who informed Hartmann of the discussion.[29] Hartmann responded in shock at the discussion informing Ford that his answer can be interpreted as a consideration for a pardon deal by President Nixon.[30] Hartmann made it clear to Ford that Haig was probing for a reaction concerning a pardon for President Nixon.[31] Hartmann warned Vice President Ford to remain removed from the situation as much as possible.[32] Later that night, in a telephone conversation with Haig, Ford had informed the chief of staff that as vice president, he needed to remain outside of President Nixon's decision-making procedure concerning the reaction to the release of the "smoking gun" tapes.[33][34] Despite all of the frustrations of August 1, Vice President Ford's anger towards President Nixon had not yet reached its peak.

---

[27] Ford, *A Time to Heal*, 3-4.

[28] Ibid., 4.

[29] Ibid.

[30] Hartmann, *Palace Politics*, 130-31.

[31] Ford, *A Time to Heal*, 6-7.

[32] Hartmann, *Palace Politics*, 132-33.

[33] Ibid., 134-135.

[34] During a trip to Mississippi after the August 1 meetings, Ron Nessen (who would later be appointed as the Press Secretary of the Ford White House) recalled that Vice President Ford would not discuss the topic of the Watergate scandal and only mentioned it when asked at a news conference stating his opinion of the matter had not changed. From Nessen, *It Sure Looks Different from the Inside*, 6-7.

By August 5, 1974, President Nixon was still debating "between resignation and attempting to ride it out."[35] Vice President Ford felt that President Nixon's political career was over.[36] The next day President Nixon held a cabinet meeting, where he opened up with "I would like to discuss the most important issue confronting the nation and confronting us internationally too–inflation."[37] The discussions of inflation at the cabinet meeting astounded Ford, who realized that President Nixon did not want face the reality of the Watergate scandal.[38] When President Nixon steered the conservation towards the Watergate scandal, he said he never deliberately broke the law.[39] It was then, that Vice President Ford informed President Nixon in a polite manner, he privately no longer supported Nixon's stance on the Watergate scandal, he would not release his opinion to the public, and he assured Nixon that he still continued to support the President's policies, particularly in foreign affairs.[40] However, President Nixon did not want to discuss the Watergate scandal in detail.[41] Despite the hardship that President Nixon had put upon Vice President Ford within a week, Ford's stress would not decrease.

The following morning, Vice President Ford, at the advice of his long-time friend Phil Buchen, sanctioned a transition team after being personally informed by Haig "to prepare to assume the Office of President." Later, Ford had a meeting with President Nixon

---

[35] Ford, *A Time to Heal*, 16.

[36] Ibid., 17.

[37] Ibid., 18.

[38] Ibid., 18-19.

[39] Ibid., 19.

[40] Henry Kissinger, *Years of Renewal* (New York: Simon & Schuster, 1999), 21.

[41] Ford, *A Time to Heal*, 21.

who gave the soon to be President Ford advice on the running the office and the policies which Ford had claimed to support. First and foremost, President Nixon personally informed Ford that he planning to resign. Numerous issues were discussed, including economic recession, rising rates of inflation, the elimination of price controls, continued support for American allies in Southeast Asia, pursuing an additional Strategic Arms and Limitations Treaty (SALT), and to reinforce ties between North Atlantic Treaty Organization (NATO) members. Conversely, during the meeting with President Nixon, Ford was unable to be ardent towards the President, due to the attitude he had developed during the preceding week. While watching President Nixon announce his intention to resign on national television, Ford became certain that the President's mindset was anywhere but within the real world.[42] With the gargantuan stress that had been placed on his shoulders in the week leading up to his appointment to the Presidency, Ford made more than one oath to the American people during his inauguration.[43]

Sectary of State and National Security Advisor Dr. Henry Kissinger recalled that August 9, 1974 was one of the most remarkable events in the history of the U.S., since the inauguration was organized to signify a new era for the state from every aspect down to the seating.[44] In his augural address, President Ford acknowledged the fact that he came to the highest single office in the U.S. "under extraordinary circumstances," that had never occurred previously in American history and that it affected many Americans.[45] Because

---

[42] Ford concluded that President Nixon was the sole person responsible for his predicament due to Nixon's ignorance to details, passing the micro-level work to others, his preference to not work with others, and his personal ambition. From Ford, *A Time to Heal*, 34-35.

[43] Ford, *A Time to Heal*, 24-25, 28-29, 28-29, 30, 37, and 5.

[44] Kissinger, *Years of Renewal*, 25-26.

President Ford was never elected to office, nor did he make a secret compact to rise to the presidency (based on Ford's account); Ford did not have any debts to repay for past favors for the Oval Office.[46]

Next, President Ford promised to perform the role of a trustee to the American Nation. Ford brings up a quote from Thomas Jefferson who stated "the people are the only sure reliance for the preservation of our liberty."[47] Furthermore, President Ford pledged to be a trustee by expressing his opinion, but to include the American Public's voices into great consideration in Ford's decision making process.[48] Unlike Nixon in 1968, President Ford does not make the ambitious declaration to bring about peace within his presidency. Although, Ford does state that the pursuit for peace while protecting Americans as well as human freedom will be a top priority in his presidency.[49] It can only be accomplished by moving forward as a nation and leaving past grievances behind.[50]

President Ford then went into a very brief discussion on how honesty keeps society together, vowed to be open to the American Public, and uttered the most well-known line of his address: "My fellow Americans, our long national nightmare is over."[51] With above mentioned line, President Ford vows as a professional, to not govern nor behave as Nixon

---

[45] Speakers' Notes, Swearing-In Ceremony: Inaugural Address, President Gerald R. Ford, August 9, 1974, folder "8/9/74 – Swearing-in Ceremony," Box 1, from the President's Speeches and Statements: Reading Copies, 1974-1977, Gerald R. Ford Library, Ann Arbor, Michigan, 2, accessed May 24, 2015, http://www.fordlibrarymuseum.gov/library/document/0122/1252055.pdf.

[46] Ibid., 5-6.

[47] Ibid., 7.

[48] Ibid., 8.

[49] Ibid., 9-10.

[50] Ibid.

[51] Ibid., 11-12.

had done during his Presidency. Even within his speech, President Ford makes a direct connection to the Watergate scandal through the "nightmare is over" line. President Ford describes, that through Watergate, a rift in American society had developed which in turn caused "suspicion and hate" of one another due to the prolonged agony of the Watergate scandal.[52]

In a fifty page presentation developed, by President Ford's transition team, the top ambitions of the Ford Presidency, which listed the number one goal in its preface being the "restoration of confidence and trust of the American people in their political leadership, intuitions and processes."[53] Watergate had discredited the American presidency which the American public had little or no trust in the institution.[54] Clearly, President Ford recognized the distrust of government authority within American society which had expanded during the Watergate scandal and was a major concern to the President himself.

Despite the vow to not govern like Nixon, President Ford asked the American public to forgive Nixon.[55] The request to absolve Nixon may have been political on President Ford's part since he did originally feel that the "nightmare is over" line was too harsh until Hartmann convinced Ford that the line was to put things into perspective for his audience.[56] Conversely, keeping in theme with President Ford's inaugural address, that forgiving Nixon would be a way to continue on as a nation in order to fulfill the goal of restoring the

[52] Speakers' Notes, Swearing-In Ceremony: Inaugural Address, President Ford, August 9, 1974,

[53] Hartmann, *Palace Politics*, 165.

[54] William Colby with James McCargar, *Lost Victory: A First Hand Account of America's Sixteen Year Involvement in Vietnam* (Chicago: Contemporary Books, 1989), 348.

[55] Speaker's Notes, Swearing-In Ceremony: Inaugural Address, President Ford, 13-14.

[56] Ford, *A Time to Heal*, 26.

American public's faith their government. Finally, President Ford distinctly reassures Americans that their system of government set forth by the U.S. Constitution will be put to use to benefit the American Public through his efforts.[57]

President Nixon's achievement in reaching a peace agreement in Southeast Asia was short lived since he became involved in the Watergate scandal. When evidence of President Nixon's attempted cover up of the Watergate scandal was about to be released to a federal court. President Nixon had tried to save his presidency. In the end, President Nixon had chosen to resign from the presidency and allow Ford to take the responsibilities of his former position. In response to the Watergate scandal, President Ford made a vow that he would not govern as Nixon had before him. Starting a new era of American politics.

---

[57] Ford, *A Time to Heal*, page 15.

The goal of the U.S. during Nixon's presidency was for the U.S. to withdraw from the

Vietnam War and create an acceptable conclusion to the conflict for the United States. Therefore,

the Nixon Administration pursued the policy of Vietnamization, where U.S. armed forces

modernized and develop strategies to expand RVNAF. The Nixon Administration had hoped

through Vietnamization, the RVN would at the very least take on a larger role in combat

operations. Meanwhile, the U.S. held secret negotiations with the DRV for a peace agreement,

which later became known as the PPA. During the negotiations for PPA, the DRV delegation

stalled progress in the process and refused to compromise their demands. In retaliation of the

DRV's intentional delays in the PPA negotiations, President Nixon escalated American air

campaigns against the DRV until the Communist Vietnamese agreed to sign the document. A

precarious situation created by decision makers in order to achieve a peace agreement for the

RVN.

The DRV intended to continue on with their efforts to conquer the RVN, despite signing

the PPA. While the U.S. Congress made efforts to prevent American re-entry into the Vietnam

War. President Ford wanted to separate himself from Nixon by implementing new policies to

help resolve other issues that were facing the American public. However, the issues of the

Vietnam War did not fade away as many people had hoped. While the PPA was formally signed

on January 27, 1973, President Nixon's "peace with honor" quickly became hollowed words.[1]

The emptiness of President Nixon's declaration lay in part within the PPA itself.

---

[1] Willbanks, *Abandoning Vietnam*, 187-88.

One of the most prominent features of the PPA was the withdrawal of American and

other South East Asian Treaty Organization (SEATO) military forces from the RVN. Article

Five of the PPA described the withdrawal of SEATO forces as a complete extraction all the way

down to paramilitary and police units "within sixty days of the signing of" the PPA.[2] With the

PPA, American military involvement came to an end, which led many observers to believe that

peace had finally come to Southeast Asia.

The PPA alone created an extremely fragile peace. Article Three of the PPA called for all

warring Vietnamese associations to hold their then controlled territory when the ceasefire went

into effect.[3] Article Three alone does not create an incentive for the RVN, DRV, or NLF to

preserve a ceasefire. The DRV considered the circumstances created by the PPA to create a very

opportunistic period for them.[4] Since Vietnamese communist forces could legally retain their

territorial gains by the end of January 1973 within the borders of the RVN.[5] After years of

conflict between the RVN and the NLF, it is difficult to imagine that the two parties would

accept Article Three for the purpose of peace alone. Theoretically, for the Provisionary

Revolutionary Government (PRG) to finally have legal territory, it could further develop its

military wing, the People's Liberation Armed Forces (PLAF), in the open without interference.

The PRG was the governing wing of the NLF, which was founded in 1969, and was

recognized by nearly 30 different states, particularly communist states to be the legitimate

---

[2] "Protocol Concerning the Cease-fire in South Vietnam and the Joint Military Commission," *American Society of International Law* Volume 67, Number 2 (April, 1973): 390, accessed September 26, 2014, Stable URL: http://www.jstor.org/stable/2199475.

[3] Ibid., 390.

[4] Military History Institute of Vietnam, *Victory in Vietnam: The Official History of the People's Army of Vietnam, 1954-1975,* translated by Merle L. Pribbenow, (Lawrence, Kansas: University of Kansas, 2002), 333.

[5] Ibid.

government of the Vietnamese people south of the DMZ.[6] From the standpoint of the RVN, President Thieu was leery of the PPA and President Nixon because he had threatened to cut off all American aid to the RVN if Thieu did not accept the terms of the PPA.[7] However, Article Three does not give the RVN any incentive to preserve the peace since it allows the NLF to legally retain territory of the RVN. Even though other articles of the PPA placed expectations on the RVN and the NLF to create a lasting peace between them.

Articles Ten through Thirteen discuss the purpose along with the function of the National Council of National Reconciliation and Concord (NCNRC), whose two-party memberships would consist of the RVN as well as the PRG. The PPA describes the purpose of NCNRC, to resolve the conflict between the RVN and the PRG through a democratic election to determine the future of the Vietnamese nation south of the DMZ. The problem with the NCNRC as described by the PPA was the peace agreement did not form the NCNRC itself; the RVN and the PRG simply agreed to form the council shortly after the ceasefire. Both the RVN and the PRG were expected, as described by Article Thirteen, to reduce their military forces. Again, with the long history of conflict between the RVN and the PRG along with Article Three of the PPA, the success of the NCNRC seemed unlikely. Similar expectations for peace were placed on the RVN and the DRV as well.[8]

As the PPA did not create a firm peace agreement between the RVN and the NLF, the document also did not create firm peace between the two Vietnamese states. The PPA asserted that the DRV was to respect the sovereignty of the RVN and to withdraw its military forces.[9]

---

[6] R. B. St. John, "Marxist-Leninist Theory and Organization in South Vietnam," *Asian Survey* Volume 20, Number 8 (August, 1980): 826, August 18, 2014, Stable URL: http://www.jstor.org/stable/2643636.

[7] Kissinger, *Ending the Vietnam War*, 427.

[8] "Protocol Concerning the Cease-fire in South Vietnam and the Joint Military Commission," 392.

Article Fifteen of the PPA placed further expectations on the RVN and the DRV to pursue

reunification through peaceful means.[10] Reunification was a major goal of the DRV. Within the

official history of PAVN, written by the Military Institute of Vietnam, it stated the PPA allowed

the DRV to rebuild PAVN in order to "liberate" "the entire (Vietnamese) nation" from the

RVN.[11] The RVN on the other hand, had very few incentives to reunify with the DRV. Since the

DRV had introduced war into the boundaries of the RVN for several years. However, Article

Fifteen states that the RVN and the DRV had to start negotiations shortly after the PPA was

signed.[12] As with the situation of the NCNRC, peaceful reunification of the Vietnamese nation

under one state seemed unlikely in the post-PPA period. Although flawed in many respects, the

PPA did have a major strength of enforcing peace within Southeast Asia.

Another important aspect of the PPA was the fact that the document considered the DRV

to be a foreign power. Article Nine of the PPA states that both the U.S. and the DRV would not

interfere with the internal politics of the Vietnamese nation south of the DMZ.[13] Article One of

the PPA affirms that the territorial boundaries and sovereignty of the two Vietnam states shall be

honored by the international community as described in the 1954 Geneva Agreements on

Vietnam.[14] The 1954 Agreements defined the border between the two Vietnams as a five

kilometer long DMZ at the seventeenth parallel with the communist forces moving north of the

---

[9] "Protocol Concerning the Cease-fire in South Vietnam and the Joint Military Commission," 390-91.

[10] Ibid., 393.

[11] Military History Institute of Vietnam, *Victory in Vietnam*, 333.

[12] "Protocol Concerning the Cease-fire in South Vietnam and the Joint Military Commission," 393.

[13] Ibid., 391.

[14] "Protocol Concerning the Cease-fire in South Vietnam and the Joint Military Commission," 389.

DMZ, while the French forces withdrew to the south.[15] Separate agreements were made

concerning the independence of Laos and Cambodia at the 1954 Geneva Conference.[16] Further

agreements were made in Geneva concerning Laos during 1962.[17] Articles Ten through Thirteen

of the PPA specifically focus on the RVN and the NLF working together in order to establish a

lasting peace, not the DRV.[18] Tied to the strength of the PPA's view of the DRV was a technical

issue.

The status of the NLF and the interpretation of the organization by the PPA were

problematic. The NLF was founded by the ruling Lao Dong Party of the DRV in December of

1960 to form an armed united socialist organization to establish a communist regime south of the

DMZ, after some southern socialist organizations had sought greater participation in government

for the peasantry.[19] Covertly, twelve southern communists were selected by the Lao Dong Party

to partake in the membership of the party's central committee.[20] The NLF's membership was

made up of Vietnamese from Southern Vietnam located within the RVN.[21] The NLF was

directed by the DRV's Lao Dong Party and had little autonomy after the formation of the

People's Revolutionary Party (PRP), the political wing of the NLF in 1962.[22] On the other hand,

---

[15] Alan Watt, "The Geneva Agreements 1954 in Relation to Vietnam," *The Australian Quarterly*, Volume 39, Number 2, (June, 1967): 12-13, accessed November 30, 2014, Stable URL: http://www.jstor.org.ezproxy.emich.edu/stable/20634125.

[16] Kenneth L. Hill, "Laos: The Vientiane Agreement," *Journal of Southeast Asian History,* Volume 8, Number 2 (September, 1967): 259, accessed November 30, 2014, Stable URL: http://www.jstor.org.ezproxy.emich.edu/stable/20067631.

[17] "Protocol Concerning the Cease-fire in South Vietnam and the Joint Military Commission," 396.

[18] Ibid., 392.

[19] St. John, "Marxist-Leninist Thoery and Organization in South Vietnam," 817.

[20] Ibid., 817.

[21] Ibid., 818.

[22] Ibid., 818 and 821.

PPA interprets the NLF was an independent organization since the document states that the NLF could retain its armed forces, territorial gains, and was expected to form the NCNRC with the RVN for a long term peace agreement. The technical issue over the NLF within the PPA created a loophole in the sense that the DRV could claim that PAVN was a part of the NLF, which would allow PAVN forces to maintain their positions.

As a countermeasure, the PPA did establish a committee to observe the post-PPA period. The purpose of the ICCS was to create documentation that the PPA was being enforced to the U.S., the RVN, the DRV, and the PRG. Some of the focuses of the ICCS were to ensure that the ceasefire was being observed, no foreign interference occurred, and that replacement for military supplies were followed properly.[23]

Under Article Seven, both the RVN and the NLF could not import military supplies unless the supplies were replacement parts due to the wear of a goods' use on a one for one ratio. As of January 27, 1973, the ICCS consisted of four states: Canada, the Republic of Indonesia, the Polish People's Republic, and the Hungarian People's Republic, two pro-Western states working with two pro-Eastern states. However, "the organization, means of activity, and expenditures of the" ICCS was left to the group's members to decide on how to carry out its duties as described in the PPA. Since the protocol for the ICCS was left to the discretion of the group's members, the organization was highly dependent upon cooperation between its members. The function of the ICCS was solely focused on Vietnam, whereas the PPA branched out into other Southeast Asian states.[24]

---

[23] "Protocol Concerning the Cease-fire in South Vietnam and the Joint Military Commission," 390-91, and 395-96.

[24] Ibid.

The PPA had included one article on the states of the Khmer Republic (KR) and the

Kingdom of Laos (KL). Article Twenty explained that all foreign states will cease all military

activities within the KR and the KL. The sovereignty as well as security of both the KR and the

KL was to be respected by all foreign states including their internal conflicts. Essentially, the

PPA's Article Twenty banned foreign intervention into the KR and the KL. Although the PPA

has several positive passages, there was only one incentive for Southeast Asian states to uphold

the PPA.[25]

Outside of a genuine desire for peace, the only enticement for the RVN, the DRV, and

other states concerned to enforce the PPA, was American money. In order to gain the RVN's

approval for the PPA under President Thieu, President Nixon had to threaten Thieu that all

American aid to the RVN would be completely cut.[26] Under Article Seven, the RVN could

replace its military supplies on a one for one ratio.[27] The RVN could also, under Article

Fourteen, receive "economic and technical aid form any country (state) with no political

conditions attached."[28] The expectation from the RVN was that the U.S. would be a major

supplier for their aid. As for the DRV, Article Twenty-One specifies that the U.S. "will

contribute … to postwar reconstruction of the Democratic Republic of Vietnam and throughout

Indochina (Southeast Asia)."[29]

The language used in the PPA along with President Nixon's pressure on President Thieu,

both the Nationalist and Communist Vietnamese had to be bribed by the U.S. to, in theory,

---

[25] "Protocol Concerning the Cease-fire in South Vietnam and the Joint Military Commission," 396-97.

[26] Kissinger, *Ending the Vietnam War*, 427.

[27] "Protocol Concerning the Cease-fire in South Vietnam and the Joint Military Commission," 390-91.

[28] Ibid., 393.

[29] Ibid., 397.

uphold the PPA. The RVN was reluctant to accept the PPA due to fears of being enabled to defend the Nationalist Vietnamese state.[30] For the Vietnamese Communists, it was a major policy goal to conquer the RVN.[31] Since the PPA relied on American funding in order to be respected by the Vietnamese parties, it was a weak agreement, since it only created a ceasefire and stipulated that the Vietnamese parties needed to create their own formal peace agreements. When President Nixon had informed the American public that an honorable peace had been achieved in Southeast Asia, it was only on paper.[32]

The ceasefire was to be in effect by midnight Greenwich Mean Time January 27, 1973.[33] However, the ceasefire was broken by both the RVN and the DRV in an effort to control greater portions of territory.[34] The land grab campaigns began shortly before the effective date of the ceasefire, initially with PAVN and the NLF.[35] RVNAF responded to the communist land grab campaigns with counter attacks.[36] Both the Nationalist and Communist Vietnamese continued to seek out the greatest amount of territory between one another even after the agreed upon implementation of the cease-fire.[37] In a report on the validly of the Hamlet Evaluation Surveys (HES), Major Wayne A. Downing of the Office of the Assistant to the Secretary of Defense

---

[30] Kissinger, *Ending the Vietnam War*, 354.

[31] Military History Institute of Vietnam, *Victory in Vietnam*, 333.

[32] Nixon, "12 – Address to the Nation Announcing Conclusion of an Agreement on Ending the War and Restoring Peace in Vietnam, January 23, 1973."

[33] Kissinger, *Ending the Vietnam War*, 441.

[34] Ibid.

[35] Parker, "Vietnam and Soviet Asian Strategy," 106.

[36] George J. Veith, *Black April: The Fall of South Vietnam, 1973-1975* (New York: Encounter Books, 2012), 40.

[37] Kissinger, *Ending the Vietnam War*, 441.

described the ceasefire in Vietnam as "an amorphous mess," just three days after when the ceasefire went into effect.[38]

Even after another ceasefire was agreed upon for June 15, 1973, both the Nationalists and the Communist Vietnamese continued combat activities.[39] The violations of the second ceasefire were on a smaller scale.[40] The continuation of the Vietnam War during the post-PPA period was due to policy goals of the RVN and the DRV. Among the Nationalists, President Thieu insisted upon defending the greatest amount of territory within the RVN's defined international borders.[41] The DRV on the other hand, refused to abandon its goal of conquering the RVN and reunifying the Vietnamese nation under a communist state.[42] The violations made by the Vietnamese parties were tests on the strength of the PPA.

In order to enforce the PPA, the ICCS was created to monitor and report on ceasefire violations under Article Eighteen of the PPA.[43] The ICCS quickly became an international body without a meaningful function since the organization was unable to enforce the PPA.[44] The communist members of the ICCS refused to acknowledge that the DRV and the NLF were in violation of the PPA.[45] Quite often, the pro-West members' observations did not have the

---

[38] Letter, Major Wayne A. Downing to Major Jack Pellicci, January 30, 1973, Folder One, HES Question Elimination Study, 4A, Entry# A1 531: General Records; 1969 – 1975, Box Three, HES Question Elimination Study, 1973 through Reconstruction and Development Conference/ Independence Palace (Second Copy) 27 July, 1973, Record Group 472 U.S. Forces in Southeast Asia, 1950-1975, MACV, HQ CORDS/ Special Assistant to U.S. Ambassador for Field Operations (SAAFO), National Archives, College Park, Maryland.

[39] RVNAF Quarterly Assessment: Fourth Quarter, Fiscal Year, 1973, Defense Attaché, Saigon, MG John Murray, 1-8.

[40] Ibid.

[41] Quang Dan, "The Vietnam Experience," 269.

[42] Military History Institute of Vietnam, *Victory in Vietnam*, 333.

[43] "Protocol Concerning the Cease-fire in South Vietnam and the Joint Military Commission," 395-96.

[44] Willbanks, *Abandoning Vietnam,* 192.

support within the ICCS to be included in official reports, which caused Canada to leave the organization and was replaced by Imperial Iran.[46] General Thi noted that after Polish and Hungarian observers had completed their inspection of his command, his troops were quickly bombarded by communist artillery fire.[47] The observance of the pro-West members of the ICCS was furthermore hindered by the DRV and the NLF refusal to allow observers to completely inspect communist territory.[48] The weakness of the PPA became clear shortly after the effective ceasefire date, particularly since the document lacked the commitment from the RVN, the DRV, and the PRG. Thus, allowing the Vietnam War to enter another phase.

Initially, the PPA was seen as a triumph of humanity, ushering peace to a region marred by war. The hopes of peace were quickly dashed when the scheduled ceasefires failed to encourage the Nationalist and Communist Vietnamese to conclude the Vietnam War. Upon closer inspection, it is clear the PPA lacks strong incentive for the Vietnamese parties to enforce the peace. The PPA itself did not firmly establish peace, but an agreement to pursue peace. The Nationalist and Communist Vietnamese lacked a true desire to create a firm peace agreement. From the actions of the Vietnamese parties, the only clear incentive to even consider adhering to the PPA was American funding. Even by creating the ICCS, the PPA failed to create transparency in the Vietnamese peace process.

---

[45] Lam Quang Thi, *The Twenty-Five Year Century*, 295.

[46] Ibid., 295-96.

[47] Ibid.

[48] Ibid., 294-295.

Chapter Four: Money

During 1973, the Vietnam War entered into a phase of economic development. Where the two Vietnams were attempting to undermine one another through the promise of greater livelihood for the populace. Both the Saigon and Hanoi utilized economic development to strengthen their respective states. However, one Vietnam would employ its development for an offensive. Shortly after the ceasefire date, the DRV and the PRG initiated their economic development.[1] Within the DRV's politburo, the prevailing opinion was to continue on the Vietnam War through political struggle after the failure of the 1972 Easter Offensive.[2] Political struggle was a strategy utilized by the DRV which focused on guerrilla warfare, underground cells, and propaganda.[3] Through political struggle, the DRV in theory, would have time to develop a stronger economy, which in turn would aid in the material development of future military offensives.[4]

During the 1974 February National Assembly, Vice Premier Le Thanh Nghi announced the DRV's economic plans to rebuild the DRV after years of conflict that would carry through 1975 in order to prepare for a five-year economic plan set to begin in 1976. The DRV's announcement in February 1974 was a major break in the Lao Dong Party's economic planning since it was the first time the Hanoi made economic plans for more than one year based on the

---

[1] RVNAF Quarterly Assessment: Third Quarter, Fiscal Year, 1974, Defense Attaché, Saigon, Major General John Murray, 1-1, Folder One 228-07/ RVNAF Quarterly Assessment/ Third Quarter, Fiscal Year 1974, Entry #A1 1727: RVNAF Quarterly Assessment Reports: 1973-1975, Third Quarter 1974 through Second Quarter 1975, Box Two, DAO, Ops and Plans Division/ Readiness Section, Record Group 472, U.S. Forces in Southeast Asia, 1950-1975, National Archives, College Park, Maryland.

[2] Veith, *Black April*, 37-38.

[3] Ibid., 36.

[4] Ibid., 37-38.

their available military supplies. The 1974 plan called for the civilian economy to be combined with the DRV's military. An eighty-three percent increase of civilians into technical training programs in order to increase the number of skilled laborers, a fifty percent increase from the DRV state into the production of capital goods, and an increase of the Gross National Product (GNP) of the DRV by twenty-one percent. Public display of a desire for a stronger economy did not mean that the DRV had abandoned its long standing goals.[5]

When the DRV had announced their economic plans, they displayed the long-standing desire for renunciation of the Vietnamese nation under a communist state through actions as well. During the early days of the ceasefire, PAVN was still infiltrating units into Communist held territory as replacements. In 1973, the Defense Attaché Office (DAO) of the U.S. Embassy in Saigon reported that PAVN infiltration into the RVN through its international boundaries was down by thirty-seven percent from 1972 in all border areas. Except through the northern two provinces of MRI, where infiltration had increased to 9,000 men. Along the Ho Chi Minh Trail, PAVN was holding fourteen tanks in Laos in what appeared, at the time, to be held in reserve.[6]

Along with infiltration, the DRV was active in shipping military supplies into communist held territory inside the RVN.[7] Roughly running parallel to the Ho Chi Minh Trail, the DRV was active in expanding its oil pipeline to supply mechanized PAVN units in the two Northern provinces of the RVN.[8] Within the first nine months of 1973, PAVN had shipped eighty thousand tons of military supplies and forty-five thousand tons of "civilian supplies" down the

---

[5] RVNAF Quarterly Assessment: Third Quarter, Fiscal Year, 1974, Defense Attaché, Saigon, MG John Murray, 1-1 and 1-2.

[6] RVNAF Quarterly Assessment: Fourth Quarter, Fiscal Year, 1973, Defense Attaché, Saigon, MG John Murray, 1-3 and 1-4.

[7] Ibid.

[8] Ibid., 1-5.

Ho Chi Minh Trail.[9] Among the infiltrated PAVN units were two artillery regiments,[10] which were deployed within range of Pleiku City, Bein Hoa, and Tay Ninh.[11] In addition, PAVN was repairing airfields and deploying surface to air missile sites within communist territory.[12] PAVN was still launching attacks against RVNAF; conversely, the frequency and scale of the attacks had diminished.[13] Additionally, PAVN was unable to conduct a large military offensive and to critically damage RVNAF.[14] While Hanoi was solidifying its positions south of the DMZ through PAVN, the Lao Dong Party also utilizing the NLF's PRG to improve the communist hold over their newfound gains from the PPA.

Since the signing ceremony of the PPA, the PRG behaved more as a legitimate state government by carrying out the functions of a state in the open as opposed to underground cells. A major driving force behind the reasons why the PRG functioned as a legitimate government than previously was due to its interpretation of the PPA, where the organization believed that communist held territory within the RVN was sovereign land for the Communist Vietnamese.[15] The vast majority of communist-held land within the RVN was rural, lightly populated,

---

[9] Military History Institute of Vietnam, *Victory in Vietnam*, 338-39.

[10] Ibid., 339.

[11] RVNAF Quarterly Assessment: Fourth Quarter, Fiscal Year, 1973, Defense Attaché, Saigon, MG John Murray, 1-7 and 1-8.

[12] Ibid., 1-1 and 1-2.

[13] RVNAF Quarterly Assessment: Fourth Quarter, Fiscal Year, 1973, Defense Attaché, Saigon, MG John Murray, 1-11 and 1-12 and Military History Institute of Vietnam, *Victory in Vietnam*, 339.

[14] Ibid. and Ibid.

[15] Intelligence Report Draft on PRG Land, 1, October 26, 1973, Folder five, The PRG's in Vietnam, 1973, Entry # A1 531: General Records; 1969-1975, Box 3, HES Question Elimination Study, 1973 through Reconstruction and Development Conference/ Independence Place (Second Copy), 27 July, 1973, MACV, Headquarters CORDS/ Special Assistant to U.S. Ambassador for Field Operations (SAAFO), Record Group 0472 U.S. Forces in Southeast Asia, 1950-1975, National Archives, College Park, Maryland.

mountainous, and/or jungle country typically along the RVN's long Western overland border.[16]

Within Communist Vietnamese territory in the RVN, the PRG governed two percent of the total

Vietnamese population south of the DMZ, which created a weak power base of support for the

PRG.[17]

Under Hanoi's direction, the PRG participated in PAVN's solidification of communist-

held territory within the RVN.[18] Despite the fact that both organizations were in violation of the

PPA. In one aspect of solidifying its hold on territory, the PRG attempted to become self-reliant

in food production by raising rice within its territory.[19] However, the PRG was unsuccessful in

its agriculture program in 1973 due to the lack of irrigation and fertilizers.[20] Another aspect of

the PRG attempting to develop an independent economy was taxation.[21] The PRG had a goal of

collecting "an estimated 13.5 billion piasters" in taxes and goods.[22] Which by July 27, 1973, the

PRG had collected five thousand-four hundred million in taxes, consisting mostly of agricultural

products.[23] To help break its reliance on the DRV, the PRG purchased goods from local

producers near communist-held territory.[24] Which was also an attempt to undermine the

---

[16] Intelligence Report Draft on PRG Land, 1.

[17] Ibid., 1-2.

[18] Ibid.

[19] Ibid., 3.

[20] Ibid., 3.

[21] Reconstruction and Development Conference Presentations at the Independence Palace, Section G, 1-2, July 27, 1973, Folder seven, Reconstruction and Development Conference/ Independence Palace (Second Copy), July 27, 1973, Entry # A1 531: General Records; 1969-1975, Box 3, HES Question Elimination Study, 1973 through Reconstruction and Development Conference/ Independence Place (Second Copy), 27 July, 1973, MACV, Headquarters CORDS/ Special Assistant to U.S. Ambassador for Field Operations (SAAFO), Record Group 0472 U.S. Forces in Southeast Asia, 1950-1975, National Archives, College Park, Maryland.

[22] Ibid., Section G, 4.

[23] Ibid.

authority of the RVN by taking away goods that could have been taxed by Nationalist Vietnamese agency.[25] Through the efforts to function as a legitimate government, the PRG was attempting to rebuild the NLF into a formidable force in the post-Tet Offensive period.[26]

Nineteen seventy-three was a period of rebuilding for the DRV and the NLF. Despite signing the PPA, both the DRV and the NLF made numerous violations to weaken the RVN.[27] While it was clear that the Communist Vietnamese were preparing for another offensive and far-reaching political struggle, they were still unable to launch a large military offensive.[28] In light of the violations of the PPA made by the DRV and the NLF, the U.S. had the political tool of economic aid to help uphold the peace agreement.

As described in Article Twenty-One of the PPA, the U.S. would provide economic aid to rebuild the DRV in the post-PPA period.[29] In February 1973, Dr. Kissinger traveled to Hanoi to discuss with the DRV's Politburo of forming a stronger diplomatic relationship and adherence of the PPA by its signatories.[30] While conversing with DRV Prime Minister Pham Van Dong on the PPA, Dr. Kissinger picked up on the DRV's lack of commitment to the peace agreement and

---

[24] Reconstruction and Development Conference Presentations at the Independence Palace, Section G, 3-4.

[25] Ibid.

[26] Ibid., Section G, 5.

[27] Central Reconstruction and Development Council of the Republic of Vietnam, Community Reconstruction and Development Plan, 1973, 1, Folder three, 1601-11A Community Reconstruction and Local Development Plan, 1973, Entry # A1 531: General Records; 1969-1975, Box Two, 228-08/ Ceasefire Violations and Related Items/ Monthly, March – December, 1973 Through 228-08/ HES Airgram, May, 1973 – January, 1975, MACV, Headquarters CORDS/ Special Assistant to the U.S. Ambassador for Field Operations (SAAFO), Record Group 472 U.S. Forces in Southeast Asia, 1950-1975, National Archives, College Park, Maryland.

[28] RVNAF Quarterly Assessment: Fourth Quarter, Fiscal Year, 1973, Defense Attaché, Saigon, MG John Murray, 1-11 and 1-12.

[29] "Protocol Concerning the Cease-fire in South Vietnam and the Joint Military Commission," 397.

[30] Kissinger, *Ending the Vietnam War*, 433.

would continue the Vietnam War.[31] However, Dr. Kissinger found that the DRV's politburo was quick to adhere to Article Twenty-one and requested the full $7.5 billion that the Nixon Administration had budgeted for economic aid in support of all of Southeast Asia.[32] Dr. Kissinger was able to convince the DRV politburo to accept $3.25 billion in economic aid, but Prime Minister Dong insisted that the aid to the DRV was to be unconditional.[33]

Despite Dr. Kissinger's efforts to inform Prime Minister Dong about the American constitutional process concerning budget procedures. Prime Minister Dong was not persuaded until Dr. Kissinger agreed to setting up a "Joint Economic Commission," which would further develop economic agreements between the U.S. and the DRV, before American Congressional approval.[34] As the DRV continued to violate the PPA and the knowledge of the horrific treatment of American POWs by the Communist Vietnamese became public knowledge, the U.S. Congress refused to approve any form of economic aid for the DRV.[35] Thus eliminating the DRV's observance of Article Twenty-One of the PPA. While the Communist Vietnamese were gaining strength by violating the PPA and without American funding, the RVN had their own plans to create greater stability.

In response to the DRV's and the NLF's economic development in their hamlets within the RVN, the Nationalist Vietnamese responded with their own four-year economic and development plan. In 1972, the RVN launched its Four-Year National Economic Plan, by creating modest gains in the agricultural and manufacturing sectors of the Nationalist

---

[31] Kissinger, *Ending the Vietnam War*, 440-41.

[32] Ibid., 446-47.

[33] Ibid., 448-49.

[34] Ibid., 450.

[35] Ibid., 469.

Vietnamese economy at the expense of the service sector within the GNP.[36] While drafting plans

for the economy, the RVN sought to create economic reforms while the plans were being

implicated in Nationalist Vietnamese policy.

The overall goal of the economic plans and reforms of the Nationalist Vietnamese

economy was to slowly dismantle the state's strong control over the economy to a more open

market system.[37] Economic reforms were carried out by the RVN due to the growth of the black

market, Vietnamization, a rising inflation rate, the desire to reduce the state's budget, poor

economic planning by the state officials, and the lack of public funds for economic development,

leading to the prevailing opinion amongst Nationalist Vietnamese government officials that the

private sector could fill the void that the state created in economic development, if enabled to do

so.[38] Through economic planning and reforms, the RVN state government sought to create an

economically independent state.[39]

The Nationalist Vietnamese intellectual Le Hoang Trong strongly supported the goals

that the RVN state government had set.[40] However, Trong argued the RVN should seek out loans

from the U.S. to create greater incentive for the RVN to utilize the funds more wisely, while

continuing American aid to address the threat the Nationalists faced from the Communist

Vietnamese.[41] The RVN went as far as to write an Eight-Year National Economic Plan to not

---

[36] Nguyen Anh Tuan, *South Vietnam Trial and Experience: A Challenge for Development* (Athens, Ohio: Ohio University Center for International Studies, 1988), 190-91.

[37] Ibid., 195.

[38] Ibid., 195-96.

[39] Nguyen Anh Tuan, *South Vietnam Trial and Experience*, 184.

[40] Le Hoang Trong, "Survival and Self-Reliance: A Vietnamese Viewpoint," *Asian Survey* Volume 15, Number 4 (April, 1975): 281-82, accessed January 12, 2014, Stable URL: http://www.jstor.org/stable/2643234.

[41] Ibid.

only induce economic development, but to repair the damages caused by the Vietnam War during the "peace" expected after the signing of the PPA.[42] Despite the optimism of the RVN, the grim reality quickly clashed the with RVN's outlook.

No matter how well thought-out the economic plans of the RVN were, the plans failed to anticipate later developments. Some of the developments were the American military withdrawal from Southeast Asia and the continuation of the Vietnam War. The Four-Year Economic Plan was still dependent on foreign aid, particularly from the U.S.[43] Additionally, the Four-Year Plan was not initially developed for a period after an American military withdraw, described within the PPA.[44] In 1972, American aid for the RVN totaled 32.8 million in U.S. dollars; whereas, American aid decreased to a total of 16.9 million U.S. dollars in 1974.[45] During 1973, the GNP of the RVN was believed to be 1,250 billion piasters, while the RVN's consumption level at the same time was at 1,350 billion piasters, which created a shortfall of 250 billion piasters after subtracting investment expenditures.[46] With the American military withdraw from the Vietnam War, the RVN economy lost an estimated $300 to $400 million U.S. dollars in its Gross Domestic Product (GDP).[47]

While foreign aid to the RVN was decreasing, the inflation rate was increasing, which greatly diminished the standard of living for the Nationalist Vietnamese.[48] General Thi recalled

---

[42] Nguyen Anh Tuan, *South Vietnam Trial and Experience*, 191.

[43] Ibid., 190-91.

[44] Ibid.

[45] Ibid., 218.

[46] Reconstruction and Development Conference Presentations at the Independence Palace, Section I, 1.

[47] Nguyen Anh Tuan, *South Vietnam Trial and Experience*, 213.

[48] Reconstruction and Development Conference Presentations at the Independence Palace, Section I, 1-2.

that inflation became so severe that several of his soldiers of numerous ranks had to take up

second jobs in order to support their families.[49] Inflation could be seen on the official foreign

currency exchange rate, where in December of 1972 the official rate was 465 Vietnamese

piasters for one U.S. dollar.[50] Whereas, in December, 1974, the official exchange rate was 700

Vietnamese piasters for one U.S. dollar.[51] The official exchange rate had surpassed the black

market exchange rate of 1974 by fifteen piasters.[52] Nineteen seventy-three marked the first time

that the official exchange rate of Nationalist Vietnamese piasters for U.S. dollars surpassed the

black market rate.[53] The decreasing amount of foreign aid and the lack of well-constructed

economic planning were not the only causes to the RVN's economic woes; it was affected by

international developments as well.

Nineteen seventy-three was not only a pivotal year for the Vietnam War; it was also a

pivotal year in international politics. Since 1973 marked the first time a group of developing

states could challenge the industrialized West. The developing states who took on Western

supremacy in international politics were for the most part the Arabic member states of the

Organization of Petroleum Exporting Countries (OPEC) through an artificial increase in the price

of light crude oil.[54] OPEC was established to create steady as well as reasonable prices for

member states' petroleum products from consumer states during the period of decolonization of

---

[49] Lam Quang Thi, *The Twenty-Five Year Century*, 321.

[50] Nguyen Anh Tuan, *South Vietnam Trial and Experience*, 207.

[51] Ibid.

[52] Ibid.

[53] Ibid.

[54] Charles Issawi, "The 1973 Oil Crisis and After," *Journal of Post Keynesian Economic* Volume 1, Number 2 (Winter, 1978-1979): 15-16, accessed January 9, 2015, stable URL: http://www.jstor.org/stable/4537467.

the post-World War Two era and to prevent foreign oil companies from dominating the petroleum market.[55]

After the Yom Kippur War in 1973, several Southwest Asian OPEC member states choose to increase the price a barrel of oil from $3.01 to $5.12 in U.S. dollars on October 16, 1973.[56] The OPEC price increase was quickly followed by reduced production, among Arabic member states by twenty-five percent and an oil embargo on the U.S. and the Kingdom of the Netherlands.[57] The embargo was created due to American and Dutch political support for the State of Israel, since several Arabic OPEC members states believed that Israeli aggression was reason why the Yom Kippur War broke out.[58] By the last weeks of 1973, the price for a barrel of oil had reached $11.65 in U.S. dollars, which caused numerous states to panic and to quickly expand their oil reserves.[59] Although the oil crisis of 1973 was to target the West, the crisis also affected the developing world.

For the RVN, the 1973 Oil Crisis wreaked havoc on its economy.[60] The oil crisis had pushed the RVN economy into a recession in 1974.[61] VNAF had grounded two fighter squadrons due to aviation fuel rationing.[62] By 1975, VNAF's transportation mobility was limited to a

---

[55] "Organization of the Petroleum Exporting Countries: Brief History," Organization of the Petroleum Exporting Countries, modified 2016, accessed April 23, 2016, http://www.opec.org/opec_web/en/about_us/24.htm.

[56] Kissinger, Years of Renewal, 666.

[57] Issawi, "The 1973 Oil Crisis and After," 15.

[58] Kissinger, Years of Renewal, 666.

[59] Ibid., 666-67.

[60] Thomas Polgar as told to Larry Engelmann, Tears before the Rain: An Oral History of the Fall of South Vietnam (New York: Oxford University, 1990), 61.

[61] Lam Quang Thi, The Twenty-Five Year Century, 321.

[62] Allen E. Goodman, "South Vietnam: War without End?," Asian Survey Volume 15, Number 1 (January, 1975): 72, accessed January 9, 2015, Stable URL: http://www.jstor.org/stable/2643432.

maximum of one infantry battalion; whereas, prior to the PPA, VNAF could move one fully

manned and equipped regiment, as a result of aviation fuel shortages.[63] In 1973, alone, the RVN

had spent $82 million in U.S. dollars on imported petroleum products.[64] While the price of

gasoline in the U.S. was $1.65 per gallon in January of 1974, the Nationalist Vietnamese were

paying $245 piasters per liter of gasoline and a liter of diesel fuel reached a high of $125

piasters.[65] The situation on oil imports for the RVN was so dire the U.S. assisted the RVN in

their pursuit of oil credits from the Kingdom of Saudi Arabia for the importation of oil into the

RVN.[66] The oil crisis however, was not the only source of the RVN's economic decline.

On the issue of defense and economic development, the RVN was in a quagmire. The

RVN had to divert the vast majority of its economic resources towards national defense in order

to maintain an independent state with an economy to develop.[67] In the labor force, the RVN

required a large military force for its defense plans, which in turn required a big labor force to

support a hefty military.[68] The majority of the RVN's labor force was employed in the service

sector of the economy which was largely funded by American aid.[69] While the RVN's service

sector was expanding, the agricultural and industrial sectors' output diminished.[70] Since foreign

---

[63] Lam Quang Thi, *The Twenty-Five Year Century*, 319-20.

[64] Nguyen Anh Tuan, *South Vietnam Trial and Experience*, 220.

[65] Ibid., 217.

[66] Telegram, from Sectary of State Henry Kissinger to Ambassador Graham Martin, February 20, 1975, Folder two: VN-SD TG SECSTATE-NODIS (1), Box 21, NSA Presidential Country Files for East Asia and the Pacific: Country File: Vietnam – Department of State Telegrams, Gerald R. Ford Presidential Library, Ann Arbor, Michigan.

[67] Nguyen Anh Tuan, *South Vietnam Trial and Experience*, 212.

[68] Ibid., 211.

[69] Ibid., 211-12.

[70] Ibid.

aid funded the RVN's service sector, roughly one fifth of the Nationalist Vietnamese labor force become unemployed after the withdrawal of SEATO forces from Vietnam.[71] At a time when foreign economic aid, particularly from the U.S., was decreasing, the RVN required the economic aid for its future development since the state could not even fully support RVNAF with its own resources.[72] Not only was the economy of the RVN unable to obtain self-sufficiency to support a massively staffed RVNAF, the military was unable to defend the territory held by the RVN after the PPA.

Through the PPA, the PRG began to collect taxes and function as a state not an underground organization. While the DRV was directing its economy to fight a total war and replenish its military. PAVN continued its infiltration into Communist held territory south of the DMZ. Because the DRV violated the PPA and for its treatment of American POWs, the U.S. Congress refused to allocate any funds to assist economic reconstruction efforts in the DRV.

The RVN saw foreign aid cuts from the U.S. during the same period. The aid cuts came during a recession in the RVN. Where inflation rapidly rose after the completion of Vietnamization and the SEATO withdraw. Through privatization, the RVN hoped the economic expansion would occur. The RVN attempted to expand its economy, but the labor needed for economic expansion were serving in RVNAF. The defense of the RVN was additionally hampered by the 1973 Oil Crisis, where the price for oil rose to then unprecedented heights. In the civilian world, most Nationalist Vietnamese were employed in the service sector, making economic expansion difficult, while supporting an enlarged RVNAF.

---

[71] Lam Quang Thi, *The Twenty-Five Year Century*, 321.

[72] Nguyen Anh Tuan, *South Vietnam Trial and Experience*, 212.

Chapter Five: For What It's Worth

The national defense plan of the RVN was unfeasible for the state to support because the plan required too few resources to defend large tracks of geographic territory. In part of the RVN's economic development policy, there were plans to allocate greater amount of land for agricultural use.[1] Which in turn would have permanent military protection, instead of single sweep pacification operations that left villages unprotected at the conclusion of the mission, and greater participation in local government.[2] Initially, in the post-PPA period, RVNAF was able to provide security for more than seventy-five percent of the rural Nationalist Vietnamese population.[3] In order to accomplish the goal to increase more land for agriculture, President Thieu ordered RVNAF to defend the entire territory under Nationalist Vietnamese control.[4]

Overall, President Thieu refused to cede any territory to the Communist Vietnamese since it would, in his mindset, give the PRG Nationalist recognition as a legitimate political entity, which Thieu strongly disapproved of.[5] The RVN officially was comprised of seventeen million hectares, of which fifty-seven percent of the land was forested with a majority of it being dense jungle, and nearly "two-thirds" of the RVN was mountainous terrain.[6] General Thi argued

---

[1] Laurence E. Grinter, "How They Lost: Doctrines, Strategies and Outcomes of the Vietnam War," *Asian Survey* Volume 15, Number 12 (December, 1975): 1116, accessed January 30, 2014, Stable URL: http://www.jstor.org/stable/2643587.

[2] Ibid.

[3] Ibid., 1114-115.

[4] Phan Quang Dan, "The Vietnam Experience," 269.

[5] Veith, *Black April*, 28.

[6] Arthur H. Westing, "Environmental Consequences of the Second Indochina War: A Case Study," *Ambio* Volume 4, Number 5/6, War and Environment: A Special Issue (1975): 216-17, accessed January 16, 2015, Stable URL: http://www.jstor.org.ezproxy.emich.edu/stable/4312150.

the geography of Vietnam was the fatal flaw in any defense strategy devised by RVNAF since

the RVN was a long and narrow state with coastlines that were "less than 100 kilometers (km)

from the mountains,"[7] Because of the RVN's geography along with its defense plan, an

estimated fifty to sixty-eight percent of RVNAF personnel were assigned to defensive positions

and/or duties.[8]

By taking geography into account, President Thieu's defense policies over extended

RVNAF in order to protect territory that lacked strategic and economic importance.[9] Nineteen

seventy-four, marked a period of increased PAVN infiltration into the RVN. PAVN infiltration

reached the same level of troop strength as the communist had in 1971 at 35,000 as of the third

quarter of the American fiscal year.[10] While the DRV was building up its forces, terrorist attacks

had occurred in increasing numbers during 1974.[11] The national defense of the RVN was very

weak and poorly executed.

President Thieu was not a man of the people; he sought political power for himself and

relinquished it only when he felt there were direr alternatives. Politics in the RVN, in general,

were characterized by factional clique politics, comprised of egocentric individuals with similar

personal goals.[12] Political cliques were often based on familiar and loyal ties among social elites,

which had contributed to the lack of stability within the RVN.[13] Because of the presence of

---

[7] Lam Quang Thi, *The Twenty-Five Year Century*, 328.

[8] Goodman, "South Vietnam: War without End?," 71.

[9] Phan Quang Dan, "The Vietnam Experience," 268-69.

[10] RVNAF Quarterly Assessment: Third Quarter, Fiscal Year, 1974, Defense Attaché, Saigon, MG John Murray, 1-3 and 1-4.

[11] Ibid., 2-1.

[12] Joseph W. Dodd, "Faction and Failure in South Vietnam," *Asian Affairs* Volume 2, Number 3 (January – February, 1975): 175-76, accessed March 24, 2014, Stable URL: http://www.jstor.org/stable/30171883.

numerous elitist political cliques, the law was applied on a personal rather than a theoretical basis.[14] Because of the nature of clique politics, President Thieu was very suspicious of others and greatly feared coups ever since he came across the body of the overthrown President Ngo Dinh Diem in 1963.[15] Additionally, President Thieu felt threatened by democratic processes and worked to remove the processes from the National Vietnamese government, under the guise of state emergencies, when it best suited him.[16]

Since the law was applied when it best suited the ruling clique, the Nationalist Vietnamese populace was very resentful toward their government.[17] Because of the corruption caused by political cliques, several opposition groups emerged to protest the Thieu clique in particular, while pressuring politicians to enforce the law on theoretical basis.[18] The opposition movement against President Thieu caused concern in the Ford Administration who wanted the Nationalist Vietnamese government to maintain a stable RVN and to do so under legal means.[19] To the American Public and the U.S. Congress however, it did not matter what took place within the RVN, much less what act President Thieu committed.

---

[13] Dodd, "Faction and Failure in South Vietnam," 176.

[14] Ibid.

[15] Nguyen Tien Hung and Jerrold L. Schecter, *The Palace File* (New York: Harper and Row, 1986), 259.

[16] Grinter, "How They Lost," 1128-129.

[17] Phan Quang Dan, "The Vietnam Experience," 268.

[18] Trong, "Survival and Self-Reliance," 289-90.

[19] Telegram, Secretary of State Henry Kissinger to Ambassador Graham Martin, October 26, 1974, 7, Folder Two: VN-SD TG SECSTATE – NODIS (1), Box 21, NSA Presidential Country Files for East Asia and the Pacific: Country File: Vietnam – Department of State Telegrams, Gerald R. Ford Presidential Library, Ann Arbor, Michigan.

During the last years of the Vietnam War, the American public had entrenched itself in opposition to further American involvement in the conflict.[20] In March 1973, Gallup reported that the Vietnam War was not considered to be an issue amongst the American public.[21] Previously in August 1972, when Gallup asked respondents if the U.S. should or should not withdraw, sixty-two percent responded that the U.S. should withdraw.[22] Gallup even discovered during 1975 that more than seventy-five percent of the American public objected to send any form of military aid to the RVN.[23] CIA Director Colby speculated that after the return of American POWs from Vietnam, the American public had lost interest in the Vietnam War.[24] With the American public having a disinterested attitude towards the RVN, the U.S. Congress followed suit.

With a pessimistic outlook towards the RVN, the U.S. Congress proposed several bills to limit American involvement in Southeast Asian conflicts due to the long-term American commitment in the Vietnam War.[25] The anti-war legislation that had emerged in the 1970s was a reaction to the prevailing view that the Vietnam War was an American president's war, not an American war since a formal declaration of war was never made by congress.[26] Quite often in

---

[20] Lunch and Sperlich, "American Public Opinion and the War in Vietnam," 29.

[21] Veith, *Black April*, 47.

[22] Lunch and Sperlich, "American Public Opinion and the War in Vietnam," 28.

[23] Ibid., 32.

[24] Colby with McCargar, *Lost Victory*, 344.

[25] William G. Howell and Jon C. Pevehouse, "When Congress Stops Wars: Partisan Politics and Presidential Power," *Foreign Affairs* Volume 86, Number 5 (September – October, 2007): 101-02, accessed September 9, 2014, Stable URL: http://www.jstor.org/stable/20032436.

[26] John G. Tower, "Congress Versus the President: The Formulation and Implementation of American Foreign Policy," *Foreign Affairs*, Volume 60, Number 2 (Winter, 1981): 244-45, accessed September 9, 2014, Stable URL: http://www.jstor.org/stable/20041078.

American politics, when a rival party has a majority in congress opposite from the President's political party, congress is more likely to contest presidential decisions and can make use of congressional powers over military conflicts.[27]

Even as early as 1971, congress curtailed the scope of American war effort in Southeast Asia through the Cooper-Church Amendment, which did become law.[28] The Cooper-Church Amendment ceased funding for the American war effort to assist the KR and stated that any future American aid of any form to the KR was to not be translated as a formal obligation.[29] As part of the Second Appropriations Act (SAA) for the 1973 fiscal year, the Fulbright Amendment sought to force the U.S. into a complete withdraw from conflicts in Southeast Asia.[30] The SAA with the Fulbright Amendment ceased American funding for all combat activities in Southeast Asia.[31] On June 4, 1973, the U.S. Senate passed the Case-Church Amendment, which caused concern for Dr. Kissinger who feared that the U.S. would lose the ability to create incentives for a peace agreement in Cambodia through pressure bombing similar to the Linebacker II campaign.[32] The Case-Church Amendment stated that no American funding could be sent to any Southeast Asia state directly or indirectly.[33] Senator John G. Tower argued that the Nelson-

---

[27] Howell and Pevehouse, "When Congress Stops Wars," 96-97.

[28] Tower, "Congress versus the President," 237.

[29] Amy Belasco, Lynn J. Cunningham, Hannah Fischer, and Larry Niksch, "Congressional Restrictions on U.S. Military Operations in Vietnam, Cambodia, Laos, Somalia, and Kosovo: Funding and Non-funding Approaches," (Congressional Research Service Report for Congress presented to Members and Committees of Congress on January 16, 2007), 31, http://fas.org/sgp/crs/natsec/RL33803.pdf.

[30] Tower, "Congress versus the President," 237.

[31] Belasco, Cunningham, Fischer, and Niksch "Congressional Restrictions on U.S. Military Operations In Vietnam, Cambodia, Laos, Somalia, and Kosovo," 31.

[32] Kissinger, *Ending the Vietnam War*, 486-87.

[33] Belasco, Cunningham, Fischer, and Niksch "Congressional Restrictions on U.S. Military Operations in Vietnam, Cambodia, Laos, Somalia, and Kosovo," 37.

Bingham Amendments of the Foreign Assistance Act of 1974 required all sales of American arms greater than $25 million to have Congressional approval after receiving presidential notice of the sale before twenty calendar days had passed.[34] Although he was concerned about the Foreign Assistance Act could negatively affect American aid for the RVN and the KR, President Ford believed that the act had merits to become law since he signed the bill.[35] The most significant piece of legislation, became law in 1973.

The War Powers Act of 1973 was introduced for the same reason why the Cooper-Church and Case-Church Amendments were introduced as bills, which were for the U.S. Congress to cease American participation in the Vietnam War.[36] Unlike the most pieces of anti-war legislation of the 1970s, the War Powers Act was designed to be a proactive measure as a failsafe against possible long term presidential conflicts similar to the way congress viewed the Vietnam War.[37] The War Powers Act called for the president to consult with members of congress before introducing American troops into conflict as well as for the president to gain congressional approval for troop deployment or to remove the troops from a conflict within sixty days, if congress does not grant consent for the deployment.[38] Despite President Nixon's veto, congress passed the War Powers Act with the required two thirds majority.[39]

---

[34] Tower, "Congress versus the President," 234.

[35] Ford, *A Time to Heal*, 226.

[36] Tower, "Congress versus the President," 237-38.

[37] Ibid., 238.

[38] "War Powers Resolution," Yale Law School: Lillian Goldman Law Library's Avalon Project, last modified 2008, accessed January 19, 2015, http://avalon.law.yale.edu/20th_century/warpower.asp.

[39] Ford, *A Time to Heal*, 251-52.

While serving as a member of the House, Ford voted against the War Powers Act on three separate occasions: the joint conference between the House and the Senate, when the House voted for the Act, and when the Act came up for vote again to override President Nixon's veto.[40] Originally, Ford believed that the War Powers Act was unconstitutional since it allowed congress to have a veto in security policy and cited the U.S. Supreme Court case *Immigration and Naturalization Service v. Chadha*, where the Supreme Court found the use of a veto by a legislator was found to be unlawful.[41] While serving as President, Ford discovered the War Powers Act to be "impractical," since the executive office had to deliberate with twenty-five members of congress, which he discovered were unavailable in times of emergency.[42] Overall, Ford believed that the War Powers Act allowed congress to have too much control over national security which created an imbalance of political power between the legislature and the executive.[43] Unlike the opinions of congress during the 1970s towards Vietnam, President Ford's personal opinions differed.

Before ascending to the American presidency, Ford had been a strong supporter and believer in the American war effort in Southeast Asia.[44] Even as early as 1953, Ford expressed his support for the American war effort in Southeast Asia to his family and the planned "end use" of military supplies for American allies in the region.[45] Additionally, in the same 1953

---

[40] Gerald R. Ford, "Congress, the Presidency and National Security Policy," *Presidential Studies Quarterly* Volume 16, Number 2, Congress, the Court, and the Presidency in National Security Policy (Spring, 1986): 201, accessed January 11, 2014, Stable URL: http://www.jstor.org/stable/40574643.

[41] Ford, "Congress, the Presidency and National Security Policy," 202.

[42] Ibid., 201-02.

[43] Ibid., 200-01.

[44] Ford, *A Time to Heal*, 248-50.

letter, Ford expressed his belief that with autonomy, the Southeast Asian states could successfully resist communist forces.[46] Ford argued further in the 1953 letter that American economic aid for refugees was needed to help rebuild their lives after fleeing from communist aggression.[47]

During the 1960s Ford was an advocate of widespread use and increased intensity of the USAF bombing missions as an effective means to win the Vietnam War.[48] In 1965, Ford once informed a reporter that he would not support an American disengagement from Southeast Asia.[49] Being a strong supporter of Nixon's policies towards the Vietnam War, President Ford shaped his policy on that of his predecessor.[50] Because he openly supported the Vietnam War, congress during the mid-1970s saw President Ford "as the hawk of Vietnam hawks."[51] Since the President had been vocal about his approval for the Vietnam War, Ford's criticism on the strategies utilized by the United States have often been forgotten.

Although a supporter of the American war effort in the Vietnam War, President Ford was also a major critic on the conduct of the war. Once he became persuaded that the Johnson Administration did not actively pursue a momentous victory in the Vietnam War, Ford no longer considered himself to be a Vietnam hawk.[52] While serving as a congressman, Ford felt if the

---

[45] Letter, Gerald R. Ford to Betty, Mike, and John "Jack" Ford, September 3, 1953, Congressional Papers of Gerald R. Ford, 1, accessed May 25, 2015, Gerald R. Ford Presidential Library, Ann Arbor, Michigan, http://www.fordlibrarymuseum.gov/library/exhibits/vietnam/005400673-001.pdf.

[46] Ibid., 1-2.

[47] Ibid., 2.

[48] Ford, *A Time to Heal*, 82-83.

[49] Anderson, "Gerald R. Ford and the Presidents' War in Vietnam," from *Shadow on the White House*, 186.

[50] Ibid., 185-86.

[51] Hartmann, *Palace Politics*, 318.
[52] Hartmann, *Palace Politics*, 210.

USAF was being deployed to Vietnam, bombing campaigns needed to have regular raids and not be ordered by President Johnson to have intermittent halts to the bombing campaigns.[53] Ford even opposed the introduction of American infantry into the Vietnam War in 1965.[54] In 1968, Ford once commented to a reporter that unless President Johnson was planning to use a full military effort in Vietnam, "there was 'no justification for sending one more American over there.'"[55]

Ford strongly believed that the conflicts in Southeast Asia could be won by American proxy war efforts, where the U.S. supplied materials as well as information to the RVN and the KR.[56] According to President Ford, in order for an American proxy war effort to be successful in Southeast Asia, Ford's plans required that RVNAF successful defend the state of the RVN, the Nationalist Vietnamese populace support RVNAF, and the U.S. Congress would continue to approve aid budgets for the RVN.[57] Ford's criticism on the conduct of the Vietnam War and its damaging effects on the U.S. continued well into his presidency.

Ignorance of the needs of the American public and its issues was not an attribute of President Ford. Since President Ford was generally concerned on what issues were afflicting the nation. President Ford recognized that the Vietnam War was dividing American society. Hence President Ford introduced conditional amnesty for roughly 50,000 individuals charged with desertion and/or failure to be inducted after being drafted into the U.S. Armed Forces.[58]

---

[53] Ford, *A Time to Heal*, 82-83.

[54] Anderson, "Gerald R. Ford and the Presidents' War in Vietnam," from *Shadow on the White House*, 184.

[55] Ibid., 186.

[56] Ibid., 187.

[57] Ford, *A Time to Heal*, 249.

[58] Ibid., 141-42.

When President Ford was ready to announce his amnesty program, he stated that he wanted to announce the program at the national convention of the Veterans of Foreign Wars (VFW) in Chicago.[59] Hartmann suggested to President Ford that he would be better received at Ohio State University's summer commencement.[60] With a prediction the amnesty announcement would be well received by collegiate graduates.[61] President Ford replied, it was students he did not need to persuade, it was Ford's generation of World War II veterans who were often characterized as idealists who were also and considered to be Vietnam hawks, who needed to be convinced to support the program.[62] When President Ford announced his amnesty program at the VFW convention, members of the VFW initially met his declaration with silence.[63] In his VFW speech, President Ford only supported conditional amnesty by stating "as I reject amnesty, so I reject revenge."[64] At the end of his speech, President Ford was received by a standing ovation for the members of the VFW.[65] A few weeks later, President Ford proclaimed that the conditional amnesty was for individuals in question to report to the U.S. Attorney General, swear allegiance to the U.S., and complete a twenty-four month tour of public service outside of military duty.[66]

---

[59] Hartmann, *Palace Politics*, 211.

[60] Ibid.

[61] Ibid.

[62] Ibid.

[63] Ibid., 214-15.

[64] "16 – Remarks to the Veterans of Foreign Wars Annual Convention, Chicago, Illinois, August 19, 1974," President Gerald R. Ford, from *the American Presidency Project*, last modified by Gerhard Peters and John T. Woolley, last modified 2015, accessed January 24, 2015, http://www.presidency.ucsb.edu/ws/index.php?pid=4476.

[65] Hartmann, *Palace Politics*, 215.

[66] "78 – Proclamation 4313 – Announcing a Program for the Return of Vietnam Era Draft Evaders and Military Deserters, September 16, 1974," President Gerald R. Ford, from *the American Presidency Project*, last modified by Gerhard Peters and John T. Woolley, last modified 2015, accessed January 24, 2015, http://www.presidency.ucsb.edu/ws/index.php?pid=4714.

The criticism of the Vietnam War dividing the U.S. was one cause of social separation, which was a major issue that President Ford wanted to resolve.

When Ford was sworn into the Executive Office of the President, the American public was divided on numerous issues, except for one topic: distrust of the Federal government. Since the mid-1960s, American presidents struggled to reach a fifty percent approval rating from the public, and the Watergate scandal only encouraged further presidential disapproval from the public. The 1974 elections saw the lowest voter turnout in thirty years. Sixty-eight percent of Americans believed that the Federal government had purposely misinformed the public for the previous ten years, according to a 1975 opinion poll.[67]

Due to his strong belief that the American public had divided itself because of the changes and the events from the 1960s to the 1970s[68], along with developing a distrust of the Federal government. President Ford made bringing the American public together to solve the issues of the mid-1970s and restoring trust in the Federal government, a centerpiece of his Administration's goals.[69] Early in Ford's presidency, he was asked how he planned to prevent more presidential scandals.[70] President Ford replied his administration would be an open

---

[67] Yanek Mieczkowski, *Gerald Ford and the Challenges of the 1970's* (Lexington, Kentucky: University Press of Kentucky, 2005), 20-21.

[68] The events of the 1960s as well as the 1970s referred to, while not limited to, were the resistance that the Civil Rights movement had endured, massive societal changes, the Counter Culture, assassinations of prominent political leaders, the Cold War, military build-up, growing concern for the environment, race riots, increased crime rates, the proliferation of illicit drug use, economic recession, inflation, the 1973 Oil Crisis, underfunded Great Society programs, the resurgence of big government, draft dodging, the Alcatraz protest, resistance to the United Farm Workers, *Roe v. Wade*, the inability of Congress to pass the Equal Rights Amendment, the Watergate scandal and the Vietnam War. From "Decades of Change - 1960-1980: The Rise of Cultural and Ethnic Pluralism," United States Department of State: International Information Programs (Digital), last modified April 5, 2008, accessed October 26, 2015, http://iipdigital.usembassy.gov/st/english/publication/2008/04/20080407123655eaifas0.7868769.html#axzz3pe0tea3 e.

[69] Ford, *A Time to Heal*, 124-25.

[70] "39 – The President's News Conference, August 28, 1974," President Gerald R. Ford, from *the American Presidency Project*, last modified by Gerhard Peters and John T. Woolley, last modified 2015, accessed January 24, 2015, http://www.presidency.ucsb.edu/ws/index.php?pid=4671.

administration, which would not function like the Nixon Administration, and he would seek

recommendations from several advisors.[71] When answering the question on scandal prevention,

President Ford gave the American public a glimpse of his decision-making style.

For twenty-five years, President Ford had been a member of Congress before his

appointment to the vice presidency.[72] Therefore, it was normal for Ford to seek the opinions of

other officials and deliberate on possible solutions to issues before reaching a decision. President

Ford's preference in decision-making was to consider all possible options.[73] At times within the

Ford White House, staff members had accused one another for pushing their own agendas.[74]

Quite frequently, President Ford took time to analyze documents and facts before coming to a

decision, but, there were times when Ford felt that deliberation had continued long enough.[75]

Conversely, in Hartmann's opinion, President Ford "never wavered on essential matters."[76]

However, President Ford's deliberative approach to decision making greatly affected the

President's resolution making process.

During President Ford's first news conference on August 28, 1974, reporters questioned

Ford several times on the topic of the Watergate scandal.[77] After the first news conference,

President Ford consulted his advisors who stated that the press will continue to ask questions

related to Watergate until the scandal is formally concluded.[78] Causing President Ford to realize

---

[71] "39 – The President's News Conference, August 28, 1974," President Ford.

[72] Anderson, "Gerald R. Ford and the Presidents' War in Vietnam," from *Shadow on the White House*, 185.

[73] Hartmann, *Palace Politics*, 178.

[74] Ibid., 307-08.

[75] Ibid., 269.

[76] Ibid., 421.

[77] "39 – The President's News Conference, August 28, 1974," President Ford.

the Watergate scandal had no end in sight.[79] When Ford had inherited the presidency, there were numerous ongoing issues that were facing the U.S. including the fact that the Vietnam War was still ongoing, rising rates of inflation, growing trade deficit, the Yom Kippur War, the energy crisis, etc.[80]

While seeking answers to abundant of legal questions over Watergate, President Ford began to consider pardoning Nixon, since questions of jurisdiction over the scandal documents were increasingly consuming his time.[81] After several days of inquiry, President Ford's legal aides informed him that a trial of Nixon could take years, excluding an appeal and other investigations of corruption.[82] If the U.S. was going to move on from the Watergate scandal to grapple with other issues, then the legal matters of the scandal had to come to a close.[83] With a pardon of Nixon, President Ford believed that his administration could give full focus on resolving the issues that faced the U.S. during the mid-1970s.[84]

Finally, on September 8, 1974, President Ford signed the proclamation that pardoned Nixon for all crimes committed and participated in during his presidency.[85] In his announcement, President Ford cited that the prosecutions of Nixon for his connection to the Watergate scandal

[78] Ford, *A Time to Heal*, 158-59.

[79] Ibid.

[80] Ibid., 150-51.

[81] Ibid., 159.

[82] Ibid., 167.

[83] Hartmann, *Palace Politics*, 269.

[84] Ford, *A Time to Heal*, 178.

[85] "60 – Remarks on Signing a Proclamation Granting Pardon to Richard Nixon, September 8, 1974," President Gerald R. Ford, from *the American Presidency Project*, last modified by Gerhard Peters and John T. Woolley, last modified 2015, accessed January 25, 2015, http://www.presidency.ucsb.edu/ws/index.php?pid=4695.

would take years, the question of could Nixon receive a fair trial, and that the national nightmare

needed to conclude in order to insure the tranquility of the United States.[86] Initially, President

Ford felt he had made the right choice by pardoning Nixon, but he had second thoughts when

faced with the American public's reaction to the pardon.[87] In response to President Ford's choice

to pardon Nixon, the American public reduced its approval rating of Ford from "72 to 49 percent

less than a month coming into office."[88] Despite the public reaction to and the reasons for

Nixon's pardon, the Ford Administration sought to face other concerns, including the conflict in

Southeast Asia.

By the end 1974, the DRV had observed the developments in Southeast Asia since the

signing of the PPA. Since the first ceasefire, PAVN units had been training in combined arms

warfare.[89] In the DRV's military and political circles, the opinion of a rapid, massive scale

offensive would lead to a complete victory over the RVN was slowly gaining support.[90] While

PAVN was building up its forces and mechanizing many of its units, RVNAF on the other hand

was de-mechanizing its units due to economic restraints.[91]

The DRV had made the improvements to the Ho Chi Minh Trail their top priority.[92] The

Ho Chi Minh Trail was the primary supply route of the Communist Vietnamese, which began in

---

[86] "60 – Remarks on Signing a Proclamation Granting Pardon to Richard Nixon, September 8, 1974," President Ford.

[87] Ford, *A Time to Heal*, 178.

[88] T. Christopher Jespersen, "Kissinger, Ford, and Congress: The Very Bitter End in Vietnam," *Pacific Historical Review* volume 71, number 3 (August 2002): 446, accessed January 10, 2014, stable URL: http://www.jstor.org/stable/10.1525/phr.2002.71.3.439.

[89] Military History Institute of Vietnam, *Victory in Vietnam*, 336-37.

[90] Ibid., 341-42.

[91] Lam Quang Thi, *The Twenty-Five Year Century*, 328.

[92] Military History Institute of Vietnam, *Victory in Vietnam*, 348.

the DRV and filtered into other areas of Southeast Asia with the prime destination being the

RVN.[93] By the end of construction in 1975, the Ho Chi Minh Trail consisted of 6,810 km of

main road ways, 4,980 km of connecter roads, and 5,000 km of detour pathways for a total of

16,790 km of roadway, and a 1,712 km pipeline that ran parallel to the trail, that began sending

fuel south, down to PAVN units in January 1975.[94] Additionally, the road surface of the Ho Chi

Minh Trail was designed to be an all-weather roadway.[95]

On September 3, 1974, the DRV's Politburo met to discuss future military strategy along

with the concerns about the RVN.[96] American aid had decreased significantly, while the

Nationalist Vietnamese morale lowering due to the issues generated or expanded by the lack of

aid.[97] The RVN, since the signing of the PPA, had been attempting to develop stronger

diplomatic ties with the PRC and Japan.[98] Japan had been a state that was able to reconstruct its

economy from near non-existence to an average annual growth rate of 8.2 percent per capita of

income, which lasted until 1972 and became a highly developed state, which continues to be

referred to as an economic miracle.[99] Additionally, the DRV's politburo discussed the possibility

of American intervention, which caused Lao Dong Party members to stress a rapid military

---

[93] George J. Veith and Merle L. Pribbenow II, "Fighting is an Art: The Army of the Republic of Vietnam's Defense of Xuan Loc, 9-21 April 1975," *The Journal of Military History* Volume 68, Number 1 (January, 2004): 169, accessed April 17, 2014, Stable URL: http://www.jstor.org/stable/3397252.

[94] Military History Institute of Vietnam, *Victory in Vietnam*, 348-49.

[95] Colby with McCargar, *Lost Victory*, 344-45.

[96] Military History Institute of Vietnam, *Victory in Vietnam*, 357.

[97] John C. Donnell, "South Vietnam in 1975: The Year of Communist Victory," *Asian Survey* Volume 16, Number 1, A Survey of Asia in 1975: Part One (January, 1976): 10-11, accessed January 30, 2014, Stable URL: http://www.jstor.org/stable/2643276.

[98] Veith, *Black April*, 8.

[99] Benigno Valdes, "An Application of Convergence Theory to Japan's Post-WWII Economic 'Miracle,'" *The Journal of Economic Education* Volume 34, Number 1 (Winter, 2003): 61, accessed January 18, 2015, Stable URL: http://www.jstor.org/stable/30042525.

offensive.[100] Despite its concerns, the Politburo of the DRV felt that the time to conquer the RVN was before the Nationalist Vietnamese state could reorganize itself.[101] Causing the Politburo to order a draft of 108,000 men for a two-year large military offensive called the Ho Chi Minh Offensive (aka the Spring or Finial Offensive), with a goal of concluding in 1976 with the fall of the RVN.[102]

In the post-PPA period the overall effectiveness of RVNAF weakened over time. Vietnamization developed a Nationalist Vietnamese economy that was highly dependent on foreign aid, particularly from the United States. However, the U.S. Congress no longer wanted to support the RVN and wanted to reduce the American commitment to the Nationalist Vietnamese. The 1973 Oil Crisis which led to an increase of oil prices further reduced the economic output of the RVN as well as effectiveness of a mechanized RVNAF. With the events that transpired during the post-PPA period, the DRV believed that they had the opportunity to conquer the RVN.

---

[100] Military History Institute of Vietnam, *Victory in Vietnam*, 357.

[101] Ibid., 356-57.

[102] Ibid.

Administrative Divisions and Military Regions in South Vietnam

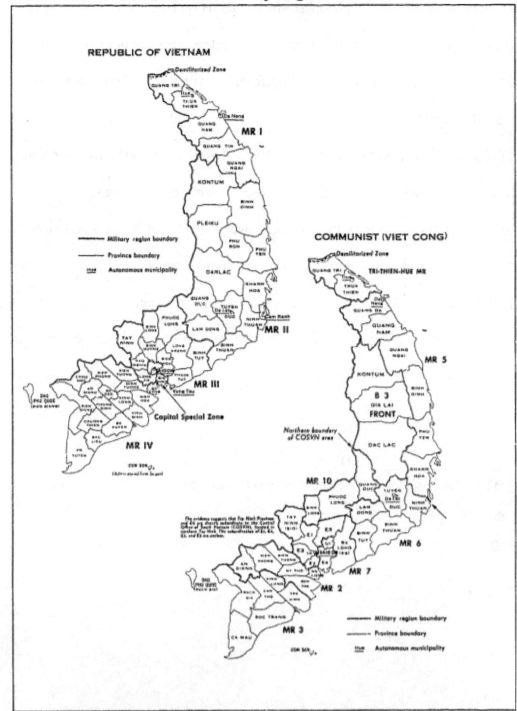

Courtesy of the *Central Intelligence Agency* from Central Intelligence Agency: Directorate of Intelligence, *Intelligence Handbook: Guide to a Viet Cong Province*, May 1971, 2, accessed January 11, 2019, https://www.cia.gov/library/readingroom/docs/CIA-RDP85T00875R001500200004-6.pdf.

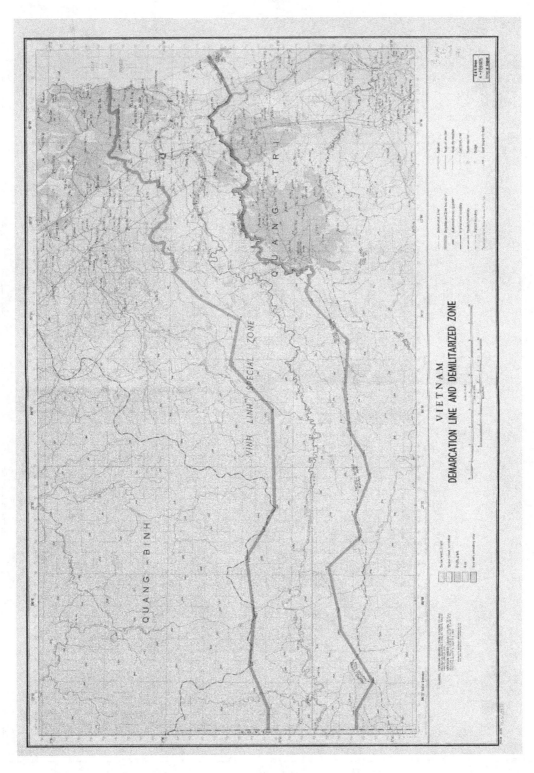

Demarcation line and Demilitarized Zone of Vietnam Map, 1966. Courtesy of the
Library of Congress, Geography and Map Division

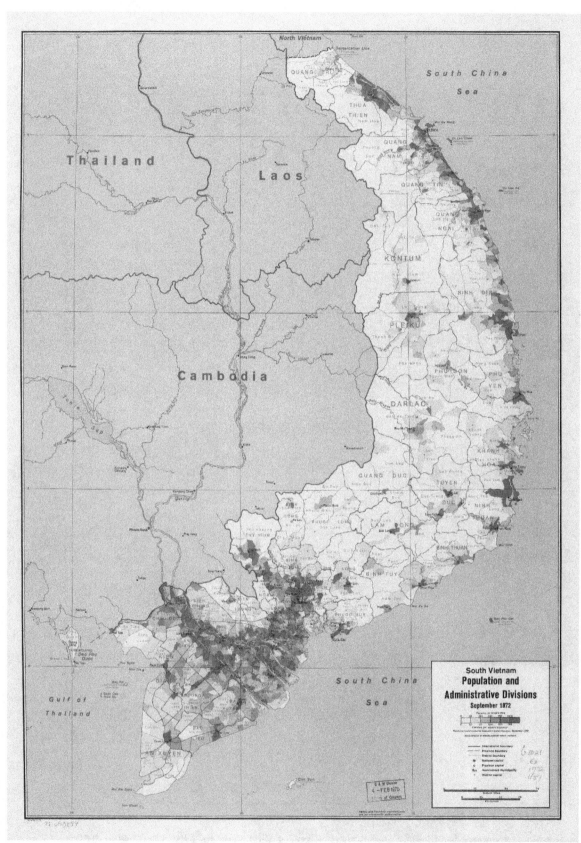

Courtesy of the *Library of Congress, Geography and Map Division*

Photo from IPS   (67-3796)

Inauguration of Nguyen Van Thieu as President of the Republic of Vietnam, October 21, 1967. Then Vice President
Nguyen Cao Ky can be seen on the far left. Courtesy of the *U.S. Information Agency*

Nationalist Vietnamese President Nguyen Van Thieu, 1968. Courtesy of the *Lyndon B. Johnson Presidential Library*

President Richard M. Nixon with General William C. Westmorland. Courtesy of the *U.S. Information Agency*

ARVN soldiers with a captured PAVN T-59 tank during the Easter Offensive, 1972.
Courtesy of *National Archives, Records of the Office of the Chief Signal Officer*

Three F-4D Phantom II Fighters and Three Corsair II attack aircraft dropping Loran
bombs, 1973. Courtesy of *National Archives, General Records of the Department of
the Navy*

Gerald R. Ford Presidential Swearing-in ceremony. From left to right, Gerald R. Ford, Betty Ford, and Chief Justice of the Supreme Court Warren Burger. Courtesy *Gerald R. Ford Library*

From left to right, Ambassador Graham Martin, General Frederick Weyand, Dr. Henry Kissinger, and President Gerald R. Ford, March 25, 1975. Courtesy *Gerald R. Ford Library*

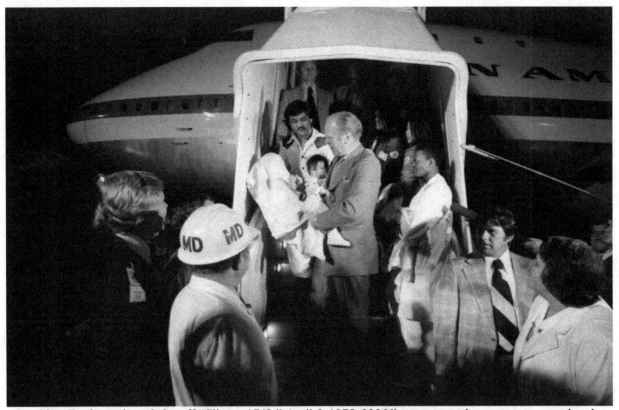

President Ford carrying a baby off "Clipper 1742," April 5, 1975. 325 Vietnamese orphans were evacuated to the U.S. in Operation Babylift. Courtesy *Gerald R. Ford Library*

President Gerald R. Ford at Tulane University, April 23, 1975. Courtesy *Gerald R. Ford Library*

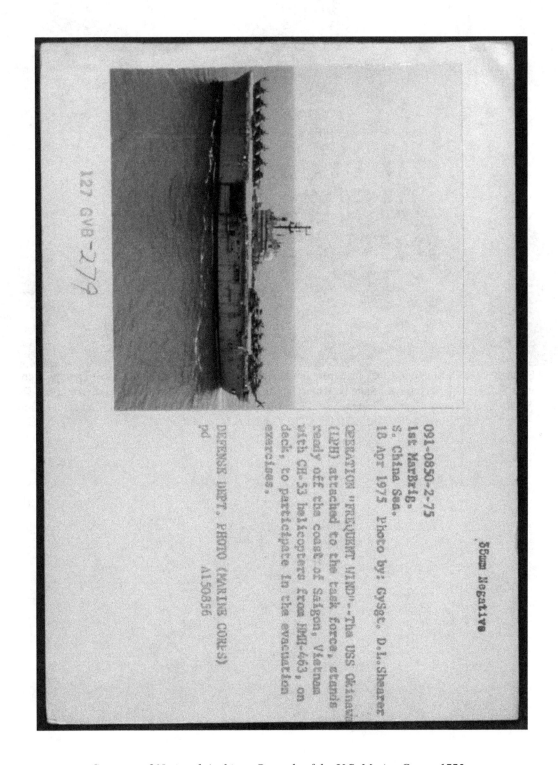

127 GVB-279

35mm Negative

091-0850-2-75
1st MarBrig.
S. China Sea.
18 Apr 1975   Photo by: GySgt. D.L.Shearer

OPERATION "FREQUENT WIND".--The USS Okinawa
(LPH) attached to the task force, stands
ready off the coast of Saigon, Vietnam
with CH-53 helicopters from HMH-463, on
deck, to participate in the evacuation
exercises.

DEFENSE DEPT. PHOTO (MARINE CORPS)
pd   A150856

Courtesy of *National Archives, Records of the U.S. Marine Corps, 1775 –*

National Security Council Meeting. Clockwise from left to right, CIA Director William Colby, Deputy Secretary of State Robert S. Ingersoll, Secretary of State Dr. Henry Kissinger, President Gerald R. Ford, Secretary of Defense James Schlesinger, Deputy Defense Secretary William Clements, Vice President Nelson Rockefeller, General George S. Brown, April 28, 1975. Courtesy *Gerald R. Ford Library*

Courtesy of *National Archives, Records of the U.S. Marine Corps, 1775 –*

Crewman of the *USS Blue Ridge* push a Vietnamese Air Force HU-1 helicopter off the landing deck into the sea. Allowing other escaping helicopters full of refugees to land, April 29, 1975. Courtesy of *National Archives and Record Administration*

American sailors of the *USS Durham* in the South China Sea assisting Vietnamese refugees, 1975. Courtesy of *National Archives, General Records of the Department of the Navy*

Nationalist Vietnamese refugees approaching the *USS Durham*, April 4, 1975. Courtesy of *National Archives and Records Administration*

Courtesy of *National Archives, Records of the U.S. Marine Corps, 1775 -*

35mm Negative

124-762-14-75
3rd MarDiv
Aboard USS HANCOCK
29 Apr 1975 Photo by: Cpl M.A. Abrham

OPERATION "FREQUENT WIND"--A South
Vietnamese helicopter pilot and
his family, safely aboard the USS
HANCOCK, are escorted by a Marine
Security Guard to the refugee area
during the evacuation of Saigon,
Republic of Vietnam.

DEFENSE DEPT. PHOTO (MARINE CORPS)
pd   A801617

127 GVB-279

Courtesy of *National Archives, Records of the U.S. Marine Corps, 1775 -*

35mm Negative

091-0850-40-75
1st MarBrig.
Aboard USS Hancock
29 Apr 1975 Photo by: GySgt.D.L.Shearer

OPERATION "FREQUENT WIND"--A Vietnamese
woman, carrying her son, is given a
numbered tag as she arrives onboard
the USS HANCOCK. Her belongings will
be tagged with the same number due to
the language barrier between the refugees
and marines during evacuation of
civilians in Saigon.

DEFENSE DEPT.PHOTO (MARINE CORPS)
pd   A150894

127 GVB-279

Courtesy of *National Archives, Records of the U.S. Marine Corps, 1775 –*

110

President Gerald R. Ford in a meeting with bipartisan congressional leaders discussing the evacuation from the Republic of Vietnam, April 29, 1975. Courtesy *Gerald R. Ford Library*

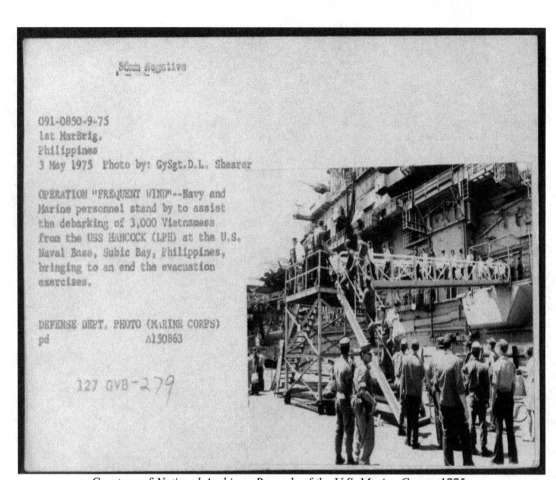

Courtesy of *National Archives, Records of the U.S. Marine Corps, 1775 -*

Chapter Six: Run Through the Jungle

After observing the political and military landscape of Southeast Asia, the DRV chose to launch another full military offensive. At first the DRV begins with a limited offensive to test the American reaction to the extreme violations to the PPA. Since the U.S. did not re-enter the Vietnam War, the DRV pushed on with a full military offensive. During the DRV's last offensive, the RVN fought for its very survival. In response to RVNAF's setbacks, President Thieu made several requests for additional American aid. Based on the political climate in the U.S., the events in the Vietnam War that took place in the conflict's final years, and President Thieu's requests, President Ford made his decision on how the U.S. was to react to in the final months of the war that began with the DRV's choice to renew large scale military warfare.

For the final or Ho Chi Minh Offensive, the DRV had poured large amounts of its resources into the military campaign. In manpower, the Lao Dong Party Politburo requested 108,000 men to be drafted for the Offensive.[1] Some of the individuals drafted for Ho Chi Minh Offensive were as young as sixteen years of age, in order to fill the demand for manpower made by the DRV Politburo.[2] By March 1975, PAVN had become the fifth largest army in the world.[3] Numerous PAVN units underwent extended training programs during 1974, with the focus on combined arms, urban combat, and assaulting fortified positions.[4] Shortly before the commencement of the final offensive, PAVN had succeeded in infiltrating

---

[1] Military History Institute of Vietnam, *Victory in Vietnam*, 357.

[2] Veith and Pibbenow II, "'Fighting is an Art,'" 175.

[3] Mieczkowski, *Gerald Ford and the Challenges of the 1970s*, 290.

[4] Military History Institute of Vietnam, *Victory in Vietnam*, 351.

"over 200,000 combat troops" and fielded up to ten divisions by the end of the Offensive, of

which, six were deployed South of the DMZ.[5] PAVN had developed a highly effective

logistic system to resupply units in the field.[6] After Viktor Kulikov, the Chief of the Soviet

General Staff made an official visit to Hanoi in December 1974, shipments of Soviet military

goods increased four times more than before his trip.[7] Despite all the preparations made by

the DRV for their Ho Chi Minh Offensive, top political and military officials of the

Communist Vietnamese wanted to test their opponents.

For PAVN, the first of many conquests during the Ho Chi Minh Offensive occurred

in the RVN province of Phoc Long. The capital city of the same name of the province of

Phoc Long was captured by PAVN in December 1974, which was only seventy-five miles

away from the RVN capital of Saigon.[8] During an urgent meeting on January 2, 1975, with

the senior officers of RVNAF, President Thieu essentially ceded Phoc Long province to the

Communist Vietnamese.[9] President Thieu did not order a counter offensive or to reinforce

current RVNAF units deployed in the province, due to the severe lack of reserves.[10] RVNAF

---

[5] RVNAF Final Assessment: January through April, Fiscal Year, 1975, Defense Attaché, Saigon, Major General H.D. Smith, 1-1 and 1-2, Folder Three 228-07/ RVNAF Final Assessment/ January Through April, Fiscal Year, 1975, Entry # A1 1727: RVNAF Quarterly Assessment Reports; 1973-1975, Final Assessment January –April, 1975 Through Final Assessment January-April, 1975, Box 3, DAO, Operations and Plans Division/ Readiness Section, Record Group 472, U.S. Forces in Southeast Asia, 1950-1975, National Archives, College Park, Maryland.

[6] Ibid.

[7] Kissinger, *Ending the Vietnam War*, 500-01.

[8] Tien Hung and Schecter, *The Palace File*, 248.

[9] Ibid., 249.

[10] Ibid.

supply depots could only provide at full capacity for forty percent of needed fuel and ammunition for its units during the early days of 1975.[11]

By January 6, 1975, PAVN's Forth Corps had conquered the province of Phoc Long, the first time in the Vietnam War the Communist Vietnamese occupied an entire province south of the DMZ.[12] PAVN had made some small gains in the latter days 1974.[13] The offensive in Phoc Long was a probe attack to test the reactions of RVNAF and the U.S. to determine if the DRV Politburo should order the general mobilization for the Ho Chi Minh Offensive.[14] With a groundbreaking victory to start their offensive, the Communist Vietnamese waited for the U.S. to respond.

In response to the news of PAVN's conquest of Phoc Long province, the Ford Administration authored a press release. Before the briefing, Press Secretary Ron Nessen wanted to meet with a member of the NSC, in order to present an accurate report since many press secretaries had lost their creditability to the press after being caught for supplying false information.[15] President Ford's first Press Secretary, Jerald terHorst, had resigned over Ford's choice to pardon Nixon, a decision with which terHorst strongly disagreed.[16]

Previously, Nessen was employed as a journalist for twenty years and worked as a television correspondent on an assignment covering the White House for National

---

[11] Parker, "Vietnam and Soviet Asian Strategy," 108.

[12] Military History Institute of Vietnam, *Victory in Vietnam*, 359.

[13] Ibid.

[14] Ibid.

[15] Nessen, *It Sure Looks Different from the Inside*, 91.

[16] Ford, *A Time to Heal*, 175-76.

Broadcasting Company's (NBC) "Nightly News."[17] When interviewing for the position of

press secretary, Nessen requested and was informed that he would be a high ranking aide

with unrestricted access to the White House.[18] Nessen was notified that he would not have

the responsibility of being a salesman for the Ford Administration's policies, President Ford

stated that it was the President's job to sell his own programs to the public.[19] While Nessen's

job was to make accurate announcements on the president's decisions and he was not

required to agree with Ford's every decision.[20] In fact, President Ford only offered the

position of press secretary to Nessen.[21]

During the press briefing on Phoc Long, Nessen was asked the question of whether

President Ford would re-introduce American armed forces into the Vietnam War, he

responded that the President was "forbidden by law" to do so, including bombing raids. After

the press briefing, Nessen was scolded by NSC liaison officer to the Press Office Les Janka

for his answer on the re-introduction of American combat forces into Vietnam. Despite the

answers Nessen had received from Janka before he had met with the press. Regardless of the

Nessen statement during the press conference, the Ford Administration discussed what

actions the U.S. could make in response to the news of Phoc Long.[22]

In response to the news of Phoc Long, the Washington Special Actions Group

(WSAG) met on formulating an effective response. One of the first topics introduced at the

---

[17] Nessen, *It Sure Looks Different from the Inside*, 11.

[18] Ibid., 13.

[19] Ibid., 13-14.

[20] Ibid.

[21] Ford, *A Time to Heal*, 184.

[22] Nessen, *It Sure Looks Different from the Inside*, 91-92.

January 7, 1975 WSAG meeting was President Ford's choice of requesting supplemental aid

for the RVN from Congress.[23] During the WSAG meeting, Sectary of State Dr. Kissinger

recommended sending other U.S. military units to the region such as, B-52s to Thailand or a

carrier fleet to the Gulf of Tonkin.[24] A day later, Dr. Kissinger informed President Ford of

the possible courses of action the U.S. could take to pressure the DRV.[25] During the WSAG

meeting, President Ford agreed to sending supplemental aid to the RVN and for deploying

military units to the region of Southeast Asia.[26] These deployment orders included B-52

bombers to Thailand and an aircraft carrier in the Gulf of Tonkin.[27] However, due to the

timing of congressional budget hearings, the Department of Defense did not order

redeployment of American military forces to Southeast Asia for fear of budget cuts from war

weary legislators.[28] The Ford Administration requested $300 million in supplemental aid for

the RVN, since it was the amount of aid that was removed from the 1975 fiscal year.[29] After

the Armed Services Committee had previously authorized $1 billion in aid for the RVN,

---

[23] Telegram, Deputy National Security Advisor Brent Scowcroft to Ambassador Graham Martin, 14, January 7, 1975, 1, Folder Two VW CD-1, August 9, 1974 – March 3, 1975, Box 38, National Security Advisor, Kissinger – Scowcroft West Wing Office Files, 1969-1977, General Subject File: Vietnamese War – 'Camp David File,' Gerald R. Ford Presidential Library, Ann Arbor, Michigan.

[24] Ibid., 1-2.

[25] Meeting Minutes, Memorandum of Conversation, President Gerald Ford, Secertary of State Henry Kissinger, and Deputy National Security Advisor General Brent Scowcroft, January 8, 1975, 5-6, Box 8, National Security Advisor Memoranda of Conversations – Ford Administration, Gerald R. Ford Presidential Library, Ann Arbor, Michigan, http://www.fordlibrarymuseum.gov/library/document/0314/1552907.pdf.

[26] Ibid.

[27] Ibid.

[28] Kissinger, *Ending the Vietnam War*, 505-06.

[29] Ibid.

which created the hope for a quick process to appropriate aid.[30] President Ford then took action to obtain aid for the RVN.

President Ford first revealed his request for congress to send supplemental aid for the RVN along with the KR in a televised interview and later formally in a meeting with members of congress on January 23 and 26, 1975 respectively.[31] President Ford began his address to members of congress that many states and nations had hoped the Vietnam War would have come to a conclusion with the PPA.[32] President Ford stated the violations of the DRV including the capture of Phoc Long province, the infiltration of PAVN soldiers along with large amounts of heavy equipment, Communist Vietnamese raids, and the DRV refusal to negotiate a formal peace agreement with the RVN as described in the PPA.[33] Without the supplemental aid, the RVN would struggle to stabilize the front lines through the purchase of military equipment as described by President Ford.[34] Therefore, it was necessary for congress to approve the additional $300 million.[35]

President Ford went on to discuss the lack of military supplies available to RVNAF and the desperate need for supplemental aid. By supporting the RVN, President Ford argued that politically the U.S. needed to demonstrate that it is a reliable ally and would continue to support previous agreements made with other states all over the world. While appealing for

---

[30] Kissinger, *Ending the Vietnam War*, 508.

[31] Ibid.

[32] "53 – Special Message to Congress Requesting Supplemental Assistance for the Republic of Vietnam and Cambodia, January 28, 1975," President Gerald R. Ford, from *the American Presidency Project*, last modified by Gerhard Peters and John T. Woolley, last modified 2015, accessed February 24, 2014, http://www.presidency.ucsb.edu/ws/index.php?pid=5216.

[33] Ibid.

[34] Ibid.

[35] Ibid.

supplemental aid for the RVN in the message, President Ford stressed the U.S. would only

assist the RVN through proxy endeavors and not combat endeavors. Additionally, President

Ford stated that Americans longed for the U.S. to cease its task with the RVN, mentioning he

himself wanted this as well.[36]

When President Ford sent his message to congress, Dr. Kissinger ordered

Ambassador Graham Martin to return to Washington, D.C. to assist in the Ford

Administration efforts to obtain congressional approval for additional aid for the RVN.[37] Dr.

Kissinger stated to a group of bipartisan congressional leaders if the DRV was forced into

another stalemate similar to 1972 Easter Offensive, the DRV's Politburo would return to

peace negotiations with the RVN.[38] However, congress followed its course of apprehension

towards Vietnam.

Upon receiving the special message from President Ford requesting additional aid for

the RVN, Congress had a muddled response.[39] Privately, Speaker of the House Carl Albert

agreed with President Ford's attitude towards Vietnam, but Albert was unsure that the House

would support the President's request.[40] In a cabinet meeting on January 29, 1975, Secretary

of Defense James R. Schlesinger estimated without supplemental aid the RVN would fall by

---

[36] President Ford, "53 – Special Message to Congress Requesting Supplemental Assistance for the Republic of Vietnam and Cambodia, January 28, 1975."

[37] Telegram, Sectary of State Henry Kissinger to Ambassador Graham Martin, January 28, 1975, folder two, VN-SD TG SECSTATE-NODIS (1), box 21, NSA Presidential Country Files for East Asia and the Pacific: Country File: Vietnam - Department of State Telegrams, Gerald R. Ford Presidential Library, Ann Arbor, Michigan.

[38] Meeting Minutes, Memorandum for the Record with Bipartisan Congressional Leadership, page three, January 28, 1975, box 8, National Security Advisor's Memoranda of Conversation Collection, Gerald R. Ford Library, Ann Arbor, Michigan, Accessed May 25, 2015, http://www.fordlibrarymuseum.gov/library/document/0314/1552931.pdf.

[39] Ford, *A Time to Heal*, 250.

[40] Ibid.

the end of spring because of the strict rationing of essential military goods including ammunition and fuel.[41] In another meeting later that day, President Ford stressed that other parts of the world are no more important than Southeast Asia and the U.S. would continue supporting its allies in Southeast Asia as a demonstration of the state's commitment to its allies around the world.[42] Senator Hugh Scott stated he supported the Ford Administration's request and judgment for additional aid.[43] On the other hand, Congressman Albert Ullman felt the U.S. would be sending aid to a state destined to collapse.[44] Congressman Charles Melvin Price affirmed if the Ford Administration publically assured the American public the U.S. would not re-introduce American military forces into Vietnam then the public and members of congress would support additional aid.[45]

The mixed reaction from members of congress caused President Ford to consider requesting congress to send a delegation to Southeast Asia.[46] A consideration which delayed Ambassador Martin from returning to the Washington.[47] Furthermore, President Ford's supplemental aid request was not assisted by NBC news report broadcasted on the Today

---

[41] Cabinet Meeting Minutes, Notes of the Cabinet Meeting, 1, January 29, 1975, 1975/01/29 Cabinet Meeting, box 4, James Conner Files, Gerald R. Ford Library, Ann Arbor, Michigan, http://www.fordlibrarymuseum.gov/library/exhibits/cabinet/cm750129.pdf.

[42] Meeting Minutes, Memorandum of Conversation: Cabinet Meeting, page 2, January 29, 1975, National Security Advisor's Memoranda of Conversation Collection, Gerald R. Ford Library, Ann Arbor, Michigan, accessed May 25, 2015, http://www.fordlibrarymuseum.gov/library/document/0314/1552932.pdf.

[43] Meeting Minutes, Memorandum for the Record with Bipartisan Congressional Leadership, 7, January 28, 1975.

[44] Ibid., 6.

[45] Ibid., 7.

[46] Telegram, Sectary of State Henry Kissinger to Ambassador Graham Martin, January 30, 1975, folder two, VN-SD TG SECSTATE-NODIS (1), box 21, NSA Presidential Country Files for East Asia and the Pacific: Country File: Vietnam – Department of State Telegrams, Gerald R. Ford Presidential Library, Ann Arbor, Michigan.

[47] Ibid.

Show.[48] Just days earlier from President Ford's meeting with some congressional leaders, stating a few staff members of the American Embassy in Saigon have claimed, in the material sense, additional aid is not required, but any attempts to send more aid would be to restore Nationalist Vietnamese confidence in the United States.[49] Therefore, President Ford awaited a response from congress.

While members of congress were unsure of approving supplemental aid for the RVN. President Ford encouraged congress to send a delegation to Southeast Asia in hopes the Congressional team would convince their colleagues to approve the supplemental aid for the RVN.[50] Senator Hubert Humphrey proposed a congressional delegation which President Ford accepted with disinclination.[51] Since many of the proposed members of the delegation were either unwilling to commit to the mission or were too recently elected to have political clout in congress.[52] President Ford accepted Senator Humphrey's proposed delegation because of his high respect for the senator had not changed since Ford had requested advice on the vice presidency from Humphrey back in 1973.[53] Additionally, President Ford stated in an interview with the *Chicago Tribune* that he would be willing to completely discontinue aid

[48] Telegram, 25, Deputy Assistant to the President for National Security Affairs Brent Scowcroft to Ambassador Graham Martin, January 27, 1975, folder nine, Washington to Saigon January 5, – April 1, 1975 (1), box 7, NSA, Saigon Embassy Files Taken by Ambassador Graham Martin (Copies), 1963-1975 (1976), Gerald R. Ford Presidential Library, Ann Arbor, Michigan.

[49] Ibid.

[50] Paul Norton "Pete" McCloskey as told to Larry Engelmann, *Tears before the Rain: An Oral History of the Fall of South Vietnam*, 26.

[51] Kissinger, *Ending the Vietnam War*, 512.

[52] Ibid.

[53] Letter, Senator Hubert Humphrey to Gerald Ford, October 30 1973, 1, Opening Statement: Experts View the Vice Presidency, box 242, Gerald R. Ford Presidential Library, Ann Arbor, Michigan, and letter, Gerald Ford to Senator Hubert Humphrey, November 5, 1973, Opening Statement: Experts View the Vice Presidency, box 242, Gerald R. Ford Presidential Library, Ann Arbor, Michigan, http://www.fordlibrarymuseum.gov/library/document/25thamend/humphreyletter.pdf.

for the RVN after three fiscal years with a ceiling of $6 billion dollars to persuade congress

to approve more funds of aid for the RVN.[54] After some time of debate congress finally sent

a congressional delegation to the RVN.[55]

The congressional delegation consisted of Paul Norton "Pete" McCloskey, John

Flynt, William V. Chappell, Jr., Bella Abzug, John Murtha, Donald M. Fraser, and Millicent

Fenwick.[56] Having previously traveled to the RVN on four separate occasions, McCloskey

had considered himself to be a dove and believed that the U.S. was the sole reason for the

existence of the RVN, after the assassination of President Diem in 1963.[57] Flynt was a long-

serving Democrat from the American South who had been a strong supporter of gun

ownership, a veteran of World War II, a member of the Appropriations and House Ethics

Committees.[58] Congressman Chappell was first elected to the House in 1969, a naval veteran

of World War II, and later became a member of the Armed Forces Committee where he

advocated for American military equipment expansion.[59]

Before Abzug was first elected to the House of Representatives in 1970 on a platform

that supported feminist values and called for the cession of the American role in the Vietnam

---

[54] Telegram, 27, Deputy Assistant to the President for National Security Affairs Brent Scowcroft to Deputy Ambassador Wolf Lehmann, folder nine, Washington to Saigon January 5, – April 1, 1975 (1), box 7, NSA, Saigon Embassy Files Taken by Ambassador Graham Martin (Copies), 1963-1975 (1976), Gerald R. Ford Presidential Library, Ann Arbor, Michigan.

[55] Kissinger, *Ending the Vietnam War*, 512.

[56] McCloskey as told to Larry Engelmann, *Tears before the Rain*, 26.

[57] Ibid., 27-28.

[58] The Associated Press, "John J. Flynt Jr., Georgia Democrat, Is Dead at 92," *New York Times*, June 25 2007, accessed October 26, 2015, http://www.nytimes.com/2007/06/25/us/25flynt.html?_r=0.

[59] The Associated Press, "Bill Chappell Jr. is Dead at 67; erved in the House for 20 Years," *New York Times*, March 31, 1989, accessed October 26, 2015, http://www.nytimes.com/1989/03/31/obituaries/bill-chappell-jr-is-dead-at-67-served-in-the-house-for-20-years.html.

War.[60] Abzug was a prominent leader in the social activist organization called Women Strike

for Peace, which regularly held protests against American policy in the Vietnam War.[61]

Murtha was a freshman and the first Vietnam Veteran to serve in congress, when he was

requested to join the congressional delegation, while serving as a reservist in the United

States Marine Corps with strong views of service being connected to patriotism.[62] With

interests in human rights as well as international politics, Frasier was a long serving associate

of the Members of Congress for World Peace through Law.[63] Frasier "held hearings on the

Vietnam War" in his home state of Minnesota, and at the 1968 National Democratic

Convention he advocated against continuing the American war effort in Southeast Asia.[64]

One of the major concerns of Fenwick was human rights; she spoke out against hatred and to

human rights violations as early as the 1930s, when she joined the National Conference of

Christians and Jews.[65]

Deputy Ambassador Wolf Lehmann felt that the majority of the congressional

delegation took their duties seriously.[66] With the exceptions of Abzug and Frasier who

---

[60] "Abzug, Bella Savitzky," Office of the Historian of the United States House of Representatives, from History, Art, and Archives, U.S. House of Representatives, accessed July 10, 2015, http://history.house.gov/People/Detail/8276.

[61] Ibid.

[62] "Murtha, John Paterick," Lauren Borsa, last modified Spring 2010, accessed July 10, 2015, http://pabook.libraries.psu.edu/palitmap/bios/Murtha__John.html.

[63] "Donald McKay Frasier," Minnesota Historical Society, last modified 2015, accessed July 10, 2015, http://www2.mnhs.org/library/findaids/00290.xml.

[64] Ibid.

[65] "Fenwick, Millicent Hammond," Office of the Historian of the United States House of Representatives, from History, Art, and Archives, U.S. House of Representatives, accessed July 10, 2015, http://history.house.gov/People/Listing/F/FENWICK,-Millicent-Hammond-(F000078)/.

[66] Wolf Lehmann as told to Larry Engelmann, *Tears before the Rain*, 34.

according to Lehmann were pursuing their own agendas.[67] Dr. Nguyen Tien Hung President Thieu's Special Assistant felt the congressional delegation was very hostile, particularly towards Thieu.[68] While interviewing General Ngo Quang Truong commander of MR I and I Corps, Truong openly omitted to McCloskey that his forces were deployed over such a large geographic area that PAVN could easily overwhelm his forces in large numbers.[69] McCloskey believed the additional aid for the RVN was to be a wasted effort due to the flaws of Vietnamization and the Nationalist Vietnamese defense plan.[70]

McCloskey advocated for supplemental aid for the KR instead.[71] McCloskey based the argument on his observations of the horrific conditions while touring the frontlines outside of KR's capital Phnom Penh.[72] McCloskey had predicted if the Khmer Rouge captured Phnom Penh there would be massive massacres of the two million refugees in the city.[73] McCloskey argued for at least enough funds needed to be allocated for refugees to reach a safe haven.[74]

While traveling back to Washington, the congressional delegation discussed whether or not to advocate to their colleagues to approve President Ford's request for supplemental

---

[67] Wolf Lehmann as told to Larry Engelmann, *Tears before the Rain*, 34.

[68] Nguyen Tien Hung and Schecter, *The Palace File*, 256.

[69] McCloskey as told to Larry Engelmann, *Tears before the Rain*, 28-29.

[70] Ibid.

[71] Ibid.

[72] Ibid., 30-31.

[73] Ibid.

[74] Ibid.

aid for the RVN.[75] The eight members of the congressional delegation were split in half.[76] An observation of the congressional delegation found it was more interested in the political sins of President Thieu as opposed to the predicament the RVN was in.[77] Dr. Kissinger described the congressional delegation to be a successful waste of time.[78]

The DRV understood the economic, political, and military quagmire the RVN faced. The RVN was experiencing economic downturn, struggling to support RVNAF. The Nationalist Vietnamese economy was so severe, RVNAF could not fulfill President Thieu's defense plan. To test the severity of the quagmire the RVN faced, PAVN conquered the entire providence of Phoc Long. Americans across the political spectrum had become so strongly opposed to the Vietnam War, they were unwilling to send further support. President Ford sought to find congressional support for additional military aid for the RVN. Eventually, a congressional delegation was sent, who did not deliver the result President Ford hoped for. While the Ford Administration found little success from the Congressional delegation, PAVN was making military gains.

---

[75] McCloskey as told to Larry Engelmann, *Tears before the Rain*, 26.

[76] Ibid.

[77] Anderson, "Gerald R. Ford and the Presidents' War in Vietnam," from *Shadow on the White House*, 193.

[78] Kissinger, *Ending the Vietnam War*, 512.

Chapter Seven: All Along the Watchtower

In March 1975, after waiting for the American response to PAVN's capture of Phoc Long province, the Communist Vietnamese pushed on with their offensive. Late in the night of March 3, 1975, PAVN began its devastating assault on the Nationalist Vietnamese held city of Ban Me Thuot.[1] PAVN had chosen to begin its prong of assault in the Central Highlands at Ban Me Thuot.[2] Due to the Ban Me Thuot's location at the strategic crossroads of Routes Nationale 14 and 21, along with its lack of RVNAF defenses.[3] By fighting in the Military Regions (MRs) outside of MR 2, Communist Vietnamese decision makers hoped RVNAF would be withdrawn from the Central Highlands in order to soften RVNAF defenses in the region.[4] PAVN's attack on Ban Me Thuot caught decision makers in the RVN by surprise.[5] Since the prevailing opinion at the time was the cities of Pleiku and Kontum would be the greatest possible targets by communist forces.[6] By March 11, Ban Me Thuot and the surrounding area was under the occupation of PAVN and forced RVNAF units deployed north of the city to be dependent on air shipments for supplies.[7] The loss of Ban Me Thuot to the Communist Vietnamese was a prelude to a series of catastrophes and blunders to occur in the latter days of the Vietnam War.

---

[1] Military History Institute of Vietnam, *Victory in Vietnam*, 367.

[2] Ibid., 365.

[3] Ibid.

[4] Military History Institute of Vietnam, *Victory in Vietnam*, 363 and Veith and Pibbenow II, "'Fighting is an Art,'" 170.

[5] Wolf Lehmann as told to Larry Engelmann, *Tears before the Rain*, 33.

[6] Ibid.

[7] Military History Institute of Vietnam, *Victory in Vietnam*, 372-73.

Unlike Phoc Long, President Thieu believed RVNAF could retake Ban Me Thuot which would in theory prevent PAVN a route to reach the coast of the RVN, eliminate PAVN's battle hardened 320th division, and to save several Nationalist Vietnamese units from being lost behind enemy lines.[8] A day after the fall of Ban Me Thuot, 145 helicopter sorties introduced a RVNAF counter attack to the then recently lost city.[9] The RVNAF reinforcements were defeated by the Communist Vietnamese within a few short days.[10] While the RVNAF counter attack was under way, President Thieu came to the conclusion, after conferring with ARVN Major General Pham Van Phu.[11] The Nationalist Vietnamese forces needed to be withdrawn from MR II.[12]

There was minimal planning for the RVNAF withdrawal and it was kept secret until large numbers of soldiers began to leave the city of Pleiku.[13] The withdraw caused numerous civilians to flee in panic with the soldiers along the unmaintained Interprovincial Route LTL-7B.[14][15] Due to the poor condition of Interprovincial Route LTL-7B, RVNAF along with the

---

[8] Nguyen Tien Hung and Schecter, *The Palace File*, 267-68.

[9] Military History Institute of Vietnam, *Victory in Vietnam*, 373-74.

[10] Ibid.

[11] Wolf Lehmann as told to Larry Engelmann, *Tears before the Rain*, 35.

[12] Ibid.

[13] Hung and Schecter, *The Palace File*, 268.

[14] Ibid.

[15] The panic that spread among the Nationalist Vietnamese during the DRV's final offensive was not unfounded because the Communist Vietnamese not relied on propaganda as well as the control of resources needed to survive, they also utilized terror as a means of control to prevent resistance against communist forces. A common horrific tactic used by the NLF when conducting raids on entrenched positions, was to place the families of RVNAF personal in front of advancing waves of Communist Vietnamese combatants in the hope of causing RVNAF defenders to hesitant to fire and to prevent casualties among the communists from Nguyen Cong Luan, *Nationalist in the Viet Nam Wars: Memoirs of a Victim turned Solder* (Bloomington: Indiana University Press, 2012), 550 and 253 respectively.

refugees fleeing from Pleiku, had to fight for one hundred miles against PAVN and took friendly fire from VNAF.[16] When the surviving RVNAF servicemen from Pleiku reached the coast, their units were no longer considered fit for combat. Despite the fact that the Communist Vietnamese, in the month of March, had suffered thousands more causalities than RVNAF, the Nationalist Vietnamese had still lost MR II.[17]

Shortly before withdrawing from Pleiku began, Deputy Ambassador Lehmann consulted with President Thieu on the situation in MR II. Deputy Ambassador Lehmann was never fully informed of the withdrawal but, he did pick up hints on Thieu's intentions from the President's use of language. Deputy Ambassador Lehmann's suspensions of a RVNAF withdraw from MR II, were confirmed from the American Consulate in Nha Trang. Causing Lehmann to order the Consulate to evacuate. While one catastrophe was unfolding in MR 2, another catastrophe began to develop in MR I.[18]

In MR I, on March 8, 1975, PAVN launched another prong of assault into Nationalist Vietnamese held territory.[19] The DRV's goal through the capture of MR II was to cut off ARVN's I Corps located north in MR I from the rest of Nationalist Vietnam.[20] Thousands of refugees had fled from Quang Tri province for the cities of Hue and Danang to seek safety

---

[16] Hung and Schecter, *The Palace File*, 268.

[17] Statistical Trends: Security Situation from SAAFO Studies, Research and Analysis (SRA), March, 1975, MR II-2, Folder Four, 228-08/ Stat. Trends (SAAFO Studies) January through March 1975, Entry# A1 531: General Records; 1969-1975, 228-08/ Hamlet by Military Region, January – February 1975 through 228-08/ Villages by RVN, January – February 1975, Box Nine, Record Group 472, U.S. Forces in Southeast Asia, 1950 – 1975, MACV, HQ CORDS/ Special Assistant to U.S. Ambassador for Field Operations (SAAFO), National Archives, College Park, Maryland.

[18] Wolf Lehmann as told to Larry Engelmann, *Tears before the Rain*, 35.

[19] Lam Quang Thi, *The Twenty-Five Year Century*, 335-36.

[20] Military History Institute of Vietnam, *Victory in Vietnam*, 381.

from the Communist Vietnamese.[21] In a few short days after PAVN began their prong of assault into MR I, President Thieu had ordered the redeployment of elements from the Airborne Division to Saigon.[22] In a meeting with President Thieu, General Truong was ordered to abandon the two Northern most provinces of Quang Tri and Thua Thien in order to enforce a new defense strategy.[23] President Thieu's defense strategy called for three separate enclaves within MR I to be supported by RVNAF.[24] VNAF, due to fuel and ammunition rationing along with the limited number functioning aircraft could not effectively support three Nationalist Vietnamese enclaves.[25] Additionally, Danang airport was within range of PAVN missiles.[26] Faced with overwhelming opposition, General Truong had to defend the greatest amount of territory of the RVN from the Communist Vietnamese on limited resources including the city of Hue.

When the question to defend the city of Hue came up in the meeting with General Truong, President Thieu was indecisive about the continuation of the city's defense. By March 13, President Thieu settled on continuing the defense of Hue while insisting the Marine and Airborne Divisions be redeployed to the two southern most MRs. By March 18, massive waves of refugees were pouring into the Nationalist Vietnamese held cities of MR I.

---

[21] Lam Quang Thi, *The Twenty-Five Year Century*, 337-38.

[22] Ibid., 341.

[23] Ibid., 341.

[24] Ibid., 342.

[25] Ibid., 344

[26] Ibid.

Mixed reports on RVNAF morale from some units determined to defend the region to high rates of desertion were filed.[27]

Troubles mounted even further when Prime Minister Tran Thien Khiem informed General Truong his command would not receive reinforcements. The defense of Hue was crumbling in the face of two PAVN fronts from the north and the south. After listening to pessimistic reports of the defense of Hue, General Thi ordered preparations for an evacuation of the city. Several RVNAF personnel had deserted due to rumors that MR I would be ceded to the Communist Vietnamese and civilians would not be evacuated with the Nationalist military.[28]

By March 27, the four day evacuation of RVNAF from Hue was completed, with 1st Division being comprised of only 2,000 men, while 2nd and 3rd Divisions of I Corps had experienced even greater depletion of strength due to desertion.[29] During the evacuation of Hue, President Thieu had ordered the city to be abandoned, but RVNAF was to prevent Danang from falling under PAVN occupation.[30] The Joint General Staff (JGS) of RVNAF and President Thieu had neither an emergency nor secondary defense plans for the RVN in a time of a military crisis.[31] In the latter half of the month of March, President Thieu had to make efforts and solid decisions, if the RVN was to be saved from the DRV's conquest.

With disastrous defeats in MRs I and II, President Thieu could no longer afford to wait for foreign aid to come to the RVN's rescue without Nationalist Vietnamese persuasion.

---

[27] Lam Quang Thi, *The Twenty-Five Year Century*, 342 and 347-48.

[28] Ibid., 350-51, 355, and 357-58.

[29] Ibid., 358-59.

[30] Hung and Schecter, *The Palace File*, 288.

[31] Ibid., 288.

On March 22, President Thieu held a meeting with his ministers and members of the Vietnamese legislator to develop a strategy to obtain desperate needed aid from the United States. President Thieu asked the attendees of the strategy meeting if it would be wise to go public with their quest for additional aid from the U.S. or to "work quietly" with the Ford Administration as suggested by U.S. Ambassador Martin. Everyone in attendance at President Thieu's strategy meeting, with the exemption of Thieu's Dr. Hung, agreed to pursue the option recommended by Ambassador Martin. After discussing the assurances made by the Nixon Administration around the time period of the signing of the PPA of American intervention on the condition of Communist Vietnamese violation of the peace document. President Thieu and the Nationalist Vietnamese legislative leaders agreed to begin a letter campaign to their American colleagues to up hold the commitments made by the Nixon Administration. Despite the defeats the RVN had suffered, President Thieu was determined to make his defense plan succeed.[32]

President Thieu's overall defense strategy was weak; it overextended RVNAF units over large areas of territory and was dependent on foreign intervention. When President Thieu had learned Nixon resigned from the American presidency, the news caused Thieu to be concerned.[33] Since the defense agreement made between Nixon and President Thieu was in question.[34] The Nixon–Thieu defense agreement allowed the U.S. to intervene on the RVN's behalf on the condition that the DRV made extreme violations of the PPA.[35] In his last meeting with the JGS of RVNAF on August 16, 1974, Major General John E. Murray of

---

[32] Hung and Schecter, *The Palace File*, 282-83, and 283-84.

[33] Ibid., 238.

[34] Ibid.

[35] Letter, President Nixon to President Thieu, December 17, 1972, 2, PDF page 6.

the U.S. Defense Attaché Office in Saigon stated RVNAF needed to redeploy its units to defend areas of high population density within the RVN and for practical reasons unofficially cede rural areas to the Communist Vietnamese.[36]

President Thieu had considered a defense plan similar to the one proposed by Major General Murray before receiving his first letter from President Ford. President Thieu had feared President Ford would not support the understandings to which Nixon had agreed to. Therefore, President Thieu had considered ceding MRs I and II to create a greater defense of the two southern MRs. By ceding the northern two MRs, the RVN would have lost an estimated thirty percent of its population to the Communist Vietnamese, nearly twenty percent decrease in its GNP, the primary economic industries particularly the collection of raw materials was expected to suffer the greatest economic decline, and President Thieu would have forfeited his political doctrine of never to cede territory to the communists. Nevertheless, President Thieu perceived that he had received encouragement on the RVN's defense from the delivery of a letter from President Ford.[37]

Shortly before Ford was sworn in as President of the U.S. (August 8, 1974), he held a meeting with Dr. Kissinger to discuss foreign policy.[38] Both of Ford and Dr. Kissinger agreed to inform American allies despite the change in American leadership of the executive office, the U.S. would not abandon its allies nor would was it going to modify its foreign policy.[39] Shortly after his swearing in ceremony, President Ford sent a letter to President Thieu to reassure the Nationalist Vietnamese leader the U.S. would continue its commitments

---

[36] Hung and Schecter, *The Palace File*, 241.

[37] Ibid., 239-40, 238-39, and 240-41.

[38] Ford, *A Time to Heal*, 33-34.

[39] Ibid.

to the RVN.[40] In the letter, President Ford stressed his understanding that the DRV had made

violations of the PPA and it was his hope through foreign aid the RVN was obtaining would

help the state to transition to a self-sufficient economy.[41] President Ford stated it was his

desire RVNAF to persuade the DRV's politburo to pursue the policy of peace as described in

the PPA and the U.S. supplying the aid the RVN required.[42] After reading President Ford's

letter, President Thieu's morale was raised under the belief Ford planned to uphold the

promises previously made by Nixon, causing Thieu to abandon his plans of consolidation of

the RVN and the redeployment of RVNAF.[43] As March 1975 was reaching a close, Dr. Hung

began to question President Ford's word.

On March 22, 1975 President Ford sent another letter to President Thieu, where Ford

not only acknowledged the situation of the RVN, but he stressed that his Administration

would continue their efforts to obtain additional aid for the RVN within the law.[44] President

Thieu took the letter as a sign that President Ford would support the promises made by

Nixon.[45] Dr. Hung interpreted the line "the law permit" as a negative indication congress had

---

[40] Telegram, President Gerald R. Ford to President Nguyen Van Thieu via the U.S. Embassy in Saigon, August, 1974, 1, Folder Two, VW CD-1 August 9, 1974 – March 3, 1975, Box 38, National Security Advisor Kissinger – Scowcroft West Wing Office Files, 1969-1977, General Subject File: Vietnamese War – 'Camp David File,' Gerald R. Ford Presidential Library, Ann Arbor, Michigan.

[41] Ibid., 1-2.

[42] Ibid., 2.

[43] Hung and Schecter, *The Palace File*, 240-41.

[44] Letter, President Gerald R. Ford to President Nguyen Van Thieu, March 22, 1975, 55-56, PDF, Box 5, National Security Advisor, Presidential Correspondence with Foreign Leaders, 1974-1977, accessed May 25, 2015, http://www.fordlibrarymuseum.gov/library/document/0351/1555873.pdf.

[45] Hung and Schecter, *The Palace File*, 285.

planned to resist further requests of additional aid for the RVN from the Ford Administration.[46]

Shortly before President Ford had sent his March 22 letter, President Thieu asked Dr. Hung how he could persuade the U.S. to send supplemental aid. Dr. Hung stated that Thieu's best option would be to release the American-Nationalist Vietnamese correspondence to the public as a way to appeal to the American public at large. Dr. Hung made two suggestions for a final desperate measure since, the use of military supplies was estimated to be exhausted by June of 1975. The desperate attempts to appeal for additional aid from the U.S., Dr. Hung had proposed were to purchase air time on American television for President Thieu to release the American-Nationalist Vietnamese presidential correspondence or to have a televised exclusive interview with the American Broadcasting Company (ABC). Where the ABC interviewer could be primed to inquire about the contents of the correspondence from Thieu who could then position himself to appeal for more aid. President Thieu was not persuaded by Dr. Hung's proposals, and feared releasing the letters to the public would be construed as a sign of betrayal from the White House. Therefore, President Thieu decided to be more direct with President Ford.[47]

After conferring with his legal advisors, President Thieu chose to write another letter of appeal for additional aid from the U.S. to President Ford.[48] President Thieu's legal advisors concluded under the War Powers Act, President Ford could send B-52 bombers on raids against PAVN divisions south of the DMZ for a total of two weeks.[49] In the final days

---

[46] Hung and Schecter, *The Palace File*, 285.

[47] Ibid., 278-79.

[48] Ibid., 281-82.

[49] Ibid., 280-81.

of March 1975, President Thieu made his first request for American B-52 bomber strikes to be used for the defense of the RVN.[50]

In his March 25 letter, President Thieu began the letter informing President Ford the military situation of the RVN has reached crisis levels, particularly in MRs I and II.[51] President Thieu stated the RVN signed the PPA under the belief the agreement could through "the common resolution of" the two Vietnamese states reach a peace and the U.S. had pledged to assist the RVN, if Communist Vietnamese violations of the peace agreement.[52] Because the DRV had clearly violated the PPA with a full military offensive, President Thieu stressed President Ford needed to uphold the commitments made by the U.S. to the RVN through a brief bombing campaign and additional material aid of military goods.[53] President Thieu made an emotional as well as creditability appeals to President Ford, unless the American pledges to the RVN were to be kept, generations of Nationalist Vietnamese would live under a communist system.[54] Through his March 25 letter, President Thieu demanded President Ford fulfill the promises to intervene in the Vietnam War on the RVN's behalf with American airpower. However, there was miscommunication between Presidents Ford and Thieu.

---

[50] Hung and Schecter, *The Palace File*, 286-87.

[51] Telegram, President Nguyen Van Thieu to President Gerald Ford via Deputy Ambassador Wolf Lehmann to Deputy National Security Advisor General Brent Scowcraft, March 26, 1975, 1-2, Folder Twelve: Saigon to Washington, January 5, 1975 – April 1, 1975 (3), Box 7, National Security Advisor, Saigon Embassy Files Taken by Ambassador Graham Martin (Copies), 1963-1975 (1976), Gerald R. Ford Presidential Library, Ann Arbor, Michigan.

[52] Ibid., 2.

[53] Ibid., 2-3.

[54] Ibid., 3-4.

While President Thieu's March 25 letter was being drafted, Hung came up with a theory concerning the American and Nationalist Vietnamese Presidential correspondence. The theory was President Ford did not have full knowledge of the contents of the Nixon-Thieu letters.[55] Dr. Hung came to this conclusion after he finally reviewed President Thieu's prized secret file of correspondence letters from Nixon and President Ford, while comparing the actions that the Ford White House had taken since the fall of Phoc Long.[56] In fact, President Ford did not have full knowledge of the Nixon-Thieu letters when he entered office and when he sent his first letter to President Thieu to assure the Nationalist Vietnamese President the Ford Administration would uphold American commitments to the RVN.[57]

Before President Ford had sent his first letter to President Thieu, he had not reviewed the entire Nixon-Thieu correspondence.[58] All of Nixon's letters to President Thieu were kept secret from not only the American public, but his cabinet as well.[59] President Ford had mirrored Nixon's action on keeping presidential correspondence with President Thieu secret from his cabinet as well.[60] However, Ford had never made controversial pledges to the RVN as Nixon had before him.[61] President Ford's letters to President Thieu were prepared by his

[55] Hung and Schecter, *The Palace File*, 290.

[56] Ibid.

[57] Anderson, "Gerald R. Ford and the Presidents' War in Vietnam," from *Shadow on the White House*, 188.

[58] Hung and Schecter, *The Palace File*, 291.

[59] Jerrold L. Schecter, "The Final Days: The Political Struggle to End the Vietnam War," from Gerald R. Ford and the Politics of Post-Watergate America, volume two, edited by Bernard J. Firestone and Alexej Ugrinsky (Westport, Connecticut: Greenwood Press, 1993), 541.

[60] Ibid., 542.

[61] Ibid.

NSC staff.[62] While Nixon served as President, his correspondence was drafted by his NSC which included Dr. Kissinger.[63]

President Ford had often attempted to make policies that were designed to interact with disheartened Americans in an effort to contrast from the strategies developed by the Nixon Administration.[64] However, many of the Ford White House staff members had remained from the Nixon Administration were usually worked to carry out the strategies sent forth by Nixon rather than Ford's policies.[65] When President Ford accepted Jack Marsh's suggestion of expanding the number of key White House staff members to contact the president directly after office hours with Hartmann and Marsh screening messages of questionable importance outside of the list of individuals approved by Ford himself.[66] Remnants of the former Nixon Administration aides informed the White House switchboard operators the order of communication to remain through then Chief of Staff General Haig.[67] Press Secretary Nessen believed Dr. Kissinger had been attempting to preserve Nixon's policy on Southeast Asia largely because it was Dr. Kissinger who had helped develop the strategy.[68]

---

[62] Anderson, "Gerald R. Ford and the Presidents' War in Vietnam," from *Shadow on the White House*, 188.

[63] Schecter, "The Final Days: The Political Struggle to End the Vietnam War," from Gerald R. Ford and the Politics of Post-Watergate America, volume two, 540-41.

[64] Hartmann, *Palace Politics*, 217-18.

[65] Ibid.

[66] Ibid., 219-20.

[67] Ibid.

[68] Nessen, *It Sure Looks Different from the Inside*, 101.

The RVN was an ally with strong ties to the U.S. and President Ford could not simply ignore President Thieu's March 25 request. President Ford had to make a noteworthy response to express the claims of American support for the Nationalist Vietnamese. The American response had to be made quickly for the RVN because of the severe losses in the central highlands of MR 2. President Thieu sought to bring additional military aid from the U.S. through the Nixon-Thieu correspondence. The contents of the Nixon-Thieu correspondence was fully unknown to President Ford who wanted to fulfill American obligations around the world.

Chapter Eight: Keep Searchin'

By the end of March 1975, PAVN had captured thirteen provinces south of the DMZ, which caused President Ford to fear if the U.S. did not act, the state's foreign policy creditability would suffer around the world, and felt he was not receiving the correct information on the Vietnam War.[1] Therefore President Ford sent a research team to Southeast Asia.[2] In a meeting on March 25, Dr. Kissinger insisted that President Ford send anything RVNAF required.[3]

President Ford wanted General Frederick C. Weyand give him a full assessment on the military needs of the RVN and options that would be "shocking to the North (DRV)," a mission in which Weyand accepted with high confidence.[4] General Weyand's formal team of researchers consisted of Vietnam experts from the Department of Defense and the CIA, who acted as President Ford's response to President Thieu's March 25 letter.[5] A unique volunteer for General Weyand's mission was White House photographer David Kennerly, who had not only worked in Southeast Asia as a photographer for "two and a half years," but had

---

[1] Ford, *A Time to Heal*, 250-51.

[2] Ibid.

[3] Meeting Minutes, Memoranda of Conversation: President Gerald R. Ford with General Frederick C. Weyand and U.S. Ambassador to the Republic of Vietnam Graham Martin, March 25, 1975, Central File Code: 036600012, box 10, Memoranda of Conversations – Ford Administration, PDF, 3, Gerald R. Ford Presidential Library, Ann Arbor, Michigan, accessed May 25, 2015, http://www.fordlibrarymuseum.gov/library/document/0314/1553000.pdf

[4] Ibid., 3-4.

[5] Schecter, "The Final Days: The Political Struggle to End the Vietnam War," from Gerald R. Ford and the Politics of Post-Watergate America, volume two, 544.

President Ford's upmost trust that the information he would bring back.[6] For reasons

unexplained in President Ford's autobiography, he did have strong reasons to trust Kennerly.

President Ford's trust in Kennerly was most likely based on their personal friendship.

When President Nixon was searching for a new vice president, Kennerly went to Ford's

congressional office to get an exclusive photograph of the then new vice president based on a

hunch from Kennerly's editor. The two had a humorous exchange about how they were

wasting each other's time. Kennerly's assignment from Time Magazine to cover the vice

President of the U.S., included Ford after he was appointed to the Vice presidency. Since

Vice President Ford heavily campaigned for other Republican candidates in 1974, Kennerly

followed Ford on his travels, and Kennerly was welcomed to accompany Ford on his

journeys.[7]

After Ford was sworn in as president, he offered Kennerly the position of White

House photographer. Kennerly agreed under the condition that he have unlimited access to

the Ford White House. The next day, Kennerly received a phone call from President Ford to

report to the White House for work and was given a top secret security clearance for

unlimited access in the White House. While President Ford's wife, Betty, was resting in the

hospital after an operation, Kennerly accompanied President Ford every day to visit Betty.

Additionally, Kennerly, with the assistance of President Ford's daughter Susan, gave the

Fords their golden retriever, Liberty, who can be seen in photographs as the unofficial

member of the NSC.[8]

---

[6] Ford, *A Time to Heal*, 251.

[7] David Hume Kennerly, *Shooter* (New York: Newsweek Books, 1979), 112-13 and 113-14.

[8] Ibid., 127-28, 128-29, and 155-156.

Kennerly felt that President Ford had trusted him in a similar manner as he had trusted one of his sons.[9] Before Kennerly had left for the RVN with General Weyand, he needed money for the trip.[10] Kennerly asked President Ford if he could borrow some money, and Ford gave Kennerly all the cash he had on him.[11] Despite President Ford's trust in Kennerly, General Weyand's research team would bring back information that would create more trials for the Ford Administration.

General Weyand and his team of researchers arrived on March 28, 1975. Increasing morale amongst some Nationalist Vietnamese decision makers along with high ranking RVNAF personnel who believed that Weyand could obtain the aid the RVN required to defeat PAVN. On the first night General Weyand's team in the RVN, Dr. Hung met with a member of Weyand's team Eric Von Marbod to discuss the purpose of Weyand's visit. It was at this meeting where Dr. Hung showed Von Marbod, President Thieu's files of the Nixon-Thieu correspondence. Von Marbod was shocked, not only at the letters' contents, but the fact the letters were hidden from decision makers. A short time later, Dr. Hung gave copies of four letters from President Thieu's correspondence file to Von Marbod. Dr. Hung hoped the Nixon-Thieu correspondence copies would persuade President Ford to intervene in the Vietnam War with military force as described in Nixon's letters. With knowledge of the Nixon-Thieu letters General Weyand's team traveled north to the city of Danang to continue on with their research.[12]

---

[9] Kennerly, *Shooter*, 193.

[10] Ford, *A Time to Heal*, 251.

[11] Ibid.

[12] Hung and Schecter, *The Palace File*, 290, 292-93, 294-95, and 296-97.

When General Weyand's team reached the city of Danang, the metropolis was in the process of collapsing. PAVN had launched its assault into MR I, the population of Danang grew from three hundred thousand, to an estimated two million due to the influx of refugees into the city.[13] Because the population of Danang was rapidly growing in the latter days of the Vietnam War, the Nationalist Vietnamese authorities in the city exhausted all of their resources to feed and provide shelter to two million people.[14] Since January 1, 1975, the National Police Force (NPF) of the RVN had suffered high casualities with the majority being wounded.[15] In the month of March however, large numbers of NPF officers became MIAs.[16] The lack of internal security, shortages of necessities, and overcrowding led to the growth of armed gangs roaming around Danang.[17]

By March 25, 1975, PAVN had surrounded Danang from every direction with the expectation of the South China Sea.[18] Shortly before the fall of Hue, President Thieu had informed Deputy Ambassador Lehmann, he planned to evacuate MR I due to the bleak military situation in the region.[19] In a telephone conversation with the JGS on March 27, General Truong reported his forces could no longer defend Danang and requested to begin an evacuation.[20] General Truong was ordered to discuss the Danang situation with President

---

[13] Lam Quang Thi, *The Twenty-Five Year Century*, 360.

[14] Ibid., 362.

[15] Statistical Trends: Security Situation from SAAFO Studies, Research and Analysis (SRA), March, 1975, 7.

[16] Ibid.

[17] Lam Quang Thi, *The Twenty-Five Year Century*, 360.

[18] Military History Institute of Vietnam, *Victory in Vietnam*, 388.

[19] Lehmann as told to Larry Engelmann, *Tears before the Rain*, 36.

[20] Lam Quang Thi, *The Twenty-Five Year Century*, 363.

Thieu, who could not be reached until 10 PM.[21] When General Truong informed the

Nationalist Vietnamese president "he would act according to the development of the

situation."[22] When General Truong hung up the phone, he ordered his staff to begin the

evacuation of Danang.[23]

Panic had flared up amongst the civilian population of Danang and RVNAF once the

U.S. Consulate began to evacuate.[24] Despite the panic the American Consulate staff caused,

they did make efforts to evacuate refugees from Danang.[25] At Danang airport, Nationalist

Vietnamese authorities struggled to maintain order, while roads to the airport and Marble

Mountain pier were heavily congested.[26] In response to the plight of the refugees, the U.S.

Department of Defense deployed naval vessels to Danang for offshore evacuation of

refugees.[27]

While in Danang, Kennerly took pictures from an Air America helicopter en-route to

retrieve Alan Francis, the American Consul General of Danang, from the *Pioneer*

Commander.[28] The helicopter took friendly fire from a nearby VNN ship leaving the city,

---

[21] Lam Quang Thi, *The Twenty-Five Year Century*, 363.

[22] Ibid.

[23] Ibid.

[24] Ibid., 360.

[25] Lehmann as told to Larry Engelmann, *Tears before the Rain*, 37.

[26] Telegram, U.S. Ambassador to the Republic of Vietnam Graham Martin to Secretary of State Henry Kissinger, March 27, 1975, Folder six, VN SD TG to SECSTATE EXDIS (3), Box 21, National Security Advisor, Presidential Country Files for East Asia and the Pacific; Country File: Vietnam Department of State Telegrams, Gerald R. Ford Presidential Library, Ann Arbor, Michigan.

[27] Telegram, Secretary of State Henry Kissinger to U.S. Ambassador to the Republic of Vietnam Graham Martin, March 30, 1975, Folder one, VN-SD TG to SECSTATE-EXDIS, Box 21, National Security Advisor, Presidential Country Files for East Asia and the Pacific; Country File: Vietnam Department of State Telegrams, Gerald R. Ford Presidential Library, Ann Arbor, Michigan.

[28] Kennerly, *Shooter*, 170-71.

which Kennerly theorized the incident was out of frustration and sense of abandonment from the Nationalist Vietnamese.[29] When a world Airways Boeing 727 landed at Danang airport, fleeing RVNAF personnel fired upon the 727 to cease taxiing before being swarmed by refugees and fleeing military persons.[30] Some of the refugees and military personnel used violence to board the aircraft.[31] When the World Airways Boeing 727 took off from Danang with 358 passengers in an aircraft designed to carry a maximum of 133 passengers, the aircraft was fired upon again during takeoff.[32] After swimming out into the open sea to reach the evacuation fleet, General Truong was ordered without artillery or air support to retake Danang by means of only one diminished division.[33] By March 29, the entire city of Danang was under PAVN's occupation.[34] The information of the events which occurred in Danang and the RVN did spread to other parts of the world.

The major events transpiring within Southeast Asia during the early months of 1975 were public knowledge. Different news agencies covered the traumatic events that occurring within the RVN. In a March 29, 1975, CBS News broadcast, an anchor described the panic in Danang as PAVN was approaching the city before introducing reporter Bruce Dunning's graphic footage of the last flight from Danang aboard a World Airways Boeing 727.[35] Shortly after she left the World Airways Boeing 727 from Danang, Jan Wollett was

---

[29] Kennerly, *Shooter*, 170-71.

[30] Jan Wollett as told to Larry Engelmann, *Tears before the Rain*, 4-5.

[31] Ibid.

[32] Ibid., 6-7.

[33] Lam Quang Thi, *The Twenty-Five Year Century*, 365-66.

[34] Military History Institute of Vietnam, *Victory in Vietnam*, 393.

[35] CBS, "Dunning's Frantic Flight, March 29, 1975," *CBS News*, online streaming video file, 0:05, last modified 2015, accused July 20, 2015, http://www.cbsnews.com/videos/dunnings-frantic-flight/.

interviewed by NBC News and later interviewed by a Los Angeles radio station.[36] As PAVN continued on with its conquest of the RVN, news reporters in general were remaining inside Saigon rather than documenting events on the battlefields.[37] ABC News correspondent Ken Kashiwahara was assigned to cover stories outside of Saigon where he documented civilians fleeing by the hundreds from PAVN in Qui Nhon and Nha Trang, before travel restrictions were enforced due to the PAVN advance.[38] Shortly after the fall of Danang, General Weyand and his team were ready to complete their mission.

On the last day of General Weyand's research mission, his team met with President Thieu and several of his advisors.[39] In the final meeting, General Cao Van Vien requested B-52 bomber strikes or Daisy Cutter bombs to at least stop the momentum of PAVN's invasion of the RVN.[40] A Daisy Cutter bomb is a 15,000 pound conventional explosive device designed to clear an area with a 600 foot radius and shock waves which can be felt for several miles away, and was originally utilized by the U.S. to clear dense jungle in Southeast Asia for landing zones.[41] Throughout the mission, General Weyand and his team were informed that the best option to halt the Communist Vietnamese advance were B-52 bomber strikes.[42]

---

[36] Jan Wollett as told to Larry Engelmann, *Tears before the Rain*, 11-12.

[37] Daniel Schwartz, "The Fall of Saigon: How CBC, CTV covered the 1975 Events," *CBC News*, April 30, 2015, accessed July 20, 2015, http://www.cbc.ca/news/world/the-fall-of-saigon-how-cbc-ctv-covered-the-1975-events-1.3055237.

[38] Ken Kashiwahara as told to Larry Engelmann, *Tears before the Rain*, 159-60.

[39] Hung and Schecter, *The Palace File*, 298.

[40] Ibid., 300.

[41] "The Daisy Cutter Bomb: Largest Conventional Bomb in Existence," Carolyn Lauer, last modified by Jim Maher and John Maschmayer of the University of Notre Dame, accessed July 3, 2015, https://www3.nd.edu/~techrev/Archive/Spring2002/a8.html.

While his team was still conducting research, General Weyand was ordered to report to President Ford in Palm Springs, California when his team had concluded their mission.[43] In response to his orders, General Weyand confirmed his intention to follow through with President Ford's command and remarked about how the revised defense plan of the RVN after the fall of MR I had left a positive impression on him.[44] A discussion with a U.S. Department of State Official on the developments in the Vietnam War around to time of his mission, convinced Kennerly that the RVN was about to fall.[45] During the flight to Palm Springs, General Weyand and his team wrote their report while Kennerly wrote his own statement.[46] Kennerly sent his film to be developed in Washington, D.C., where he would receive it the following day for his presentation to President Ford.[47] It was from General Weyand's and Kennerly's presentations of their fact finding mission would be a major influence on President Ford's decision making on the Vietnam War.

In Palm Springs, on the afternoon of April 5, 1975, President Ford had met with General Weyand and Kennerly in separate briefings for each of the presenters, knowing the military situation of the RVN was becoming increasingly desperate, Ford still had hope the

---

[42] Hung and Schecter, *The Palace File*, 297.

[43] Telegram, Deputy National Security Advisor General Brent Scowcroft to General Frederick C. Weyand, March, 1975, Folder nine, Washington, D.C. to Saigon January 5, 1975 – April 1, 1975 (1), Box 7, National Security Advisor, Saigon Embassy Files Taken by Ambassador Graham Martin (Copies), 1963-1975 (1976), Gerald R. Ford Presidential Library, Ann Arbor, Michigan.

[44] Telegram, General Frederick C. Weyand to Deputy National Security Advisor General Brent Scowcroft, March 28, 1975, Folder twelve, Saigon to Washington, D.C. January 5, 1975 – April 1, 1975 (3), Box 7, National Security Advisor, Saigon Embassy Files Taken by Ambassador Graham Martin (Copies), 1963-1975 (1976), Gerald R. Ford Presidential Library, Ann Arbor, Michigan.

[45] Kennerly, *Shooter*, 173.

[46] Ibid., 173-74.

[47] Ibid.

state of affairs for the Nationalist Vietnamese could improve.[48] To which President Ford

eagerly awaited to review Weyand's report.[49] For the first meeting, President Ford met with

General Weyand, who gave the President his report.[50] Although General Weyand did make a

copy of his report available for Secretary of Defense Schlesinger, Weyand insisted he hand

President Ford a copy during his meeting with Ford.[51]

In the report, General Weyand discusses the events which led to the Ho Chi Minh

Offensive. Intelligence available to General Weyand on the Communist offensive, the

situation the RVN was in during Weyand's mission, deficiencies, along with the defense

plans of the RVN as early as April, 1975, possible outcomes, and recommendation options

for the U.S. to pursue all included in the report. General Weyand briefly converses on how

the DRV blatantly violated the PPA by not only building up their forces, but the state

launched a major military offensive. American aid for the RVN declined with RVNAF spare

parts and fuel reduced by fifty percent, ammunition shrinking down to thirty percent, all the

while PAVN was reconstructing itself. General Weyand describes how MRs I and II fell to

the Communist Vietnamese. President Thieu's defense plan for the remainder of Nationalist

Vietnamese held territory as of April 4, 1975 are included. With a background of the military

situation of the RVN established, General Weyand moved on to describe the circumstances

of RVNAF shortly before he left the area. [52]

---

[48] Ford, *A Time to Heal*, 252-53.

[49] Ibid.

[50] Ibid., 253.

[51] Memorandum, Clinton E. Granger to Deputy National Security Advisor Brent Scowcroft, April 5, 1975, "A Second Opinion on General Weyand's Visit to South Vietnam" from Selected Documents on the Vietnam War, PDF, 1, Gerald R. Ford Presidential Library, Ann Arbor, Michigan, accessed May 25, 2015, http://www.fordlibrarymuseum.gov/library/exhibits/vietnam/032400082-001.pdf.

General Weyand stated in his report RVNAF was able to hold off PAVN assaults in MR III, particularly in the cities of Tay Ninh and Xuan Loc. PAVN outnumbered RVNAF "just under three to one in size." Outlined in General Weyand's report are two possible outcomes of the DRV's Ho Chi Minh Offensive. Possibility A articulates that the DRV would push on for a total victory over the RVN. On the other hand, possibility B confers in order to consolidate communist gains in the two northern MRs, the Communist Vietnamese enter negotiations for a coalition government to be established in the RVN. With a prospect of the DRV mounting another military offensive if President Thieu declines the Communist Vietnamese surrender terms during negotiations. Next, General Weyand moved into some of the most problematic issues of the RVN.[53]

Although numerous issues faced the RVN, General Weyand focused on the immediate problems threatening the survival of the state in his report. First and foremost was the sheer size of the PAVN invasion force compared to that of RVNAF, along with PAVN's ability to resupply itself after conducting hard line assaults. Second, there was the issue of the care and resettlement of the large number of refugees. The lack of firm and compelling leadership with the RVN when compared to the political guidance that was exercised in the United Kingdom during World War II was the third issue listed by General Weyand. The fourth problem General Weyand listed was the sense of hopelessness among the Nationalist Vietnamese, i.e. low morale.[54]

---

[52] Report to the President of the United States on the Situation in South Vietnam, General Frederick C. Weyand to President Gerald R. Ford, April 4, 1975, "Vietnam Assessment Report by General Frederick C. Weyand" from Selected Documents on the Vietnam War, PDF, 1-2 and 3-4, PDF pages 3-4 and 5-6, Gerald R. Ford Presidential Library, Ann Arbor, Michigan, accessed May 25, 2015, http://www.fordlibrarymuseum.gov/library/exhibits/vietnam/032400081-001.pdf.

[53] Ibid., 3-4 and 5-6, PDF pages 5-6 and 7-8.

[54] Ibid., 7-8 and 9, PDF pages 9-10 and 11.

General Weyand did state the RVN had a plan to defend the state from PAVN by holding territory in MRs III and IV along with Cam Ranh in MR II. With surviving RVNAF units from MRs I and II, the JGS planned to quickly reorganize the units for combat. General Weyand had noted earlier in his report, that due to the large loss of equipment, several surviving RVNAF units lacked the means to defend the RVN. General Weyand stated the RVN did have a plan to defend itself with the loss of MRs I and II. Although, General Weyand affirmed the leadership of the RVN did not clearly understand the magnitude of the situation. With a sense of the situation on the Vietnam War as of April 4, 1975, General Weyand then informed President Ford of possible action the U.S. could take to aid the RVN.[55]

Based on the information he had gathered, General Weyand concluded that the RVN would fall to the DRV if PAVN's offensive was not brought to a halt either through the orders of the DRV's Politburo or by other means. Meanwhile, for the RVN to achieve victory, the state needed to utilize its military forces to hold their ground against PAVN. With the rate of PAVN's advance, time was not in favor of the RVN's rate of mobilization. Therefore, General Weyand made a controversial recommendation.

> The action which the U.S. could take which would have the greatest immediate effect on Vietnamese perceptions —North and South— would be the use of U.S. air power to blunt the current NVA (PAVN) offensive. Even if confined to South Vietnam (RVN) and carried out for only a limited time, such attacks would take a severe toll on the North Vietnamese (PAVN) expeditionary force's manpower and supplies, and have a dramatic morale impact on North Vietnam's (DRV's) invading troops. These attacks would also give Hanoi's leaders' pause and raise concerns, which do not now exist, about the risks involved in ignoring a formal agreement made with the United States.

---

[55] Report to the President of the United States on the Situation in South Vietnam, Weyand to President Ford, April 4, 1975, 10-11, PDF pages 12-13.

General Weyand understood the recommendation was solely based on military matters, not political concerns, of which he was aware of. Additionally, General Weyand made a long-term recommendation of a list of equipment needed to supply the remanding RVNAF units, which amounted to an aid package of $722.2 million. With the expectations of the supplies reaching their assigned units in a period of forty-five days. Finally, General Weyand concluded his report with the fact, American creditability as an ally was at stake along with the longstanding goal of maintaining an RVN as "free and independent." General Weyand's report, was not the only topic of discussion during the meeting between President Ford and General Weyand.[56]

During his meeting with President Ford, General Weyand briefly discussed political matters. Before Dr. Kissinger arrived to the meeting, General Weyand brought up the Nixon-Thieu correspondence and handed him the four copies that were given to Von Marbod by Dr. Hung.[57] It is believed President Ford discovered the contents of the Nixon-Thieu letters during his meeting with General Weyand.[58] Based on his team's research, General Weyand attempted to persuade President Ford to re-introduce B-52s into the Vietnam War.[59] Dr. Kissinger remarked that the American public would not stand for the American re-entry into the war, a comment that echoed a remark made by President Ford earlier in the year.[60]

---

[56] Report to the President of the United States on the Situation in South Vietnam, Weyand to President Ford, April 4, 1975, 10-11, 12, and 14-15, PDF pages 12-13, 14, and 16-17.

[57] Hung and Schecter, *The Palace File*, 302.

[58] Anderson, "Gerald R. Ford and the Presidents' War in Vietnam," from *Shadow on the White House*, 188.

[59] Hung and Schecter, *The Palace File*, 304.

[60] Ibid.

In February 1975, Supreme Allied Commander Europe, General Haig insisted that

President Ford behave more like Harry S. Truman and launch a bombing campaign against

the DRV in retaliation for the Communist Vietnamese capture of Phoc Long province.[61]

President Ford responded that the American public did not want additional involvement in

the Vietnam War and would not support American re-entry into the conflict.[62] Dr. Kissinger

felt any form of aid for the RVN would only buy the state a little time before it collapsed.[63]

Hartmann agreed with Dr. Kissinger although, American aid was justifiable, it would not be

used effectively in the time it was needed.[64] When the meeting with Weyand concluded,

President Ford wanted to discuss the findings of another report on the RVN.

Shortly after he had met with General Weyand, President Ford conferred with

Kennerly about his report. Kennerly gave his pictures from the Weyand mission to President

Ford. As President Ford sadly shook his head at the images of masses of fleeing Nationalist

Vietnamese civilians and the hospitals in Phnom Penh, the capital of the KR.[65] President

Ford even studied the photographs of fleeing soldiers.[66] President Ford had noted Kennerly

was very cynical, with Kennerly stating that the KR was about to fall at any moment.[67] While

on the subject of the RVN, Kennerly stated to President Ford anyone would be "bullshitting

you if they say that Vietnam has got more than three or four weeks left."[68]

---

[61] Hung and Schecter, *The Palace File*, 251.

[62] Ibid.

[63] Kissinger, *Ending the Vietnam War*, 537-38.

[64] Hartmann, *Palace Politics*, 318.

[65] Kennerly, *Shooter*, 174.

[66] Ford, *A Time to Heal*, 253.

[67] Ibid.

After viewing the photographs and hearing Kennerly's assessment, President Ford felt distressed.[69] Later when President Ford returned to the White House, Kennerly's photos from the Weyand mission where displayed throughout the building, and Ford replied to complaints about the graphic pictures the White House staff needed to understand the nature of the situation in Southeast Asia.[70] After the meetings with General Weyand and Kennerly, President Ford stopped in San Francisco to aid volunteers in the transfer Vietnamese orphans from the aircraft to ground transportation to someplace to stay.[71]

President Ford was faced with many difficult decisions concerning the Vietnam War, particularly additional military aid. President Ford felt he needed more information and firsthand accounts from trusted advisors. Therefore, General Weyand was sent with a research team, who were accompanied by White House photographer Kennerly. It was during the fact finding mission, where Dr. Hung gave copies of the Nixon-Thieu correspondence to the Weyand team. When General Weyand and Kennerly returned, they presented their findings to President Ford. Both reports were discussed the demise of the RVN at length. General Weyand's report states American air power and additional military aid the save the remainder of the RVN. With information on PAVN's Ho Chi Minh Offensive collected first hand by General Weyand and Kennerly, President Ford waited to make a decision on the RVN.

---

[68] Ford, *A Time to Heal*, 253.

[69] Kennerly, *Shooter*, 174.

[70] Ibid.

[71] Nessen, *It Sure Looks Different from the Inside*, 98-99.

Chapter Nine: Who'll stop the Rain?

Concerning the RVN, President Ford strongly felt action needed to be taken to aid the innocents affected by the Vietnam War. President Ford wanted to ponder on the course of action the U.S. was to take in reaction to the major defeats the RVN had recently experienced. All decisions on Southeast Asia were to be made after he returned to Washington. However, action needed to be made soon, if the RVN was to survive. President Ford wanted to make fully informed decisions. Which is why President Ford sought advice from many individuals he respected.[1]

While consulting advisors on a possible course of action, President Ford sought the advice of individuals associated with the NSC along with numerous other persons.[2] Press Secretary Nessen strongly opposed American re-entry into the Vietnam War and encouraged President Ford not to send additional aid to the RVN.[3] Because Press Secretary Nessen believed supplemental aid would only delay the conclusion of the Vietnam War.[4] Hartmann reflected on the situation of the RVN and the political landscape in the U.S. during 1975.[5] To Hartmann, American bombing and additional aid to the RVN was politically unrealistic which would only postpone the inevitable fall of the RVN.[6] Dr. Kissinger argued the U.S.

---

[1] Nessen, *It Sure Looks Different from the Inside*, 99-100.

[2] Ibid., 100-01.

[3] Ibid., 101.

[4] Ibid.

[5] Hartmann, *Palace Politics*, 318.

[6] Ibid.

had a moral obligation to assist the RVN against the Communist Vietnamese offensive.[7]

However, Dr. Kissinger had doubts additional aid could be utilized in time by RVNAF.[8] CIA

Director Colby saw no issues for the U.S. to renew bombing in Southeast Asia.[9] After

President Ford requested a supplemental aid package of $300 million for the RVN, he

received a letter signed by eighty-two members of Congress demanding that the U.S. make a

complete withdrawal from Southeast Asia.[10] The percentage of Congressmen who signed the

demand for a total American withdraw, from Southeast Asia was nineteen percent out of 435

members of Congress.[11] Late in the Vietnam War, Gallup, Inc. found more than seventy-five

percent of Americans opposed additional aid for the RVN.[12] With various opinions and a vast

amount of information weighing on President Ford, he had come to a decision.

After returning from Palm Springs, President Ford met with Dr. Kissinger and Deputy

National Security Advisor Brent Scowcroft on April 3. During the meeting, Dr. Kissinger

responded to an old request from President Ford, which was how past presidents would have

reacted to the military setbacks in the RVN of 1975. Dr. Kissinger argued Dwight D.

Eisenhower would have sent American air power and diplomatic notes stating his intent to

the major communist powers along with the DRV. Dr. Kissinger went on to say that

President Ford could simply withdraw American personnel from the RVN, a

---

[7] Kissinger, *Ending the Vietnam War*, 537-38.

[8] Ibid.

[9] Colby with McCargar, *Lost Victory*, 8.

[10] Anderson, "Gerald R. Ford and the Presidents' War in Vietnam," from *Shadow on the White House*, 191-92.

[11] "Congressional Profiles: Ninety-Fourth Congress, 1975-1977," Office of the Historian of the United States House of Representatives, from History, Art, and Archives, U.S. House of Representatives, accessed July 13, 2015, http://history.house.gov/Congressional-Overview/Profiles/94th/.

[12] Lunch and Sperlich, "American Public Opinion and the War in Vietnam," 32.

recommendation President Ford disliked. Dr. Kissinger then replied the PPA worked well enough for the U.S. until the summer 1974.[13]

On one hand, President Ford wanted to move past the Vietnam War.[14] President Ford knew the Vietnam War divided the American public and dishonored the United States.[15] On the other hand, President Ford felt he needed to fulfill an obligation to aid an ally in need, while maintaining American creditability as an ally.[16] In response to Dr. Kissinger's comment, President Ford declared his decision to Dr. Kissinger, where he planned to follow through with the PPA.[17] President Ford announced his intentions to persuade congress for additional aid to be sent to the RVN, while he pursued an evacuation plan and authority to conduct such an operation.[18] With all the information he had absorbed, President Ford had chosen to get as many refugees out of Southeast Asia as possible.[19] President Ford had declined to launch a bombing campaign in Southeast Asia because due to the anti-war climate in the U.S. during 1975 and having previously pardoned Nixon. President Ford knew by ordering American re-entry into the Vietnam War, he would have isolated himself politically for an ally he could not save.

---

[13] Meeting minutes, Memorandum of Conversation, April 3, 1975, Central File Code: 0366001113, Box 10, Memoranda of Conversations – Ford Administration, PDF, 1-2, Gerald R. Ford Presidential Library, Ann Arbor, Michigan, accessed May 25, 2015, http://www.fordlibrarymuseum.gov/library/document/0314/1553015.pdf.

[14] Schecter, "The Final Days: The Political Struggle to End the Vietnam War," from Gerald R. Ford and the Politics of Post-Watergate America, volume two, 545.

[15] Ford, *A Time to Heal*, 249.

[16] Ibid., 249-50.

[17] Meeting minutes, Memorandum of Conversation, April 3, 1975, 2.

[18] Ibid.

[19] Ford, *A Time to Heal*, 253.

During March 1975 President Ford was at his lowest job approval rating from the American public according to Gallup, Inc. at thirty-seven percent.[20] President Ford focused on long-term political objectives such as his goal of reconciliation of the American nation from the trauma which occurred in the previous administration, continuing Détente, or even his desire to pursue a long lasting peace agreement to the Yom Kippur War.[21] Détente being a period of in the Cold War were the U.S. and the USSR attempted to cooperate with one another on security as well as economic concerns.[22] In President Ford's mindset, a short bombing campaign in Vietnam would have little effect in the War's final outcome. Bombing campaigns required political objectives to maximize the lethality of air power in order to be effective.[23] If political objectives do match the designed application of air power, it still does not guarantee success due to the large amount of factors that influence political outcomes through military means.[24] Although President Ford had made a decision, his choice needed to be implemented.

On April 9, 1975, President Ford informed his staff and some members of congress, his plans for the situation the RVN was facing at the time. In a meeting with congressional leaders, Dr. Kissinger informed the members of congress the Ford Administration was in the process of developing plans concerning the 6,000 Americans in the RVN. Due to security

---

[20] "Presidential Approval Ratings – Gallup Historical Statistics and Trends," Gallup, Inc., last modified 2015, accessed July 13, 2015, http://www.gallup.com/poll/116677/presidential-approval-ratings-gallup-historical-statistics-trends.aspx.

[21] Ford, *A Time to Heal*, 245-46.

[22] David Reynolds, *Summits: Six Meetings that Shaped the Twentieth Century* (New York: Basic Books, 2007), 223.

[23] Clodfelter, *The Limits of Air Power*, 203-04.

[24] Ibid.

concerns, the plans could not be revealed at the meeting. President Ford did give a hint of his plans for the RVN when he was discussing his orders to reduce the number of Americans in the KR. While on the topic of anti-American sentiment in the RVN, President Ford affirmed in announcing an evacuation and to publicly declare the RVN was bound to fall would create anti-American sentiment through the panic caused by the pessimistic declarations. President Ford requested Congressman George Mahon to delay his final hearing on supplementary aid for the RVN, sensing there was not much of a chance for the approval for the additional aid.[25] Intelligence briefings concerning the fate of the RVN were taking place in other Washington circles.

In a NSC meeting CIA Director Colby briefed the NSC members that PAVN was slowly approaching Saigon, Communist Vietnamese activity in MR IV had increased, and the DRV's Politburo revised of their plans for a complete military victory in 1975 instead of 1976 as previously stated in intelligence reports.[26] In Cambodia, CIA Director Colby reported the KR defenses around Phnom Penh were weakening, KR ammunition stocks were expected to be depleted by April 25 even with ammunition resupply from the U.S., and Phnom Penh was expected to fall to the Khmer Rouge when the month.[27] Dr. Kissinger stated if the Ford Administration does not make a public effort for supplemental aid for the

---

[25] Meeting minutes, Memoranda of Conversation: Joint Leadership Meeting, Early April, 1975, Box 10, Memoranda of Conversations – Ford Administration, PDF, 3-4, Gerald R. Ford Presidential Library, Ann Arbor, Michigan, accessed May 25, 2015, http://www.fordlibrarymuseum.gov/library/document/0314/1553017.pdf.

[26] Meeting minutes, National Security Council Meeting, April 9, 1975, Central File Code: 031200012, Box 1, National Security Advisor, National Security Council Meeting File, 2-3, Gerald R. Ford Presidential Library, Ann Arbor, Michigan, accessed May 25, 2015, http://www.fordlibrarymuseum.gov/library/document/0312/1552383.pdf.

[27] Ibid., 15-16.

RVN or if Congress votes against the aid proposal for the RVN.[28] Pandemonium would erupt

in the RVN causing the state to fall before the DRV completed its conquest, thereby

complicating matters for an evacuation.[29] However, President Ford had already chosen to

request $722 million in additional aid from Congress the day before he met with the NSC.[30]

President Ford still wanted to hold deliberation on the subject of aid along with evacuation

with members of the NSC.[31] With Dr. Kissinger's recommendations in mind, President Ford

planned to reveal his request to the public.

On April 10, 1975, President Ford spoke before a joint session of congress to discuss

the foreign policy of the United States.[32] Dr. Kissinger wanted President Ford to make a

speech with the theme of making a doomed last stand metaphor in order to place the blame

on congress for the fall of the RVN.[33] President Ford refused Dr. Kissinger's

recommendation on the April 10 address, in fact, Ford thanked congress for their hard work

---

[28] Meeting minutes, National Security Council Meeting, April 9, 1975, 8-9.

[29] Ibid., 1975, 8-9.

[30] Meeting Minutes, Memoranda of Conversation, April 8, 1975, Box 10, National Security Advisor, Memoranda of Conversations – Ford Administration, 2-3, Gerald R. Ford Presidential Library, Ann Arbor, Michigan, accessed May 25, 2015, http://www.fordlibrarymuseum.gov/library/document/0314/1553016.pdf.

[31] Ibid.

[32] Ford, *A Time to Heal*, 253-54.

[33] Ibid.

on his proposals for Federal economic and energy policy.[34] Additionally, President Ford

stated he sought the cooperation of congress, while respecting its opinion.[35]

President Ford declared in order to resolve foreign policy issues during his

presidency, he was required to maintain the trust that exists between citizens and their

government.[36] President Ford then reminds his audience of his belief that the U.S. does have

a role to create peace and stability in the world by allowing people around the world.[37] A

duty to allow all peoples to enjoy the same freedoms many Americans benefit from the

cooperative efforts of the branches of the U.S. Federal government.[38] President Ford then

moved on to list several accomplishments of the U.S. had achieved since World War II, such

as the rebuilding of the former Axis powers, negotiating an agreement to curb nuclear

weapons stockpiles with the USSR, and opening dialogue to improve relations between non-

aligned states.[39]

Moving on, President Ford described the high price the U.S. had made to support an

independent RVN from the DRV's conquest.[40] The DRV who after signing the PPA, chose to

---

[34] Speaker's reading notes, President Gerald R. Ford's Foreign Policy address to a joint session of Congress, April 10, 1975, April 10, 1975 – Foreign Policy Address, Joint Session of Congress, Box 7, President's Speeches and Statements: Reading Copies, 3-4, Gerald R. Ford Presidential Library, Ann Arbor, Michigan, accessed May 25, 2015, http://www.fordlibrarymuseum.gov/library/document/0122/1252280.pdf.

[35] Speaker's reading notes, President Ford's Foreign Policy address to a joint session of Congress, April 10, 1975, 3-4.

[36] Ibid., 4.

[37] Ibid., 5-6.

[38] Ibid.

[39] "179 – Address Before a Joint Session of the Congress Reporting on United States Foreign Policy, April 10, 1975," President Gerald R. Ford, from *the American Presidency Project*, last modified by Gerhard Peters and John T. Woolley, last modified 2015, accessed April 17, 2015, http://www.presidency.ucsb.edu/ws/index.php?pid=4826.

[40] Ibid.

carry on their plans for the domination of the RVN.[41] After discussing several options to respond to the DRV's Ho Chi Minh Offensive, President Ford requests congress to approve an additional military aid package of $722 million and $250 million in humanitarian aid for the RVN.[42] In the middle of his speech, President Ford noticed that two members of congress walked out, as an act of defiance towards the president.[43]

Congressional attitudes towards additional aid for the RVN was negative and most likely to vote against President Ford's request for nearly one billion in supplemental aid for the Nationalist Vietnamese. For most of 1975, Congress consisted of 291 Democratic and 144 Republican politicians.[44] On April 14, President Ford met with the Senate Foreign Relations Committee at the Committee's calling.[45] The Senators of the Foreign Relations Committee expressed their opinions for the U.S. to leave Southeast Asia by extending their cooperation for an evacuation of Americans from the region.[46] However, the Senators would oppose further military aid for the RVN, with the most outspoken Senators being Frank Church, Joseph Biden, and Jacob Javits.[47] The negative attitude of congress caused concern for President Ford.

---

[41] "179 – Address Before a Joint Session of the Congress Reporting on United States Foreign Policy, April 10, 1975," President Ford.

[42] Ibid.

[43] Ford, *A Time to Heal*, 254.

[44] "Congressional Profiles: Ninety-Fourth Congress, 1975-1977."

[45] Ford, *A Time to Heal*, 255.

[46] Ibid.

[47] Ibid., 255.

Since the RVN was facing a dire situation and if congress did vote against the supplemental aid, it could have caused the RVN to collapse as a state.[48] Putting Americans in the RVN in an even greater perilous situation then they were already in during mid-April 1975.[49] Secretly, high ranking members of the White House staff, the U.S. Department of State, and the Department of Defense appealed to key congressional leaders to postpone the vote on additional aid for the RVN.[50] Even President Thieu not only understood the attitude the U.S. Congress towards the RVN, he was also wise to the possible implications of a negative vote for supplemental aid for his state.[51] Therefore, President Thieu sent Dr. Hung to the U.S. to seek out a way to postpone the additional aid vote in Washington D.C., and an attempt to obtain a three billion dollar loan from the U.S. over the course of three years.[52] Even Ambassador Martin knew the implications of a negative additional aid vote would have on the RVN and attempted to persuade Dr. Kissinger to find ways to delay the vote.[53] While the efforts to delay the additional aid vote were under way in an attempt to keep the RVN from collapsing, the KR faced its doom.

After the cessation of American combat activity in Southeast Asia, the Communist Khmer Rouge with their well-trained, highly disciplined in General Secretary of the Communist Party of Kampuchea Pol Pot's political philosophy, and well supplied forces

---

[48] Ford, *A Time to Heal*, 255.

[49] Ibid.

[50] Schecter, "The Final Days: The Political Struggle to End the Vietnam War," from Gerald R. Ford and the Politics of Post-Watergate America, volume two, 545-46.

[51] Hung and Schecter, *The Palace File*, 319-20.

[52] Ibid., 319-20.

[53] Ibid., 322.

occupied an estimated eighty percent of the territory of Cambodia. Due to the brutal tactics of the Khmer Rouge, an approximation of eighty percent of the civilian population fled to the major urban areas held by the KR. The Force Armee' Nationale Khmer (FANK) of the KR lacked training while being highly dependent on foreign aid particularly from American sources. However, FANK was able to roughly maintain lines of defense against the Khmer Rouge when supplied. After February 3, 1975, the KR had been unable to resupply the meager portions of the Cambodian territory it held through its primary supply route, the Mekong River. The Khmer Rouge positions along the river and mines within the body of water. With the Mekong River closed to the KR, the only way for FANK to receive supplies were through air shipments at Phnom Penh's airfield. Khmer Rouge rocket and artillery bombardments reduced Phnom Penh's airfield capacity shortly after the Mekong River was mined.[54]

The Khmer Rouge poured a greater effort into its siege of Phnom Penh causing FANK to redeploy more units for the defense of the city from smaller outposts. Many of these small outposts later fell to the Khmer Rouge after the shift in FANK's deployment. With the Khmer Rouge wearing down FANK's defenses of Phnom Penh, the U.S. Ambassador to the KR John Gunther Dean ordered Operation Eagle Pull to go into full motion on April 3. After the Phnom Penh airfield was bombarded by Khmer Rouge artillery fire on April 10, the helicopter evacuation of the then remaining U.S. Embassy staff began and was completed on April 12. Operation Eagle Pull lasted two hours to evacuate a total of "eighty-two Americans, one hundred fifty-nine Cambodians, and thirty-five other nationals"

---

[54] Sydney H. Batchelder and D. A. Quinlan, "Operation Eagle Pull," *Marine Corps Gazette* volume 60, number 5 (May, 1976), accessed April 18, 2015, https://www.mca-marines.org/gazette/1976/05/operation-eagle-pull.

from Phnom Penh. By April 17, 1975, the Khmer Rouge had gained access to Phnom Penh, which brought about the fall of the KR and intensification in the Khmer Rouge's atrocities. As the KR was collapsing, the situation for the RVN was deteriorating.[55]

With the loss of MRs I and II, the RVNAF scrambled to maintain order, while defending the remainder of the Nationalist Vietnamese state from the DRV. Several RVNAF officers had become disgruntled from the defeats the organization had suffered in the Northern MRs.[56] The military defeats gave some validation to rumors of a coup against President Thieu.[57] Towards the end of April 1975, Ambassador Martin met with Nguyen Cao Ky who inquired if the U.S. would support his planned coup d'état of the RVN.[58] Ambassador Martin informed Ky the U.S. would not support his coup d'état.[59] Ambassador Martin later reflected a coup d'état in the RVN during 1975 would only serve for the satisfaction of an individual's ego.[60] Even the Independence Palace the residence of President Thieu was bombed by a VNAF pilot, which rendered no harm to Thieu.[61] The pilot responsible for the Independence Palace bombing landed at a Communist Vietnamese airfield in Phoc Long and claimed to have been a DRV agent who infiltrated VNAF.[62]

---

[55] Batchelder and Quinlan, "Operation Eagle Pull."

[56] Lam Quang Thi, *The Twenty-Five Year Century*, 368-69.

[57] Ibid.

[58] Ambassador Graham Martin as told to Larry Engelmann, *Tears before the Rain*, 55.

[59] Ibid.

[60] Ibid.

[61] Hung and Schecter, *The Palace File*, 305-06.

[62] Military History Institute of Vietnam, *Victory in Vietnam*, 405.

In early April, 1975, Prime Minister Khiem resigned from office, to which President Thieu took personally and had to form a new cabinet.[63] The surviving units from MR II had lost ninety percent of their equipment while the infantry units from the MR maintained only "thirty percent of their M-16 rifles."[64] Units had no more than fifteen days to be refitted, with equipment diverted from training facilities to field units.[65] RVNAF still lacked the military supplies to maintain a defense line from PAVN's invasion of the RVN.[66] General Thi was appointed to command I Corps after General Truong checked into a hospital at a time when skilled officers were needed for the RVN's defense.[67] Even in his new command, General Thi was forced to scrounge and "reissue" military gear to re-equip I Corps, including the standard issue M-16.[68] Despite the bleak outlook, RVNAF was able to briefly maintain a defense perimeter in the MRs III and IV.

With the MRs I and II under their occupation, PAVN moved on to the organization's next major objective, to capture Saigon. To complete the conquest of the RVN's capital city of Saigon, PAVN sent fifteen divisions.[69] PAVN faced against RVNAF's three divisions in MR III along with the remaining units that had withdrew from the two MRs north of MR III.[70] VNAF even had converted their C-130 cargo aircraft to bombers from carrying

---

[63] Hung and Schecter, *The Palace File*, 318-19.

[64] General Cao Van Vien, *The Final Collapse* (Washington, D.C.: Center of Military History, United States Army, 1985), 123, PDF, accessed April 20, 2015, http://www.history.army.mil/html/books/090/90-26/CMH_Pub_90-26.pdf.

[65] Ibid., 125-26.

[66] Ibid.

[67] Lam Quang Thi, *The Twenty-Five Year Century*, 370.

[68] Ibid., 372.

[69] Cao Van Vien, *The Final Collapse*, 129-30.

improvised bombs containing waste oil to a 15,000 pound daisy cutter strapped to pallets.[71] Preparations for a desperate battle.

By April 9, 1975 the battle for the territory around Xuan Loc located at the strategic intersections of Routes 1, 20, and 15 which led to Saigon began.[72] If RVNAF could hold the town of Xuan Loc with ARVN's 18th Division against PAVN's IV Corps, then the RVN could starve off defeat for one more year due to the rainy season and force the DRV into negotiations.[73] After the first day of the battle at Xuan Loc, PAVN's IV Corps was shocked they had suffered hundreds of casualties, lost more than fifty percent of their armor, and expended a sufficient portion of their artillery shells to make very little gains.[74] From an enemy who was expected to flee in the opening monuments of the battle.[75] However, PAVN moved into MR III on four different fronts.[76] Unlike the battle at Xuan Loc, PAVN was making quick advances along the coast of the RVN.[77] Causing the Nationalist Vietnamese to place a greater hope on RVNAF at Xuan Loc.

Brigadier General Le Minh Dao's 18th Division was wearing down due to two weeks of the repeated PAVN assaults on the town of Xuan Loc.[78] By April 20, General Dao was

---

[70] Cao Van Vien, *The Final Collapse*, 129-30.

[71] Ibid., 127.

[72] Military History Institute of Vietnam, *Victory in Vietnam*, 406.

[73] Veith and Pibbenow II, "'Fighting is an Art,'" 165 and 167.

[74] Ibid., 190-91.

[75] Ibid.

[76] Cao Van Vien, *The Final Collapse*, 129.

[77] Veith and Pibbenow II, "'Fighting is an Art,'" 207.

[78] Cao Van Vien, *The Final Collapse*, 132.

ordered to immediately evacuate from Xuan Loc for the defense of Saigon.[79] With the

expectation of General Dao's rear guard, his remaining forces and civilian refugees left Xuan

Loc with few incidents.[80] RVNAF also evacuated units from the areas of An Loc and Chon

Thanh, which left several routes open for PAVN's advance to the consolidated Nationalist

Vietnamese defense lines outside of Saigon.[81]

President Ford desperately wanted to asset the RVN in its time of need. However,

President Ford could not use General Weyand's recommendation of even a brief bombing

campaign. The American public and Congress were strongly against American re-entry into

the Vietnam War. President Ford could not abandon his ambitions to finding long term

solutions to American foreign policy issues and restoring public trust in the federal

government. President Ford recognized the RVN was severely deteriorating and needed to

prepare for an evacuation, not a bombing campaign. While the RVN was disintegrating, the

Ford Administration sought the assistance of an Eastern state that the U.S. had previously

had successful rapprochement with.

---

[79] Veith and Pibbenow II, "'Fighting is an Art,'" 207-08.

[80] Ibid., 209-10.

[81] Cao Van Vien, *The Final Collapse*, 133 and 136.

Chapter Ten: Back in the USSR

Since diplomatic relations between the U.S. and the PRC had slowly improved since President Nixon's "Opening the Door to China" after over two decades of no diplomatic contacts between the two states; the PRC had an incentive to preserve the PPA.[1] With two Vietnams, Chairman to the Central Committee of the Communist Party of China aka the Chinese Communist Party (CCP) Mao Tse-tung believed the U.S. would keep their military forces out of Southeast Asia, while containing Soviet influence in the region.[2] The PRC had supported communist forces in Vietnam since the closing months of 1950.[3] The PRC although a communist state, was independent from the direct influence of the USSR.

In 1957, Chairman Mao pursued a course of development away from a Soviet client state in the path of true Maoism, i.e. the Great Leap Forward.[4] Maoist theory stresses rural development particularly in agrarian states, mobilization of the peasantry, participation of the proletarian/peasantry, the ongoing continuation of the revolution to avert a bourgeoisie takeover of the state, and the revolution being carried out through closely related stages.[5] Leninism on the other hand, emphasized technical expertise particularly in political leadership to lead the masses to bring about a revolution and establish a socialist government

---

[1] Parker, "Vietnam and Soviet Asian Strategy," 103-04.

[2] Ibid.

[3] Howard R. Simpson, *Dien Bien Phu: The Epic Battle America Forgot* (Washington, D.C.: Brassey's, 1994), 34.

[4] Parker, "Vietnam and Soviet Asian Strategy," 94-95.

[5] Bernard D'Mello, "What is Maoism?," *Economic and Political Weekly* Volume 44, Number 47 (November 21-27, 2009): 46-47, accessed September 1, 2014, Stable URL: http://www.jstor.org/stable/25663811.

to eventually in theory transition into a communist state under the expertise of the leading party.[6] The ideological divided between Maoism and Leninism would have consequences.

Mao and his supporters were suspicious of the USSR, believing General Secretary of the Communist Party of the Soviet Union (CPSU) Nikita Khrushchev lacked the leadership.[7] Particularly when Khrushchev was compared to former General Secretary of the CPSU Joseph Stalin had in their perception.[8] The CCP believed the USSR foreign policy was to dictate the PRC to remain a subordinate state to the USSR.[9] To the USSR, the PRC's independence from its sphere of influence was unacceptable.

During his tenure as General Secretary, Nikita Khrushchev had constructed a strategy to create incentives for the PRC to re-align with the USSR. Khrushchev's strategy called for the exploitation of the escalation of the Vietnam War to draw further American forces into the conflict. While the USSR worked to politically isolate the PRC, the USSR appealed to the "pro-Soviet" faction of the CCP which included Liu Shao-ch'i who were dissatisfied with the outcomes of the Great Leap Forward as a means for rapid modernization.[10]

After American ground forces were deployed into the Vietnam War in 1965, Chairman Mao launched a campaign to remove political opponents from power, known as the Cultural Revolution (CR) which became more intense as the policy continued.[11] The PRC

---

[6] D'Mello, "What is Maoism?," 42-43.

[7] Christopher Andrew and Vasili Mitrokhin, *The World was Going Our Way: The KGB and the Battle for the Third World* (New York: Basic Books, 2005), 271-72.

[8] Ibid.

[9] Ibid.

[10] Parker, "Vietnam and Soviet Asian Strategy," 95-96.

[11] Ibid., 98-99.

resisted Soviet efforts to force Sino-Soviet rapprochement by closing its rail system to Soviet military shipments to the DRV until American ground forces were introduced into the Vietnam War.[12] The situation between the USSR and PRC remained tense. Leading to a series of armed border skirmishes during 1969, beginning after a Soviet border patrol held up portraits of Chairman Mao in response to a series of repeated profane incidents by a Chinese patrol along the Ussuri River.[13] While rapprochement was under way with the U.S. and tensions along the Sino-Soviet border eased.[14] The PRC still chose to cooperate with the U.S. on Southeast Asia by restricting Soviet shipments to the DRV on its rail system.[15]

With previous PRC cooperation over the Vietnam War and its political clout in Asia, the Ford Administration sought the diplomatic assistance of the PRC to seek a peaceful solution to the conflict.[16] In a meeting on April 3, 1975, with President Ford, Dr. Kissinger reported that the PRC was unable to persuade the DRV to cease its Ho Chi Minh Offensive.[17] Despite the PRC's wish for two Vietnamese states to have with close diplomatic ties for both the U.S. and the PRC.[18] The Lao Dong Party of the DRV who worked to spread the communist system into the RVN through force, is a Marxist-Leninist party, not a Maoist party.[19] Additionally, the USSR was one of the DRV strongest supporters and supplier of

---

[12]Parker, "Vietnam and Soviet Asian Strategy," 97-98.

[13] Andrew and Mitrokhin, *The World was Going Our Way*, 279-80.

[14] Parker, "Vietnam and Soviet Asian Strategy," 103-04.

[15] Ibid.

[16] Meeting minutes, Memorandum of Conversation, April 3, 1975, 2.

[17] Ibid.

[18] Ibid.

[19] St. John, "Marxist-Leninist Theory and Organization in South Vietnam," 817.

military goods, not the PRC.[20] With the lack of the PRC's political influence over the DRV, the Ford Administration sought the assistance of the DRV's strongest ally.

In an attempt to improve the situation in Vietnam, the Ford Administration contacted the USSR to develop a situation favorable to the two warring Vietnamese factions and for the then international power brokers. During the Cold War in 1975, the aggression between the U.S. and the USSR was in the era of Détente a "relaxation of tension." Détente had begun through the Moscow Summit of 1972, where the two superpowers agreed to and signed the first Strategic Arms and Limitations Treaty (SALT I) along with other cooperative economic arrangements. Détente was an era where the U.S. and the USSR attempted to cooperate with one another after decades of high tension while trying to undermine one another. However, during the era of Détente the USSR worked to spread its influence throughout the world. By 1976, President Ford to remove the word "Détente" from official government publications. It was not until after the 1979 Soviet invasion of Afghanistan, did the era of Détente come to an end with tension surging between the U.S. and the USSR. Although the Cold War in 1975 was still ongoing in the period of Détente, it was still a difficult period.[21]

On February 7, 1975, the *Los Angeles Times* released an error-filled, but scandalous front-page story of the CIA's Project Jennifer. The purpose of Project Jennifer was to retrieve a lost Soviet Golf class submarine, by sending a "giant clawed arm" to the bottom of the Pacific Ocean from the *Glomar Explorer*. The specially constructed 360 yard long ship for the mission by the Summa Corporation owned by Howard Hughes, *Glomar Explorer* would transport the retrieve submarine to be later examined by the CIA. However, the mission was

---

[20] Andrew and Mitrokhin, *The World was Going Our Way*, 264-65.

[21] Reynolds, *Summits*, 281 and 223.

a failure. Since the Soviet submarine fell apart shortly after three damaged grasping claws came loose. Leaving only the forward section of the submarine within the giant clawed arm, while the rest of the submarine sank back into the depths of the Pacific. The grasping claws were damaged from hitting the ocean floor due to a miscalculation on the first attempt to retrieve the lost Soviet submarine. Seymour M. Hersh of the *New York Times* had been researching Project Jennifer from rumors he had heard since 1973, but a reporter from the *Los Angeles Times* had picked up the story.[22]

CIA Director Colby attempted to prevent the story of Project Jennifer from spreading by promising the editors of major newspapers more details of the project at a later date if the editors did not publish further stories on the project. Hersh published the story on Project Jennifer on the front page of the *New York Times*. Hersh's article was in greater detail than the *Los Angeles Times* article, but still contained some errors in the actual events. While Hersh pointed out how wasteful Project Jennifer was by discussing the list of criticisms during the planning stages of the project along with the failure of the mission itself. For the USSR, it was an embarrassing moment because not only did they lose a ballistic missile submarine, but the Soviets learned of its exact location from the American press. Despite being warned about the secret salvage attempt by Soviet naval officer Anatoliy Shtyrov.[23]

The Ford Administration sent notes on the identities of the Soviet sailors and their burial "with full military honors."[24] One note entitled Version B gave a detailed account on

---

[22] Sherry Sontag and Christopher Drew with Annette Drew, *Blind Man's Bluff: The Untold Story of American Submarine Espionage* (New York: Harper Collins, 1999), 258-60, 262-63, 267-68, 268-69, and 270.

[23] Ibid., 270-71, 273-74, and 274-75.

[24] Diplomatic Paper #91, 6C, Deputy Assistant to the President for National Security Affairs General Brent Scowcroft to Soviet Ambassador Anatoliy Dobrynin, April 22, 1975, Folder: Ten, Items #86-#91, circa April, 1975-April 22, 1975, Box 30, National Security Advisor Kissinger-Scowcroft West Wing Office Files,

the burial practices for the recovered bodies of the Soviet sailors.[25] The most important

diplomatic communications between the two superpowers were conducted through Dr.

Kissinger and Soviet Ambassador Anatoliy Dobrynin in Washington, D.C., a back channel

set up by the Nixon Administration on February 17, 1969.[26] After some brief exchanges on

the issue of Project Jennifer between Dr. Kissinger and Ambassador Dobrynin, including a

promise the U.S. would not make a second attempt to salvage the lost Soviet submarine, the

Soviets did not press the issue further.[27] Because Project Jennifer was a failure and was

leaked to the press, the Ford Administration refused to discuss the project publicly, which

pleased the USSR.[28] Since the issue of Project Jennifer was not widely discussed in public by

the U.S. or the USSR, both states continued on with their policies, including Détente.

Because it was the Détente period of the Cold War, the Ford Administration and the CPSU

were in the process of setting up another summit meeting since the Vladivostok Summit went

well between the participants.

Previously, while on his Far Eastern tour, President Ford met with General Secretary

of the CPSU Leonid Brezhnev and Soviet Foreign Minister Andrei Gromyko in Vladivostok,

USSR during November, 1974 for the Vladivostok Summit. The Vladivostok Summit was

the first time President Ford and General Secretary Brezhnev were introduced to one another.

1969-1977: General Subject File: USSR-'D' File (Dobrynin), Gerald R. Ford Presidential Library, Ann Arbor, Michigan.

[25] Memorandum for the Secretary #91, 6D, Helmut Sonnonfeldt to Secretary of State Henry Kissinger, April 19, 1975, Folder: Ten, Items #86-#91, circa April, 1975- April 22, 1975, Box 30, National Security Advisor Kissinger-Scowcroft West Wing Office Files, 1969-1977: General Subject File: USSR-'D' File (Dobrynin), Gerald R. Ford Presidential Library, Ann Arbor, Michigan.

[26] Reynolds, *Summits,* 230-31.

[27] Sontag and Drew with Drew, *Blind Man's Bluff,* 274-75.

[28] Ibid., 274.

Both of whom "got along well." President Ford strongly believed in the process of Détente, stating "anything that would bring the arms race under control would be a plus for the world." The purpose of the Vladivostok Summit from President Ford's view was to negotiate an enduring, widely ranging second SALT. Discussions went well at Vladivostok. However, the Summit did not lead to any momentous developments. Both President Ford and General Secretary Brezhnev showed great interest in signing an additional SALT agreement. However, the DRV and the PRG would launch another offensive against the RVN in January, 1975. The 1975 Communist offensive created a perilous situation for the RVN and Americans within Vietnam, leading to a debate about the possible assistance that the Soviets may provide to the U.S.[29]

While discussing the possible responses to the declining fortunes of the RVNAF and the FANK during a NSC meeting on April 9, 1975, the topic of communist assistance to communicate with the DRV was brought up. Dr. Kissinger was discussing the requirements of an airborne evacuation of Americans and Vietnamese from the RVN. When Secretary of Defense Schlesinger mentioned the issue of PAVN anti-aircraft weapons and the possibility of PAVN deploying the weapons within range of Saigon's Tan Son Nhut airport. Dr. Kissinger suggested that PAVN may cooperate with the U.S. on the issue of not deploying anti-aircraft weapons near Tan Son Nhut airport through the coordinated efforts with either the USSR or the PRC. The NSC discussed the possible courses of action to gain congress' approval for security of the evacuation, the limitations placed on the executive office on deploying military forces, and aid packages. When Schlesinger commented on a number of issues including Soviet behavior towards Détente.[30]

---

[29] Ford, *A Time to Heal*, 33, 213, 215, 217-18, and 218-19.

Schlesinger stated the USSR had not supported the implementation of Détente within Southeast Asia, requiring the U.S. to challenge the Soviets on the issue. Schlesinger even suggested to President Ford to clarify to the USSR in his upcoming speech "we (the U.S.) want to preserve Détente but it cannot be a one way street" while modeling the speech in the style of Winston Churchill. Schlesinger's suggestions were supported by Deputy Secretary of Defense William Clements and Chairman to the Joint Chiefs of Staff General George S. Brown. However, President Ford rejected all of Schlesinger's suggestions. President Ford went on to state his speech needed to be in his own style, and Ford thought it was considered necessary to keep the speech consistent with his previous speeches. While all decision making authority under the executive branch of the U.S. belonged to the president himself. President Ford stated to the NSC the knowledge of Schlesinger's qualms was to remain within the council. While the attendees of the NSC meeting of April 9 were pessimistic about Soviet assistance in Vietnam, the Ford Administration received a more positive note from the Soviets the next day.[31]

Since the Vladivostok Summit was a sign of a developing cooperation between the U.S. and the USSR, the two states discussed the possibility of scheduling additional meetings with one another to develop agreements on several issues. General Secretary Brezhnev sent an oral message to Dr. Kissinger for President Ford on April 10, 1975, where Brezhnev expressed great interest in easing the tensions between their respective states and stressed another summit needed to be held in order to continue Détente. The first meeting proposed by General Secretary Brezhnev was a summit in the U.S., making a reference the summit was

---

[30] Meeting Minutes, NSC Meeting, April 9, 1975, 23, 24-25, and 26.

[31] Ibid., 26-27, 27-28, and 29-30.

"an agreement in principle … was confirmed in Vladivostok." The proposed summit in the U.S. included General Secretary Brezhnev in attendance in the vicinity of two months after a conclusion of a proposed final Conference on Security and Cooperation in Europe. Additionally, General Secretary Brezhnev suggested the Geneva Conference on Southwest Asia to be confirmed with the other participating parties. Along with a separate meeting between Dr. Kissinger and Soviet Foreign Minister Gromyko on the region in Moscow during May 20 and 21. The April 10, 1975 oral message as a whole signified to the Ford Administration the USSR was willing to cooperate with the U.S. on maintaining and establishing international stability.[32]

With the situation for the Nationalist Vietnamese deteriorating rapidly in the RVN, the Soviets had displayed signs of potential cooperation from the Vladivostok Summit, the April 1975 oral message, and the lack of public condemnation for Project Jennifer. The Ford Administration decided to request the assistance of the USSR to create a ceasefire in the Vietnam War. At the very least, the Ford Administration could buy time for an evacuation through Soviet assistance. According to Dr. Kissinger, the request of Soviet assistance in establishing a ceasefire was the only realistic political option the Ford Administration believed to be available to them concerning the Vietnam War circa April 18, 1975.[33] On the other hand, CIA Director Colby and Sectary of Defense Schlesinger believed it would be a wasted effort since the DRV functioned as an independent state allied with USSR, not a puppet state of the USSR.[34]

---

[32] Oral Message #87, General Secretary Leonid Brezhnev to Secretary of State Henry Kissinger, April 10, 1975, 1, 2, and 2-3, Folder: Ten, Items #86-#91, Circa April, 1975-April 22, 1975, National Security Advisor Kissinger-Scowcroft West Wing Office Files, 1969-1977: General Subject File: USSR-'D' File (Dobrynin), Gerald R. Ford Presidential Library, Ann Arbor, Michigan.

[33] Kissinger, *Ending the Vietnam War,* 542.

Regardless of Colby's and Schlesinger's arguments, President Ford went ahead with

the diplomatic effort. In an oral message sent to General Secretary Brezhnev, President Ford

stated he was willing to look beyond past disagreements between their respective states in

order to develop a temporary ceasefire and further improve international stability.[35] President

Ford stated both the U.S. and the USSR had a responsibility to resolve the Vietnam War by

"consider(ing) the long term consequences."[36] Explicitly, President Ford requested the

establishment of a temporary ceasefire to continue the evacuation of Americans and

Vietnamese Nationalists with connections to the United States.[37] However, in the talking

points for the oral message there was another goal the Ford Administration was seeking

through Soviet assistance.

Another position expressed in the talking points for President Ford on the message to

General Secretary Brezhnev was to not only request a temporary ceasefire; it was to find a

political solution to end the Vietnam War. The talking points for the Ford to Brezhnev oral

message affirmed the U.S. was willing to cease the shipment of military supplies to the RVN

during the ceasefire and that the Vietnam War be brought to a conclusion beneficial to both

superpower states.[38] One of the talking points stated the U.S. would be ready at a moment's

---

[34] Colby with McCargar, *Lost Victory,* 4.

[35] Oral Note, #90, 5C, President Gerald R. Ford to General Secretary Leonid Brezhnev, Folder 10, Items #86-#91, circa April, 1975-April 22, 1975, Box 30, National Security Advisor: Kissinger-Scowcroft West Wing Office Files, 1969-1977: General Subject File: USSR-'D' File (Dobrynin), Gerald R. Ford Presidential Library, Ann Arbor, Michigan.

[36] Ibid.

[37] Ibid.

[38] Talking Points, #90, 5D, Talking Points for President Gerald R. Ford to General Secretary Leonid Brezhnev, Folder 10, Items #86-#91, circa April, 1975-April 22, 1975, Box 30, National Security Advisor: Kissinger-Scowcroft West Wing Office Files, 1969-1977: General Subject File: USSR-'D' File (Dobrynin), Gerald R. Ford Presidential Library, Ann Arbor, Michigan.

notice to attend the Paris Conference to negotiate a peaceful conclusion of the Vietnam War with the DRV through the intermediary efforts of the USSR.[39] The final aim of the talking points articulated that the USSR had a considerable impact on the outcome to the Vietnam War and American-Soviet diplomatic relations.[40]

Although the negotiation aims in the talking points were not explicitly requested in the oral message, there was a statement in the oral message declaring the U.S. was "prepared to discuss the special political circumstances that could make this (the ceasefire) possible."[41] Dr. Kissinger stated in his memoirs, *Ending the Vietnam War,* the "special political circumstances" were the U.S. was willing to let RVN President Thieu leave office.[42] The statement Dr. Kissinger made on the "special political circumstances" contradicts the aims within the talking points for President Ford to include in the oral message to General Secretary Brezhnev. The Dr. Kissinger-talking points' contradictions could indicate the Ford Administration wanted to keep the option of allowing President Thieu leaving office secret from the DRV and international public by keeping the idea off the record. However, the language of "special political circumstances" is ambiguous and could be interrupted to reference many different issues. Despite the Dr. Kissinger-talking points' contradictions over "special political circumstances," the phrase was meant to lure the DRV and the PRG back to the negotiation table. President Ford sought out to work some details for the evacuation of Americans and Nationalist Vietnamese through the USSR.

---

[39] Talking Points, #90, 5D, Talking Points for Ford to Brezhnev.

[40] Ibid.

[41] Oral Note, #90, 5C, Ford to Brezhnev.

[42] Kissinger, *Ending the Vietnam War,* 542.

Through Dr. Kissinger's efforts, the Ford Administration was able to describe the needs of the U.S. to the USSR's Politburo in order to create a plan for an evacuation of the U.S. Embassy in Saigon. Dr. Kissinger discussed the requirements of the American embassy with the USSR's longest serving Ambassador to the U.S. Dobrynin.[43] Ambassador Dobrynin, who despite his strong loyalty to his state, had a positive professional association with the Ford Administration due to his respectable expertise as a diplomat.[44] In a telephone conversation in reference to the oral note to General Secretary Brezhnev, Dr. Kissinger added to Ambassador Dobrynin the evacuation of Saigon would require the deployment of American military units to keep control crowds at the extraction points and would leave in the last departures of the evacuation.[45] Ambassador Dobrynin had an understanding, to be added in his message to Moscow.[46]

In another telephone conversation, Dr. Kissinger requested if the USSR could influence the DRV to order PAVN not to take Tan Son Nhut airport in Saigon for it would cause a confrontation between the American military security forces if PAVN attempted to capture the airport.[47] Ambassador Dobrynin understood why Dr. Kissinger made the request

[43] Robert D. McFadden, "Anatoly F. Dobrynin, Longtime Soviet Ambassador to the U.S., Dies at 90," *New York Times*, April 8, 2010, accessed April 25, 2015, http://www.nytimes.com/2010/04/09/world/europe/09dobrynin.html?_r=0.

[44] Ibid.

[45] Telecon, Secretary of State Henry Kissinger and Soviet Ambassador to the U.S. Anatoly F. Dobrynin, April 19, 1975, 12:10 P.M., folder 4, TP Con – (2), April 10, 1975 – May 1, 1975, Box 34, National Security Advisor Kissinger – ScowcroftWest Wing Office Files, 1969-1977, General Subject File: USSR – Dobrynin in Kissinger Exchanges, Gerald R. Ford Presidential Library, Ann Arbor, Michigan.

[46] Ibid.

[47] Telecon, Secretary of State Henry Kissinger and Soviet Ambassador to the U.S. Anatoly F. Dobrynin, April 22, 1975, 11:52 A.M., 1, folder 4, TP Con – (2), April 10, 1975 – May 1, 1975, Box 34, National Security Advisor Kissinger – Scowcroft West Wing Office Files, 1969-1977, General Subject File: USSR – Dobrynin in Kissinger Exchanges, Gerald R. Ford Presidential Library, Ann Arbor, Michigan.

and stated he would send a message to Moscow to bring the issue to the USSR's Politburo's attention.[48] However, in Moscow, Chairman to the Committee for State Security (Komitet Gosudarstvinnoi Bezopasnosti (KGB)) Yuri Andropov viewed the U.S. with suspicion in the closing days of the Vietnam War.[49] KGB Chairman Andropov stated in a special meeting, with knowledge of the Korean War, since so many PAVN units were south of the DMZ, Hanoi lacked the defenses against an American invasion before communist victory could be achieved.[50] KGB Chairman Andropov feared the DRV would suffer the same fate as the Democratic People's Republic of Korea.[51] For better or for worse, the Ford Administration awaited a response from the Politburo of the USSR.

By April 24, 1975, the U.S. Department of State received a reply from General Secretary Brezhnev of the USSR, who informed the Department of State about Hanoi's response.[52] According to General Secretary Brezhnev, the DRV has no objectives to prevent the American evacuation of Saigon along with the evacuation of RVN citizens with American connections.[53] Any hopes of the attempt to entice the DRV's and the PRG's return negotiations with the USSR as an intermediary were quickly dashed. General Secretary Brezhnev went on to say "favorable conditions have been established for such an

[48] Telecon, Kissinger and Dobrynin, April 22, 1975, 11:52 A.M., 1-2.

[49] Andrew and Mitrokhin, *The World was Going Our Way*, 12-13.

[50] Ibid.

[51] Ibid.

[52] Oral Message, #92, B1, General Secretary Leonid Brezhnev to President Gerald R. Ford, April 24, 1975, Folder 10, Items #86-#91, circa April, 1975-April 22, 1975, Box 30, National Security Advisor: Kissinger-Scowcroft West Wing Office Files, 1969-1977: General Subject File: USSR-'D' File (Dobrynin), Gerald R. Ford Presidential Library, Ann Arbor, Michigan.

[53] Ibid.

evacuation."[54] As for political solutions to resolve Vietnam War, Hanoi informed Moscow they would follow and enforce the PPA, despite the fact the DRV was conducting a large scale major military offensive, which was a blatant violation of the agreement.[55] Looking back at the attempt to gain Soviet assistance in the latter days of the Vietnam War, Dr. Kissinger felt the Ford Administration lost confidence within itself for its lack progress in the situation.[56] Nevertheless, the Ford Administration took the offer brokered by General Secretary Brezhnev in order to obtain more favorable conditions for an evacuation.[57] Still, the Ford Administration wanted to develop a political solution to the Vietnam War.

On April 19, 1975, Deputy National Security Advisor General Scowcroft received a message from the French Republic about the PRG's willingness to make a political settlement concerning the Vietnam War on certain conditions.[58] According to the Head of the PRG Mission in Paris, the PRG would be willing to establish a ceasefire in exchange for free elections of a coalition government for the RVN and the departure of President Thieu's cabinet with a temporary transition government until elections were held.[59] Even a few members of President Thieu's cabinet wanted to negotiate a settlement with the DRV to cease hostilities.[60]

---

[54] Oral Message, #92, B1, Brezhnev to Ford, April 24, 1975.

[55] Ibid.

[56] Kissinger, *Ending the Vietnam War*, 543.

[57] Graham Martin as told to Engelmann, *Tears Before the Rain*, 56.

[58] Meeting Minutes, Conversation between the Secretary General of the French Foreign Office and the Head of the PRG Mission in Paris and Relayed to General Brent Scowcroft by Minister de la Force, April 19, 1975, 1, folder 5, VW – Final Stages, April, 1975, Box 38, National Security Advisor Kissinger-Scowcroft West Wing Office Files, 1969-1977, General Subject File: Vietnamese War 'Camp David File,' Gerald R. Ford Presidential Library, Ann Arbor, Michigan.

[59] Ibid., 1-2.

Since military assistance to the RVN was an unacceptable response, the Ford Administration desperately wanted to find a political solution to the Vietnam War. A political solution could not be found amongst the U.S., Nationalist Vietnamese parties, and the Communist Vietnamese to the Vietnam War. Additional political support was needed for a political solution. At first, the Ford Administration sought the assistance of the PRC, who were unable to dissuade the DRV. The PRC had lost influence over the DRV for disrupting Communist supply lines via rail.

In the spirit of Détente, President Ford requested General Secretary Brezhnev to help broker a peace agreement to the Vietnam War. Relations between the U.S. and the USSR appeared to be cordial for the Cold War because of the ongoing second SALT negotiations. General Secretary Brezhnev responded a political agreement could not be reached concerning the Vietnam War. However, the Ford Administration was able to reach an agreement with the DRV via the USSR, to allow the evacuation of Americans and a number of Nationalist Vietnamese. The DRV was not interested in a negotiated settlement; it focused all of its concentration on the unconditional surrender of the RVN.

---

[60] Hung and Schecter, *The Palace File*, 329.

Chapter Eleven: The End

On April 11, 1975, the Ford Administration sent a diplomatic note to the DRV

Embassy in Paris through the American Embassy, stating in light of the gross violations of

the PPA made by the DRV, the U.S. demanded that the DRV cease its hostilities or to suffer

the ramifications of its actions.[1] Yet, the DRV's Embassy immediately rejected the Ford

Administration's diplomatic note, citing the note as a protest and returned it to the U.S.

Embassy in Paris.[2] In a meeting with President Ford and Dr. Kissinger, Vice President

Nelson Rockefeller mentioned to his knowledge he had gathered on the political situation on

the Vietnam War as of April 18.[3] According to Vice President Rockefeller, in order for the

Communist Vietnamese to engage in negotiations with the Nationalist Vietnamese, President

Thieu had to resign from office.[4] After receiving a report from Ambassador Martin proposing

President Thieu be allowed to step down from office, the Ford White House sent a message

granting Martin permission to carry out his proposal.[5]

---

[1] Telegram, Secretary of State Henry Kissinger to the U.S. Ambassador to the French Republic, April 11, 1975, folder 3, VW CD – 2, March 24, 1975 – December 11, 1975, Box 38, National Security Advisor Kissinger-Scowcroft West Wing Office Files, 1969-1977, General Subject File: Vietnamese War 'Camp David File,' Gerald R. Ford Presidential Library, Ann Arbor, Michigan.

[2] Telegram, U.S. Ambassador to the French Republic to Secretary of State Henry Kissinger, April 11, 1975, folder 3, VW CD – 2, March 24, 1975 – December 11, 1975, Box 38, National Security Advisor Kissinger-Scowcroft West Wing Office Files, 1969-1977, General Subject File: Vietnamese War 'Camp David File,' Gerald R. Ford Presidential Library, Ann Arbor, Michigan.

[3] Meeting Minutes, Memoranda of Conversation, April 18, 1975, 2-3, Box 11, National Security Advisor's Memoranda of Conversation Collection, Memoranda of Conversations – Ford Administration, accessed April 27, 2015, Gerald R. Ford Presidential Library, Ann Arbor, Michigan, http://www.fordlibrarymuseum.gov/library/document/0314/1553035.pdf.

[4] Ibid.

[5] Hung and Schecter, *The Palace File*, 329-30.

Ambassador Martin met with President Thieu about the situation the RVN was facing as of April 20, 1975. During the meeting Ambassador Martin informed President Thieu of not only the bleak military outlook for the RVN's survival. Ambassador Martin also updated the Nationalist Vietnamese president lacked not only popular support from the citizenry and was losing the approval of Nationalist Vietnamese politicians with a long history of supporting Thieu's policies. Ambassador Martin stated it was the popular belief a political settlement could be reached with the Communist Vietnamese if President Thieu resigned from office. President Thieu inquired Ambassador Martin's opinion if his resignation would in any way improve the situation for the RVN. Ambassador Martin stated the time to resign in exchange for the U.S. Congress to approve additional aid had passed and the DRV would oppose any president of the RVN unwilling to concede to their demands. President Thieu concluded the meeting by stating he would make an appropriate decision shortly.[6]

By April 21, President Thieu announced his resignation in a speech and accused the U.S. for abandoning the RVN.[7] Years later, Ambassador Martin stated he never actively persuaded Thieu to resign from office.[8] President Thieu cited his reasons for his resignation to Ambassador Martin, being the U.S. Congress believed he was the aggressor in the Vietnam War and the DRV refused to negotiate with him as president of the RVN.[9]

---

[6] Telegram, U.S. Ambassador to the Republic of Vietnam Graham Martin to Secretary of State Henry Kissinger, April 20, 1975, 1-2 and 3, folder 5, VW – Final Stages, April, 1975, Box 38, National Security Advisor Kissinger-Scowcroft West Wing Office Files, 1969-1977, General Subject File: Vietnamese War 'Camp David File,' Gerald R. Ford Presidential Library, Ann Arbor, Michigan.

[7] Kissinger, *Ending the Vietnam War*, 544.

[8] Ambassador Martin as told to Larry Engelmann, *Tears before the Rain*, 55.

[9] Telegram, U.S. Ambassador to the Republic of Vietnam Martin to Secretary of State Kissinger, April 21, 1975, folder 2, Saigon to Washington, D.C, April 9, 1975 – April 28, 1975 (2), Box 8, National Security Advisor, Embassy Files Taken by Ambassador Graham Martin (Copies), 1963-1976 (1976), Gerald R. Ford Presidential Library, Ann Arbor, Michigan.

Therefore, President Thieu resigned to encourage congress to send military aid for the RVN, so the state could create incentive for the DRV to negotiate.[10]

During his resignation speech, Thieu appointed Vice President Tran Van Huong to the Nationalist Vietnamese presidency.[11] Thieu's resignation did not improve the situation for the RVN. Until Thieu left the RVN with Ambassador Martin's assistance, he was still meeting with Presidential advisors and RVNAF generals on official business after his resignation.[12] In addition, the Communist Vietnamese insisted a political settlement could only be reached if former General ARVN General Duong Van Minh was appointed to the Nationalist Vietnamese presidency.[13] President Huong resigned days later on April 28, and appointed Minh to the Nationalist Vietnamese presidency.[14] As president, Minh strongly believed he could create a political settlement with the Communist Vietnamese causing many Nationalist Vietnamese to be optimistic.[15] While the RVN underwent a series of presidential succession, the Ford Administration and the U.S. Embassy in Saigon made preparations for an evacuation.

During April, 1975, the Ford Administration along with several other American governmental agencies made preparations for a large-scale evacuation from the RVN. In reality the evacuation of individuals from the RVN began late in March, 1975 through

---

[10] Telegram, U.S. Ambassador to the Republic of Vietnam Martin to Secretary of State Kissinger, April 21, 1975.

[11] Hung and Schecter, *The Palace File*, 331-32.

[12] Ambassador Martin as told to Larry Engelmann, *Tears before the Rain*, 55.

[13] Hung and Schecter, *The Palace File*, 342.

[14] Military History Institute of Vietnam, *Victory in Vietnam*, 416.

[15] Cao Van Vien, *The Final Collapse*, 144-45.

underground methods.[16] An estimated one hundred thirty-five thousand people were removed from the RVN instead of the approved thirty-five thousand.[17] Deputy Ambassador Lehmann requested Washington give him the formal authority to carry out an evacuation because of the underground departures and the growing instability caused by the DRV's Ho Chi Minh Offensive.[18]

By April 25, the U.S. Embassy finally received authority to evacuate Nationalist Vietnamese individuals and their families who were considered by the Embassy to have a high risk of execution by the Communist Vietnamese, if left behind.[19] One U.S. Embassy staff member recalled Ambassador Martin was optimistic in public as the RVN was disintegrating.[20] Both Ambassador Martin and Deputy Ambassador Lehmann refused to even mention the word evacuation for fear panic would erupt in Saigon before PAVN had captured the city, based on the collapse of Danang.[21] Ambassador Martin and Deputy Ambassador Lehmann held on to their belief on pandemonium by going as far as never packing their personal possessions at the Embassy.[22] Each American governmental agency was responsible for the departure of its personnel and dependents.[23]

---

[16] Deputy Ambassador Lehmann as told to Larry Engelmann, *Tears before the Rain*, 38.

[17] Ibid.

[18] Ibid., 38-39.

[19] Cao Van Vien, *The Final Collapse*, 148.

[20] U.S. Embassy Staff Member Lacy Wright as told to Larry Engelmann, *Tears before the Rain*, 49-50.

[21] Deputy Ambassador Lehmann as told to Larry Engelmann, *Tears before the Rain*, 39.

[22] Ibid.

[23] Ibid.

For the Ford White House sanctioned evacuation, the U.S. Embassy preferred to move people out of the RVN through commercial aircraft since the departure of major airlines from Tan Son Nhut airport would not draw attention to the passengers.[24] Otherwise the evacuation would be completed through military fixed wing aircraft before utilizing helicopters.[25] Since it was required by Nationalist Vietnamese law to obtain an exit visa before departure from the RVN, the U.S. Embassy staff encouraged the state to carry out its day to day activities as another method to not create panic amongst the populace.[26] The U.S. Embassy even made arrangements with the National Police force to stay on duty until the last minute.[27] Some police officers were to depart on barges to meet with the American evacuation fleet with their families.[28] While other police officers were believed to have been paid off to maintain order in Saigon.[29] Overall, American efforts to evacuate from the RVN were kept secret and Nationalist Vietnamese only had an idea of what the U.S. Embassy was planning if they were contacted by staff members of the Embassy.[30] While the U.S. Federal government was in the process preparing for the American evacuation from the RVN, President Ford felt he needed to send a message to the American public.

While preparations for the evacuation of Saigon were under way, President Ford was working with his speech writers about delivering a positive message to student at Tulane

---

[24] Deputy Ambassador Lehmann as told to Larry Engelmann, *Tears before the Rain*, 40.

[25] Ibid.

[26] Ibid., 39.

[27] Ambassador Martin as told to Larry Engelmann, *Tears before the Rain*, 58.

[28] Ibid., 58.

[29] U.S. Embassy Staff Member Lacy Wright as told to Larry Engelmann, *Tears before the Rain*, 51.

[30] Cao Van Vien, *The Final Collapse*, 147-48.

University in New Orleans. President Ford wanted to inform students they have a bright future to focus upon, while to Ford the Vietnam War for the most part had reached its conclusion. Hartmann replied by encouraging President Ford to declare the conclusion of the Vietnam War. President Ford responded with skepticism since the war was still ongoing, but he wanted his speechwriters to work on the idea of the declaration.[31]

On April 23, 1975, President Ford delivered his speech at Tulane University.[32] After beginning with his explanation of being honored to speak at Tulane University again, President Ford remarked its students had served the U.S. in the past with great excellence with a mindset centered on the future.[33] President Ford moved on to touch on how the city of New Orleans had transitioned from "the past to the future" to play a role in the modern development of American society.[34] One contribution made by the city of New Orleans President Ford spotlights in his speech, was the Battle of New Orleans and how the victory restored American pride after Washington, D.C. was destroyed by the British in the War of 1812.[35] Then President Ford spoke the most memorable lines of his speech at Tulane University:

> Today America can again regain in the sense of pride that existed before Vietnam. But it cannot be achieved by refighting a war that is finished as far as America is concerned. The time has come to look forward an agenda for the future, to unify, to bind up the nation's wounds and restore it to health and optimistic self-confidence.[36]

---

[31] Hartmann, *Palace Politics*, 321.

[32] Speech Notes, President Gerald R. Ford's address at Tulane University, April 23, 1975, April 23, 1975 – Tulane University, New Orleans, Louisiana, Box 8, President's Speeches and Statements: Reading Copies, PDF page 1, Gerald R. Ford Presidential Library, Ann Arbor, Michigan, http://www.fordlibrarymuseum.gov/library/document/0122/1252291.pdf.

[33] Ibid., 6-7, PDF pages 8-9.

[34] Speech Notes, President Ford's address at Tulane University, April 23, 1975, 7-8, PDF pages 9-10.

[35] Ibid., 10-11, PDF pages 12-13.

[36] Ibid., 12, PDF page 14.

The second after President Ford mentioned the word finished, the students among the audience began to cheer, hug one another, and jumping with joy, with some students chanting "it's over, it's over" as President Ford continued to speak.[37] The crowd of young students were excited their president confirmed there would not be a military solution through the use of American armed forces in the Vietnam War. Excitement over how President Ford informed the students there was a future beyond the war for the United States.

Next, President Ford stated his desire for Americans to forget the past and to reconcile their differences in order to resolve the issues facing the United States.[38] During the remainder of his speech, President Ford stated the various goals of his administration and how the objective can only be achieved by the reconciliation of the American nation.[39] Finally, President Ford concluded his speech by reiterating his request for reconciliation of the American nation, and for the idea of a confident, independent nation to be spread all over the U.S. to ensure the state's future to be without limits.[40] Days after President Ford gave his speech at Tulane University, PAVN moved closer to Saigon.

By April 26, 1975, PAVN opened its assault upon Saigon with an artillery barrage lasting nearly an hour.[41] Four different corps and the massive PAVN conglomerate unit Group 232 were assigned to move into Saigon from every direction with the exception of

---

[37] Hartmann, *Palace Politics*, 322.

[38] Speech Notes, President Ford's address at Tulane University, April 23, 1975, 15, PDF page 17.

[39] "208 – Address at Tulane University Convocation, April 23, 1975," President Gerald R. Ford, from *the American Presidency Project*, last modified by Gerhard Peters and John T. Woolley, last modified 2015, accessed April 13, 2015, http://www.presidency.ucsb.edu/ws/index.php?pid=4859.

[40] Speech Notes, President Ford's address at Tulane University, April 23, 1975, 53-54, PDF pages 55-56.

[41] Military History Institute of Vietnam, *Victory in Vietnam*, 413.

directly south of the city.[42] Department of Defense contractor von Marbod departed the RVN with VNAF F-5s for the Kingdom of Thailand.[43] Violating of the agreement between the U.S. and USSR on the evacuation of American citizens, regarding no military equipment would leave the RVN, causing Ambassador Martin concern if PAVN would allow the U.S. to leave peacefully.[44] A day after of von Marbod's actions, Tan Son Nhut airport was barraged by artillery and rocket fire.[45] While high ranking officers were sent to the front lines for Saigon's defense if they had not fled, leaving Tan Son Nhut airport essentially unprotected.[46] The U.S. Joint Chiefs of Staff had issued orders to a classified individual with authority over the evacuation to make a maximum effort to complete to the American departure from the RVN on April 29 with USAF C-130 Hercules cargo aircraft.[47] With the attack on Tan Son Nhut airport, the status quo of the evacuation of Saigon could no longer be maintained.

During the PAVN barrage on Tan Son Nhut airport, two American Marines were killed in action; both the barrage and deaths caused President Ford to call for an emergency NSC meeting. CIA Director Colby and Secretary of Defense Schlesinger stated according to intelligence reports, PAVN was still in the process of laying down an artillery barrage on Tan Son Nhut airport. While two platoons of infantry were moving towards the direction of the airport. The NSC noted a concern about PAVN's SA-7 surface to air missiles within range of

---

[42] Military History Institute of Vietnam, *Victory in Vietnam*, 411-12.

[43] Ambassador Martin as told to Larry Engelmann, *Tears before the Rain*, 55-56.

[44] Ibid.

[45] Ibid., 56.

[46] Ibid.

[47] Telegram, U.S. Joint Chiefs of Staff to Ruhohoa/ CINPAC, Honolulu, Hawaii, April 28, 1975, folder six, VN SD TG to SECSTATE Exdis (3), Box 21, National Security Advisor, Presidential Country Files for East Asia and the Pacific: Country File: Vietnam – Department of State Telegrams, Gerald R. Ford Presidential Library, Ann Arber, Michigan.

Tan Son Nhut airport and how the missiles could jeopardize the evacuation. While discussing

the need for air cover, Secretary of Defense Schlesinger stated if the U.S. fires upon PAVN,

the Communist Vietnamese would retaliate with an assault on the U.S. Embassy. During the

meeting President Ford stated April 28, was the last day to evacuate the Nationalist

Vietnamese, remanding Americans including the staff at the U.S. Embassy, and the Defense

Attaché Office (DAO). However, the NSC had apprehension about evacuating Americans

first since it could have caused panic among the Nationalist Vietnamese. It was decided

Americans and Nationalist Vietnamese would be mixed onto helicopters. At the conclusion

of the NSC meeting all attendees agreed if the C-130s could not operate at the Tan Son Nhut

then the helicopter evacuation would begin at the DAO office complex and the U.S.

Embassy.[48]

Since the debris at Tan Son Nhut covered the runways, the helicopter evacuation went

ahead.[49] Despite all efforts for a smooth extraction, the helicopter evacuation was delayed.

To mobilize the Marine security force and the helicopters, the U.S. Navy took three hours to

organize the extrication teams since the Marine units were spread out on several different

ships.[50] Adding to the logistical issues were Nationalist Vietnamese civilians massing at the

U.S. Embassy and at Tan Son Nhut airport demanding to be evacuated from the RVN.[51]

---

[48] Meeting Minutes, National Security Council Meeting, April 28, 1975, 2-3, 4-5, 6-7, 8, and 9-10, NSC Meeting, April 28, 1975, Box 1, National Security Advisor's NSC Meeting File, accessed May 2, 2015, Gerald R. Ford Presidential Library, Ann Arbor, Michigan, http://www.fordlibrarymuseum.gov/library/document/0312/1552385.pdf.

[49] Ambassador Martin as told to Larry Engelmann, *Tears before the Rain*, 56-57.

[50] Deputy Ambassador Lehmann as told to Larry Engelmann, *Tears before the Rain*, 43-44.

[51] Daniel L. Haulman, "Vietnam Evacuation: Operation Frequent Wind," from *Short of War: USAF Contingency Operations 1947-1997*, edited by A. Timothy Warnock (Air University Press, 2000), 91, accessed May 2, 2015, http://www.afhso.af.mil/shared/media/document/AFD-101027-044.pdf.

By April 30, 662 sorties flew "more than 7,800" people out of Saigon before the two

day operation code named Frequent Wind was completed at 9:00 A.M. on the last day of

April, excluding the Marine security force.[52] From the U.S. embassy in Saigon, there were

two landing zones for the helicopters flying in at intervals of ten minutes apart, one official

landing pad on the roof of the embassy building itself and a makeshift landing zone in the

parking lot of the embassy compound.[53] Ambassador Martin had deliberately delayed his

departure from the U.S. embassy in Saigon, knowing shortly after he left, Operation Frequent

Wind would be brought to a close.[54] Ambassador Martin wanted to evacuate as many

Nationalist Vietnamese as possible.[55] In addition, Ambassador Martin had ordered the

Marine guard to place no more than two Americans on each helicopter, in order to evacuate

as many Nationalist Vietnamese as possible.[56]

Several American employees at the embassy were unofficially driving various groups

of Nationalist Vietnamese to the docks of Saigon along the river of the eponymous name.[57]

In order for the refugees to obtain passage to a safe haven through a commercial vessel

heading out to sea.[58] On the open sea, the *USS Kirk* took in Nationalist Vietnamese refugees

---

[52] Haulman, "Vietnam Evacuation: Operation Frequent Wind," 91-92.

[53] "Last Days in Vietnam: The American Experience: Program Transcript," "Slate: 3:00 PM, Juan Valdez, Marine Embassy Guard," Corporation for Public Broadcasting, accessed April 25, 2016, http://www.pbs.org/wgbh/americanexperience/features/transcript/lastdays-transcript/.

[54] Lieutenant Colonel James W. Washington, "Operation Frequent Wind: South Vietnamese Refugee Evacuation Operations: How it Looked in Provisional Marine Aircraft Group 39 (ProMAG 39)," *Marine Corps Gazette* volume 99, issue 5 (May, 2015): accessed April 24, 2016, https://www.mca-marines.org/gazette/2015/05/operation-frequent-wind.

[55] Ibid.

[56] "Last Days in Vietnam," "Slate: 5:00 PM, Joseph McBride, State Department Officer."

[57] Ibid.

[58] Ibid.

who had flown out to sea on helicopters hoping the U.S. Navy would accept them.[59] The crew of the *USS Kirk* had to push several helicopters off its landing deck in order for more helicopters to land, one at a time.[60] Several hours later, the *USS Kirk* escorted thousands of Nationalist Vietnamese refugees on various vessels to the Republic of the Philippines, without orders or permission from the captain's superiors.[61] Despite the humanitarian efforts in the evacuation of Saigon, major issues had arisen on the operation's viability.

As Frequent Wind went on, helicopter crews had become exhausted with some crews who had been on duty for nearly seventeen hours straight by the conclusion of the operation.[62] Raising concerns about the viability of continuing the evacuation.[63] While in Washington, D.C., Dr. Kissinger pointed out to the Ford White House, PAVN was poised to enter the city proper of Saigon and the presidential order for Ambassador Martin to leave the U.S. embassy needed to be issued.[64] Since the evacuation could not be conducted without drawing the attention of PAVN.[65]

In the early hours of April 30, President Ford issued the order for Operation Frequent Wind to be brought to a close with Ambassador Martin to be airlifted out of the embassy

---

[59] "Last Days in Vietnam," "Slate: 2:30 PM, Paul Jacobs, Commanding Officer, *USS Kirk* and Hugh Doyle, Chief Engineer, *USS Kirk*."

[60] Ibid.

[61] "Last Days in Vietnam," "Slate: 4:00 AM, Paul Jacobs, Commanding Officer, *USS Kirk* and Richard Armitage, Special Forces Advisor."

[62] Washington, "Operation Frequent Wind."

[63] Ibid.

[64] Kissinger, *Ending the Vietnam War*, 551-52.

[65] Ibid.

compound.[66] The U.S. embassy in Saigon complied with President Ford's order with plans to close the embassy at 04:30 in its last message and destroyed all non-portable communications equipment.[67] Nearly two-hundred fifty people who were approved to be evacuated by the U.S. Embassy were left behind after the Ford White House ordered the last of the remaining embassy staff to be extracted.[68] Deputy Ambassador Lehmann argued the evacuation did not just leave two-hundred fifty people behind, it abandoned nineteen million people who made up the population of the RVN.[69] With the DAO Office and the U.S. Embassy in Saigon closed, what remained of the RVN met its fate.

As PAVN moved into the city proper of Saigon in the morning hours of April 30, 1975, the remaining detachment of eleven Marines barricaded themselves on the roof of the embassy building.[70] The Ford White House was misinformed and made a statement to the press about the evacuation of Saigon.[71] In the press release, President Ford stated after conditions had begun to deteriorate, he ordered the evacuation of the U.S. embassy in Saigon, and commended everyone who assisted in the evacuation which brought "all American personnel remaining in" the RVN, out of the state.[72] Immediately after the press conference

---

[66] "Last Days in Vietnam," "Slate: 5:00 PM, Gerald Berry, Marine Pilot and Stuart Harrington, Army Captain."

[67] Telegram, United States Embassy of Saigon to Secretary of State Henry Kissinger, April 29, 1975, box 21, National Security Advisor, Presidential Country Files: East Asia and the Pacific, Country File: Vietnam – Department of State Telegrams, Gerald R. Ford Presidential Library, Ann Arbor, Michigan, PDF, https://www.fordlibrarymuseum.gov/library/exhibits/vietnam/032400112-001.pdf.

[68] Deputy Ambassador Lehmann as told to Larry Engelmann, *Tears before the Rain*, 44-45.

[69] Ibid.

[70] "Last Days in Vietnam," "Slate: Saigon, 6:00 AM, Juan Valdez, Marine Embassy Guard and Mike Sullivan, Marine Embassy Guard."

[71] Nessen, *It Sure Looks Different from the Inside*, 111-12.

[72] Statement by the President, Statement by the President on evacuation of American personnel from South Vietnam, April 29, 1975, Gerald R. Ford Administration White House Press Releases: April 18, 1975-

on the evacuation, the Ford White House received news of a Marine security detachment had yet to be flown out of the U.S. embassy compound.[73] Approximately eight in the morning, one American helicopter flew into Saigon, landed on the U.S. embassy rooftop landing pad, and extracted the remaining eleven Marines from the city.[74]

Shortly after the last eleven Marines were flown out of Saigon, Press Secretary Nessen, made a revised statement to the press about the miscommunication and confirming all U.S. embassy staff were out of what was the RVN.[75] Around 10:45 in the morning and after the completion of Operation Frequent Wind on April 30, a tank numbered 843 of the fourth tank company drove through the gates of the Independence Palace.[76] Tank 843 was followed by PAVN infantry soldiers who stormed the Palace, capturing President Minh and his entire cabinet.[77] By May 2, the entire territory of the RVN state was under the occupation of the DRV, thereby, concluding the long and bloody Vietnam War.[78]

Before the Vietnam War came to a close and Thieu resigned from the presidency of the RVN, Dr. Hung traveled to the U.S. in an effort to obtain some form of additional aid from the United States.[79] On his trip to the U.S., Dr. Hung brought with him President

May 13, 1975, box 10, White House Press Releases, 1974-77, Gerald R. Ford Presidential Library, Ann Arbor, Michigan, PDF, https://www.fordlibrarymuseum.gov/library/document/0248/whpr19750429-011.pdf.

[73] Nessen, *It Sure Looks Different from the Inside*, 112.

[74] "Last Days in Vietnam," "Slate: Saigon, 6:00 AM, Juan Valdez, Marine Embassy Guard and Mike Sullivan, Marine Embassy Guard."

[75] Statement by Press Secretary, Statement by Press Secretary on the evacuation, April 29, 1975, Gerald R. Ford Administration White House Press Releases: April 18, 1975-May 13, 1975, box 10, White House Press Releases, 1974-77, Gerald R. Ford Presidential Library, Ann Arbor, Michigan, PDF, https://www.fordlibrarymuseum.gov/library/document/0248/whpr19750429-020.pdf.

[76] Military History Institute of Vietnam, *Victory in Vietnam*, 420-21.

[77] Ibid.

[78] Ibid., 424.

Thieu's file of correspondence letters from Nixon and President Ford.[80] After hearing no more than seventy-thousand Nationalist Vietnamese refugees would be rescued, Dr. Hung released two of the letters from the Nixon-Thieu correspondence at a press conference, in an effort to persuade the U.S. to aid and rescue more refugees.[81] Contained in the letters Dr. Hung released to the press were Nixon's vows to intervene on the RVN's behalf on the condition that the DRV violated the PPA.[82] On the same day as Dr. Hung's press release, President Ford requested $507 million for the care of one hundred twenty thousand Nationalist Vietnamese refugees.[83] However, the House voted against President Ford's request and other key congressional leaders were opposed to extending aid to the Nationalist Vietnamese refugees who had to rely on the efforts of volunteers.[84] Through his presidency and the outcome to the Vietnam War, President Ford's perspective was influenced by his political goals.

During the closing days of the Vietnam War President Ford had developed a philosophy concerning the war out of his goal of reconciliation of the American nation. Where President Ford attempted to persuade Americans not to accuse groups of people for the transpired events during and the occurrence of the war itself.[85] President Ford encouraged Americans to

[79] Hung and Schecter, *The Palace File*, 321-22.

[80] Ibid., 323-24.

[81] Ibid., 345-46.

[82] Bernard Gwertzman, "Thieu Aide Discloses Promises of Force by Nixon to Back Pact," *New York Times*, May 1, 1975, accessed May 26, 2015, http://partners.nytimes.com/library/world/asia/050175vietnam-thieu-bg.html.

[83] Ford, *A Time to Heal*, 256-57.

[84] Ibid., 257.

divert their energies to new projects as a way to defuse the emotional turmoil of the Vietnam War had developed within the American nation.[86] Years later Ford's attitude towards the Vietnam War had shifted, particularly the events that occurred during his Presidency. When the Gerald R. Ford Foundation board of directors discussed whether or not to include the rooftop ladder from the former U.S. Embassy in Saigon to be used in the evacuation of Saigon now Ho Chi Minh City in an exhibit at the Gerald R. Ford Presidential Museum.[87] Dr. Kissinger remarked the ladder was a symbol of American failure in Southeast Asia.[88] Ford, however, objected to Dr. Kissinger's argument and was able to win over the board of directors to accept the Embassy ladder in an exhibit at the Ford Presidential Museum.[89] Ford described while the fall of the RVN was not an event to take pride in, the ladder still symbolizes the human desire for freedom.[90]

To begin the Final or Ho Chi Minh Offensive, the DRV tested the military commitment of the U.S. by conquering Phoc Long province of the RVN. President Ford declined to order a bombing campaign due to the tense political atmosphere in the U.S. and his political beliefs. Instead, President Ford requested additional military funding for the RVN and agreed to a Congressional delegation to investigate the need for supplementary aid for the Nationalist Vietnamese. When it became evident the Ford Administration would not

---

[85] Robert J. McMahon, "Rationalizing Defeat: The Vietnam War in American Presidential Discourse, 1975-1995," *Rhetoric and Public Affairs*, volume 2, number 4 (Winter, 1999): 531-32, accessed April 7, 2015, doi: 10.1353/rap.2010.0041.

[86] Ibid., 532-33.

[87] Douglas Brinkley, *Gerald R. Ford: The American Presidents Series*, General Editor Arthur M. Schlesinger, Junior (New York: Time Books, 2007), 96-97.

[88] Ibid.

[89] Ibid., 97-98.

[90] Ibid.

launch a bombing campaign into the RVN in response to the DRV's capture of Phoc Long province. PAVN carried out its full offensive plans in March 1975.

In a period of roughly two months, RVNAF defenses quickly fell all over the RVN due to poor strategic defense planning, lack of supplies, poor leadership in some units, wide deployments of military units over large tracks of territory, and overwhelming numbers of PAVN forces. After MRs I and II fell to PAVN, President Thieu requested B-52 bomber strikes from President Ford as part of the American commitment to the RVN. President Ford leery of President Thieu's appeal for American intervention and sent General Weyand to investigate the matter. Based on his research, General Weyand recommended the best option for President Ford to aid the RVN was through a short bombing campaign. Additionally, Nixon's letters to President Thieu that promised American intervention on the condition of extreme Communist Vietnamese violations were presented to President Ford. However, Kennerly informed President Ford that the RVN was on the verge of collapsing in the matter of a few short weeks.

After contemplating his options and considering the political environment the U.S. was in, President Ford declined to launch a bombing campaign in favor of evacuating as many people as possible. The evacuation had to be conducted without causing panic, to avoid the trauma during the fall of Danang. The U.S. began its evacuation from the RVN quietly, in order to not raise suspicion. The evacuation was not completed until April 29, 1975, since PAVN had encircled the city of Saigon while a helicopter airlift took place. Still to this day April, 1975, is a bitter memory to numerous people.

Conclusion

When faced with the choice of whether or not to launch a bombing campaign to re-introduce U.S. armed forces back into the Vietnam War, President Ford declined to do so. The American public was strongly against American participation in the Vietnam War during Ford's Presidency. Once President Ford obtained knowledge of the contents in the Nixon-Thieu correspondence, it further complicated matters for the president. Kennerly was able to pass information on the RVN's military defenses a month before the Nationalist Vietnamese state's fall to the DRV. Convincing President Ford any form of aid for the RVN would not reach the state in time since it was expected to fall in a matter of a few short weeks. Although President Ford felt very strongly about the necessity to support American allies in dire need, such as the RVN, he could not politically afford to send American air power back into Vietnam without politically isolating himself.

As described in his transition file, his inaugural address, the amnesty program for Vietnam War era draft dodgers, the pardon of Richard Nixon, and the Tulane University speech, President Ford's top objective was for Americans to put aside their differences to resolve other major issues. In order to make progress on his objective of reconciliation of the American nation, President Ford required cooperation of other decision makers and the support of the American public, while avoiding controversy. Had President Ford launched a bombing campaign into Vietnam, he would have discredited himself and would have struggled for political support for his programs. As Nixon's successor in the Oval Office, Ford knew documented information would at some point in time become public knowledge. Ultimately, President Ford's decision to not re-introduce American bombers in the Vietnam War was influenced by the events of the early to mid-1970s.

As the Vietnam War went on, the American public became disillusioned with their state's involvement in the conflict and demanded that the U.S. Federal government end the war. In the 1968 presidential election, Nixon vowed to end the Vietnam War. Once elected to the presidency, Nixon and his staff developed the process of Vietnamization. A process where the U.S. made periodic withdrawals of its combat forces in Southeast Asia while simultaneously arming and training RVNAF. However, Vietnamization was designed and implemented for the benefit of the U.S. rather than the RVN. The U.S. was successful in building RVNAF into a large military equipped with modern weaponry, but the military model used was unsustainable for the RVN. The post-Vietnamization RVNAF required massive funding from foreign states, particularly the U.S. Since Vietnamization took too many individuals out of the civilian labor force to support a military within the Nationalist Vietnamese economy and the lack of economic development within the RVN. Vietnamization was not only hampered by American decisions; it was hampered by Nationalist Vietnamese decisions as well.

Nationalist Vietnamese decision makers failed to make contingency plans for when the Communist Vietnamese launched another offensive. President Thieu insisted the entire geographic territory under Nationalist Vietnamese control at the time of the first ceasefire was to remain under RVNAF control. It was unfeasible since RVNAF lacked the manpower to effectively patrol and maintain security in rural areas. Never did Nationalist Vietnamese decision makers make contingency plans for another PAVN offensive, outside of the hopes the U.S. would intervene on their behalf. American intervention was promised to the RVN as a means for the state to agree to the PPA.

The purpose of the PPA was to create a peaceful conclusion to the Vietnam War, but due to its many flaws the document never established peace as it was intended to. Neither the Nationalist nor the Communist Vietnamese wanted the PPA. In order for the Vietnamese parties to even agree to the PPA, the U.S. had to resort to threats. For the DRV, the U.S. launched the bombing campaign Linebacker II. After promising intervention on the Nationalist behalf if the DRV violated the peace agreement. President Nixon threatened to cut off American aid for the Nationalist Vietnamese if the RVN refused the sign the PPA. The U.S. on the other hand desired the PPA since the American involvement in the Vietnam War severely lacked popular support and many American decision makers believed that the War was a stalemate.

President Nixon was determined to fulfill his 1968 campaign pledge to conclude the Vietnam War even when Dr. Kissinger raised concerns about the PPA's viability to maintain peace in Southeast Asia. A major flaw in the PPA was that the document did not formalize a peace agreement between the Nationalist and Communist Vietnamese. The Vietnamese parties only agreed to take measures to establish a formal peace agreement. The PPA did, however, establish peace between the U.S. and the Communist Vietnamese. Leading to the final extraction of American combat forces from the Vietnam War. When President Nixon announced that the DRV and the RVN had signed the PPA, many Americans believed the Vietnam War had finally had come to a close. While President Nixon believed he had concluded the Vietnam War in an honorable way, a domestic issue had become a growing concern for many Americans.

During the 1972 presidential election, several men broke into the Democratic Party National Committee headquarters at the Watergate Office Complex to place listening devices. These men were apprehended in the act. As investigations went on, evidence the

Nixon Administration had employed the burglars and President Nixon himself had attempted

to cover up his Administration's involvement in the Watergate affair became public

knowledge. President Nixon's involvement in the Watergate scandal caused many Americans

to become disillusioned with the U.S. Federal government particularly with the executive

office. Because of his part in the Watergate scandal, Nixon resigned from the Presidency.

Thereby, allowing Ford to assume the executive office.

Like many Americans, Ford was shocked and frustrated by Nixon's actions upon

learning the truth of Nixon's role in the Watergate scandal. In his inaugural address,

President Ford vowed to the American public he would not govern in the same manner as his

immediate predecessor had. In addition, President Ford had stated in his inaugural address

his presidency was the beginning of a new era for the United States. Understanding

American society was divided on numerous issues including the Vietnam War and the

Watergate scandal. Ford felt he needed to take efforts to bring the American public together

in order for other issues faced by the U.S. to be resolved. One of the best examples of

President Ford's goal of reconciliation was the conditional amnesty program for draft

evaders. In order to make progress towards his goal, President Ford had to avoid controversy.

However, President Ford did create some confusion in his correspondence with President

Thieu.

While Nixon was president, he wrote a series of letters assuring President Thieu the

U.S. could aid the RVN militarily on the possible condition the DRV violated the PPA.

Nixon made the defense agreement with President Thieu without informing the U.S. Senate

and the Nixon White House Staff on his negotiations with Thieu. When Ford entered the presidency, he assured President Thieu all previous agreements made with the RVN would be up held by the Ford Administration. Little did President Ford knew, Nixon had made a defense agreement with President Thieu before Ford had sent his first letter to Thieu. When President Thieu received President Ford's initial letter, he believed Ford would support the defense agreement made by Nixon. President Thieu continued to base RVNAF's defense plans around the secret agreement. It was not until after the DRV launched their Ho Chi Minh Offensive, did President Ford learn of the contents of the Nixon-Thieu correspondence.

Shortly before New Year's Day of 1975, the DRV launched their probe assault of the Ho Chi Minh Offensive leading to the Communist Vietnamese conquest of Phoc Long province by early January 1975. President Ford never ordered a bombing campaign against the DRV as President Thieu expected. With a lack of response from the U.S., the DRV pressed on with their offensive leading to the control of MRs I and II, half of the Nationalist Vietnamese state.

With dwindling military supplies and a weakened RVNAF, President Thieu specifically requested B-52 bomber strikes against advancing PAVN divisions. President Ford instead sent General Weyand and White House photographer Kennerly on a fact finding mission. Through the fact finding mission, President Thieu's advisor Dr. Hung gave copies of the Nixon-Thieu correspondence to the Weyand mission who in turn presented the letters to President Ford. During the his presentation, General Weyand recommended President Ford to launch a brief bombing campaign against PAVN forces south of the DMZ. However, while touring the RVN and the KR, Kennerly learned both states were about to collapse. Kennerly's information was passed to President Ford. With the information from both presentations, President Ford had to make a decision.

The choice President Ford made was to discreetly evacuate all Americans and as many Nationalist Vietnamese as possible. While at the same time, request for supplemental aid for the RVN from congress. From the information he had studied, President Ford reluctantly accepted the fact that the RVN was on the verge of collapsing in April, 1975. President Ford wanted to aid the RVN through proxy measures and stop the flow of communism. However, at the same time, politically, President Ford could not afford to launch a bombing campaign to re-introduce the U.S. in the Vietnam War. President Ford knew well enough from his predecessor all documented information would at some point become public knowledge. Thus, President Ford never supported the defense agreement Nixon made with President Theiu, guaranteeing American intervention into the Vietnam War on the Nationalist Vietnamese behalf when the DRV violated the PPA.

Considering the political environment in the U.S. during the mid-1970s, President Ford had made the right decision to decline a bombing campaign into the Vietnam War and to evacuate as many people as possible from the RVN. Had President Ford launched a bombing campaign into the Vietnam War at President Thieu's request, Ford would have broken his vow in his inaugural address not to govern as Nixon had before him. The evacuation from the RVN, Saigon in particular, had to be conducted quietly. In order to help prevent the sense of panic that had developed in Danang before the evacuation was complete. The U.S. wanted to move away from the trauma that had developed during the Vietnam War and wanted to leave the conflict. Still, the final American withdraw from the Vietnam War came at a great cost for the U.S. and its allies.

Judging by the lack of a detailed historiography on President Ford and his decision not to launch a bombing campaign into Vietnam. Americans still struggle with the final outcome of the Vietnam War, not to mention, most likely, the Nationalist Vietnamese as well. Even as an American who had not lived through the Vietnam War era, the conclusion to the war is still a difficult subject discuss. Nonetheless, this work of history on President Ford's choice to decline the re-introduction of American bombers in the Vietnam War is not meant to bring back the emotions of the Vietnam War era. Nor is it to instill the emotions in a younger generation of people. *Over as Far as America is Concerned* is designed to bring about a conversation and understanding on the latter years of the Vietnam War. Which many people find as a difficult subject to discuss. There are still many topics that require research related to President Ford's choice to decline recommendations for a bombing campaign in the Vietnam War. Some topics include, U.S. foreign policy towards the KR during the latter days of the state, a study of American congressional leaders' attitude during the latter years of the Vietnam War, and the choices made by Nationalist Vietnamese decision makers at various levels of government.

Bibliography

Aldrich, George H. Letter, Legal Advisor George H. Aldrich, Acting to Ambassador McClosky. Memorandum for Ambassador McClosky. January13, 1975. National Security Advisor Presidential Country Files for East Asia and the Pacific: Vietnam, box 19. folder 1, document 3. Gerald R. Ford Presidential Library, Ann Arbor, Michigan.

American Merchant Marine at War. "Capture and Release of *SS Mayaguez* by Khmer Rouge Forces in May, 1975." Last modified 2000. Accessed October 23, 2015. http://www.usmm.org/mayaguez.html.

Anderson, David L. "Gerald R. Ford and the Presidents' War in Vietnam." In *Shadow on the White House: Presidents and the Vietnam War, 1945-1975*, edited by David L. Anderson, 184-207. Lawrence, Kansas: University Press of Kansas, 1993.

Andrew, Christopher. and Vasili Mitrokhin. *The World was Going Our Way: The KGB and the Battle for the Third World.* New York: Basic Books, 2005.

Associated Press, The. "Bill Chappell Jr. is Dead at 67; Served in the House for 20 Years." *New York Times*, March 31, 1989. Accessed October 26, 2015. http://www.nytimes.com/1989/03/31/obituaries/bill-chappell-jr-is-dead-at-67-served-in-the-house-for-20-years.html.

----. "John J. Flynt Jr., Georgia Democrat, Is Dead at 92." *New York Times*, June 25, 2007. Accessed October 26, 2015. http://www.nytimes.com/2007/06/25/us/25flynt.html?_r=0.

Batchelder, Sydney H. and D. A. Quinlan. "Operation Eagle Pull." *Marine Corps Gazette* volume 60, number 5 (May, 1976). Accessed April 18, 2015. https://www.mca-marines.org/gazette/1976/05/operation-eagle-pull.

Belasco, Amy. Lynn J. Cunningham, Hannah Fischer, and Larry Niksch. "Congressional Restrictions on U.S. Military Operations in Vietnam, Cambodia, Laos, Somalia, and Kosovo: Funding and Non-Funding Approaches." Congressional Research Service Report for Congress presented to Members and Committees of Congress on January 16, 2007. http://fas.org/sgp/crs/natsec/RL33803.pdf.

Bernstein, Carl and Robert Woodward. "Dean Alleges Nixon Knew of Cover-up Plan." *Washington Post*, June 3, 1973. From *Washington Post* Politics: The Watergate Story. Accessed

September 16, 2014. http://www.washingtonpost.com/politics/dean-alleges-nixon-knew-of-
cover-up-plan/2012/06/04/gJQAgpyCJV_story.html.

Borsa, Lauren. "Murtha, John Paterick." Last modified Spring 2010. Accessed July 10, 2015.
http://pabook.libraries.psu.edu/palitmap/bios/Murtha__John.html.

Brezhnev, General Secretary Leonid. Oral Message #87. General Secretary Leonid Brezhnev to
Secretary of State Henry Kissinger. April 10, 1975. Folder: Ten, Items #86-#91, Circa April,
1975-April 22, 1975. National Security Advisor Kissinger-Scowcroft West Wing Office
Files, 1969-1977: General Subject File: USSR- 'D' File (Dobrynin). Gerald R. Ford
Presidential Library, Ann Arbor, Michigan.

----. Oral Message, #92, B1. General Secretary Leonid Brezhnev to President Gerald R. Ford. April
24, 1975. Folder 10, Items #86-#91, circa April, 1975-April 22, 1975. Box 30, National
Security Advisor: Kissinger-Scowcroft West Wing Office Files, 1969-1977: General Subject
File: USSR- 'D' File (Dobrynin). Gerald R. Ford Presidential Library, Ann Arbor, Michigan.

Brinkley, Douglas. *Gerald R. Ford (The American Presidents Series: The 38th President, 1974-
1977),* General Editor Arthur M. Schlesinger Jr. New York: Henry Holt and Company, 2007.

Cabinet Meeting Minutes. Notes of the Cabinet Meeting. January 29, 1975. 1975/01/29 Cabinet
Meeting. Box 4, James Conner Files. Gerald R. Ford Library, Ann Arbor, Michigan.
http://www.fordlibrarymuseum.gov/library/exhibits/cabinet/cm750129.pdf.

Cannon, James. *Gerald R. Ford: An Honorable Life.* Ann Arbor: University of Michigan, 2013.

CBS. "Dunning's Frantic Flight, March 29, 1975." *CBS News.* Online streaming video file. Last
modified 2015. Accused July 20, 2015. http://www.cbsnews.com/videos/dunnings-frantic-
flight/.

Central Reconstruction and Development Council of the Republic of Vietnam. Community
Reconstruction and Development Plan, 1973. Folder three, 1601-11A Community
Reconstruction and Local Development Plan, 1973. Entry # A1 531: General Records; 1969-
1975. Box Two, 228-08/ Ceasefire Violations and Related Items/ Monthly, March –
December, 1973 Through 228-08/ HES Airgram, May, 1973 – January, 1975. MACV,
Headquarters CORDS/ Special Assistant to the U.S. Ambassador for Field Operations
(SAAFO). Record Group 472 U.S. Forces in Southeast Asia, 1950-1975. National Archives,
College Park, Maryland.

Clodfelter, Mark. *The Limits of Air Power: The American Bombing of North Vietnam.* New York:
Free Press, 1989.

Colby, William with James McCarger. *Lost Victory: A Firsthand Account of America's
Sixteen Year Involvement in Vietnam.* Chicago: Contemporary Books, 1989.

Corporation for Public Broadcasting. "Last Days in Vietnam: The American Experience: Program Transcript." Accessed April 25, 2016. http://www.pbs.org/wgbh/americanexperience/features/transcript/lastdays-transcript/.

Cronkite, Walter. "Walter Cronkite, 'We are Mired in a Stalemate' Broadcast, CBS News, February 27, 1968." From The Pacifica Radio/ UC Berkeley's Social Activism Sound Recording Project. Last modified March 25, 2008. Accessed September 23, 2014. http://www.lib.berkeley.edu/MRC/pacificaviet/cronkitevietnam.html.

Dan, Phan Quang. "The Vietnam Experience" *Asian Affairs*, Volume 4, Number 4 (March – April, 1977): 255-271. Accessed January 16, 2014. Stable URL: http://www.jstor.org/stable/30171484.

D'Mello, Bernard. "What is Maoism?" *Economic and Political Weekly* Volume 44, Number 47 (November 21-27, 2009): 39-48. Accessed September 1, 2014. Stable URL: http://www.jstor.org/stable/25663811.

Dodd, Joseph W. "Faction and Failure in South Vietnam." *Asian Affairs* Volume 2, Number 3 (January – February, 1975): 173-178. Accessed March 24, 2014. Stable URL: http://www.jstor.org/stable/30171883.

Donnell, John C. "South Vietnam in 1975: The Year of Communist Victory." *Asian Survey*, Volume 16, Number 1 (January, 1976): 1-13. Accessed January 30, 2014. Stable URL: http://www.jstor.org/stable/2643276.

Downing, Major Wayne A. Letter Major Wayne A. Downing to Major Jack Pellicci. January 30, 1973. Folder One, HES Question Elimination Study. 4A, Entry# A1 531: General Records; 1969 – 1975, Box Three, HES Question Elimination Study, 1973 through Reconstruction and Development Conference/ Independence Palace (Second Copy) 27 July, 1973. Record Group 472 U.S. Forces in Southeast Asia, 1950-1975, MACV, HQ CORDS/ Special Assistant to U.S. Ambassador for Field Operations (SAAFO). National Archives, College Park, Maryland.

Engelmann, Larry. *Tears before the Rain: An Oral History of the Fall of South Vietnam*. New York: Oxford University, 1990.

Ford, Gerald R. Letter. Gerald R. Ford to Betty, Mike, and John "Jack" Ford. September 3, 1953. Congressional Papers of Gerald R. Ford. Accessed May 25, 2015. Gerald R. Ford Presidential Library, Ann Arbor, Michigan, http://www.fordlibrarymuseum.gov/library/exhibits/vietnam/005400673-001.pdf.

---- Letter. Gerald Ford to Senator Hubert Humphrey. November 5, 1973. PDF page 5. Opening Statement: Experts View the Vice Presidency, box 242. Gerald R. Ford Presidential Library, Ann Arbor, Michigan. http://www.fordlibrarymuseum.gov/library/document/25thamend/humphreyletter.pdf.

----. "1 – Remarks on Taking the Oath of Office, August 9,1974." from *The American Presidency Project*. Last modified 2014 by Gerhard Peters and John T. Woolly. Accessed May 11, 2015. http://www.presidency.ucsb.edu/ws/index.php?pid=4409.

----. Speakers' Notes. Swearing-In Ceremony: Inaugural Address, President Gerald R. Ford. August 9, 1974. Folder "8/9/74 – Swearing-in Ceremony." Box 1, from the President's Speeches and Statements: Reading Copies, 1974-1977. Gerald R. Ford Library, Ann Arbor, Michigan. Accessed May 24, 2015. http://www.fordlibrarymuseum.gov/library/document/0122/1252055.pdf.

----. Telegram. President Gerald R. Ford to President Nguyen Van Thieu via the U.S. Embassy in Saigon. August, 1974. Folder Two, VW CD-1 August 9, 1974–March 3, 1975. Box 38, National Security Advisor Kissinger – Scowcroft West Wing Office Files, 1969-1977. General Subject File: Vietnamese War – 'Camp David File.' Gerald R. Ford Presidential Library, Ann Arbor, Michigan.

----. "16 – Remarks to the Veterans of Foreign Wars Annual Convention, Chicago, Illinois, August 19, 1974." From *The American Presidency Project*. Last modified by Gerhard Peters and John T. Woolley. Last modified 2015. Accessed January 24, 2015. http://www.presidency.ucsb.edu/ws/index.php?pid=4476.

----. "39 – The President's News Conference, August 28, 1974." From *The American Presidency Project*. Last modified by Gerhard Peters and John T. Woolley. Last modified 2015. Accessed January 24, 2015. http://www.presidency.ucsb.edu/ws/index.php?pid=4671.

----. "60 – Remarks on Signing a Proclamation Granting Pardon to Richard Nixon, September 8, 1974." From *The American Presidency Project*. Last modified by Gerhard Peters and John T. Woolley. Last modified 2015. Accessed January 25, 2015. http://www.presidency.ucsb.edu/ws/index.php?pid=4695.

----. "78 – Proclamation 4313 – Announcing a Program for the Return of Vietnam Era Draft Evaders and Military Deserters, September 16, 1974." From *The American Presidency Project*. Last modified by Gerhard Peters and John T. Woolley. Last modified 2015. Accessed January 24, 2015. http://www.presidency.ucsb.edu/ws/index.php?pid=4714.

----. "53 – Special Message to Congress Requesting Supplemental Assistance for the Republic of Vietnam and Cambodia, January 28, 1975." From *The American Presidency Project*. Last modified by Gerhard Peters and John T. Woolley. Last modified 2015. Accessed February 24, 2014. http://www.presidency.ucsb.edu/ws/index.php?pid=5216.

----. Letter. President Gerald R. Ford to President Nguyen Van Thieu. March 22, 1975. PDF. Box 5, National Security Advisor, Presidential Correspondence with Foreign Leaders, 1974-1977. Accessed May 25, 2015. http://www.fordlibrarymuseum.gov/library/document/0351/1555873.pdf.

----. Oral Note, #90, 5C. President Gerald R. Ford to General Secretary Leonid Brezhnev. Folder 10, Items #86-#91, circa April, 1975-April 22, 1975. Box30, National Security Advisor: Kissinger-Scowcroft West Wing Office Files, 1969-1977: General Subject File: USSR- 'D' File (Dobrynin). Gerald R. Ford Presidential Library, Ann Arbor, Michigan.

----. Talking Points, #90, 5D. Talking Points for President Gerald R. Ford to General Secretary Leonid Brezhnev. Folder 10, Items #86-#91, circa April,1975-April 22, 1975. Box 30, National Security Advisor: Kissinger-Scowcroft West Wing Office Files, 1969-1977: General Subject File: USSR- 'D' File (Dobrynin). Gerald R. Ford Presidential Library, Ann Arbor, Michigan.

----. Speaker's reading notes. President Gerald R. Ford's Foreign Policy address to a joint session of Congress. April 10, 1975. April 10, 1975 – Foreign Policy Address, Joint Session of Congress. Box 7, President's Speeches and Statements: Reading Copies. Gerald R. Ford Presidential Library, Ann Arbor, Michigan. Accessed May 25, 2015. http://www.fordlibrarymuseum.gov/library/document/0122/1252280.pdf.

----. "179 – Address Before a Joint Session of the Congress Reporting on United States Foreign Policy, April 10, 1975." From *The American Presidency Project*. Last modified by Gerhard Peters and John T. Woolley. Last modified 2015. Accessed April 17, 2015. http://www.presidency.ucsb.edu/ws/index.php?pid=4826.

----. Speech Notes. Excerpt Related to Vietnam from President Ford's address at Tulane University (Reading Copy of   Entire Speech). April 23, 1975. Under "Selected Document on the Vietnam War." Gerald R. Ford Presidential Library, Ann Arbor, Michigan. Accessed February 27, 2014. http://www.fordlibrarymuseum.gov/library/document/0122/1252291.pdf.

----. "208 – Address at Tulane University Convocation, April 23, 1975." From *The American Presidency Project*. Last modified by Gerhard Peters and John T. Woolley. Last modified 2015. Accessed April 13, 2015. http://www.presidency.ucsb.edu/ws/index.php?pid=4859.

----. Statement by the President. Statement by the President on evacuation of American personnel from South Vietnam. April 29, 1975. Gerald R. Ford Administration White House Press Releases: April 18, 1975-May 13, 1975. Box 10, White House Press Releases, 1974-77. Gerald R. Ford Presidential Library, Ann Arbor, Michigan. PDF. https://www.fordlibrarymuseum.gov/library/document/0248/whpr19750429-011.pdf.

----. *A Time to Heal: The Autobiography of Gerald R. Ford.* New York: Harper and Row, 1979.

----. "Congress, the Presidency and National Security Policy." *Presidential Studies Quarterly* Volume 16, Number 2, Congress, the Court, and the Presidency in National Security Policy (Spring, 1986: 200-205. Accessed January 11, 2014. Stable URL: http://www.jstor.org/stable/40574643.

Gallup, Inc. "Presidential Approval Ratings – Gallup Historical Statistics and Trends." Last modified 2015. Accessed July 13, 2015. http://www.gallup.com/poll/116677/presidential-approval-ratings-gallup-historical-statistics-trends.aspx.

Gartner, Scott Sigmund. "Differing Evaluations of Vietnamization." *The Journal of Interdisciplinary History*, Volume 29, Number 2 (Autumn, 1998): 243-262. Accessed April, 24, 2014. Stable URL: http://www.jstor.org/stable/207045.

Goodman, Allen E. "South Vietnam: War without End?" *Asian Survey* Volume 15, Number 1 (January, 1975): 70-84. Accessed January 9, 2015. Stable URL: http://www.jstor.org/stable/2643432.

Granger, Clinton E. Memorandum. Clinton E. Granger to Deputy National Security Advisor Brent Scowcroft. April 5, 1975. "A Second Opinion on General Weyand's Visit to South Vietnam." From Selected Documents on the Vietnam War. PDF. Gerald R. Ford Presidential Library, Ann Arbor, Michigan. Accessed May 25, 2015. http://www.fordlibrarymuseum.gov/library/exhibits/vietnam/032400082-001.pdf.

Greene, John Robert. *The Presidency of Gerald R. Ford.* Lawrence: University of Kansas, 1995.

Grinter, Laurence E. "How They Lost: Doctrines, Strategies and Outcomes of the Vietnam War." *Asian Survey* Volume 15, Number 12 (December, 1975): 1114-1132. Accessed January 30, 2014. Stable URL: http://www.jstor.org/stable/2643587.

Gwertzman, Bernard. "Thieu Aide Discloses Promises of Force by Nixon to Back Pact." *New York Times*, May 1, 1975. Accessed May 26, 2015. http://partners.nytimes.com/library/world/asia/050175vietnam-thieu-bg.html.

Hammond, William M. "The Press in Vietnam as Agent of Defeat: A Critical Examination." *Reviews in American History*, Volume 17, Number 2 (June, 1989): 312-323. Accessed September 9, 2014. Stable URL: http://www.jstor.org/2702936.

Hanhimaki, Jussi. *The Flawed Architect: Henry Kissinger and American Foreign Policy.* Auckland: Oxford University, 2004.

Hartmann, Robert T. *Palace Politics An Inside Account to the Ford Years.* New York: McGraw-Hill 1980.

Haulman, Daniel L. "Vietnam Evacuation: Operation Frequent Wind." From *Short of War: USAF Contingency Operations 1947-1997*, edited by A. Timothy Warnock. Air University Press, 2000. Pages 83-93. Accessed May 2, 2015. http://www.afhso.af.mil/shared/media/document/AFD-101027-044.pdf.

Hill, Kenneth L. "Laos: The Vientiane Agreement." *Journal of Southeast Asian History* Volume 8, Number 2 (September, 1967): 257-259. Accessed November 30, 2014. Stable URL: http://www.jstor.org.ezproxy.emich.edu/stable/20067631.

Howell, William G. and Jon C. Pevehouse. "When Congress Stops Wars: Partisan Politics and Presidential Power." *Foreign Affairs* Volume 86, Number 5 (September–October, 2007): 95-107. Accessed September 9, 2014. Stable URL: http://www.jstor.org/stable/20032436.

Humphrey, Hubert. Letter. Senator Hubert Humphrey to Gerald Ford. October 30 1973. PDF pages 1-4. Opening Statement: Experts View the Vice Presidency, box 242. Gerald R. Ford Presidential Library, Ann Arbor, Michigan. http://www.fordlibrarymuseum.gov/library/document/25thamend/humphreyletter.pdf.

Hung, Nguyen Tien and Jerrold L. Schecter. *The Palace File.* New York: Harper and Row, 1986.

Intelligence Report Draft on PRG Land, October 26, 1973. Folder five, The PRG's in Vietnam, 1973. Entry # A1 531: General Records; 1969-1975. Box 3, HES Question Elimination Study, 1973 through Reconstruction and Development Conference/Independence Place (Second Copy), 27 July, 1973, MACV, Headquarters CORDS/ Special Assistant to U.S. Ambassador for Field Operations (SAAFO). Record Group 0472 U.S. Forces in Southeast Asia, 1950-1975. National Archives, College Park, Maryland.

Issawi, Charles. "The 1973 Oil Crisis and After." *Journal of Post Keynesian Economic* Volume 1, Number 2 (Winter, 1978-1979): 3-26 Accessed January 9, 2015. Stable URL: http://www.jstor.org/stable/4537467.

Institute of Medicine (U.S.) Committee on Blue Water Navy Vietnam Veterans and Agent Orange Exposure. *Blue Water Navy Vietnam Veterans and Agent Orange Exposure: Historical Background.* Washington, D.C.: National   Academies Press, 2011. Accessed July 26, 2015. http://www.ncbi.nlm.nih.gov/books/NBK209598/.

Jespersen, T. Christopher. "Kissinger, Ford, and Congress: The Very Bitter End in Vietnam." *Pacific Historical Review*, Volume 71, Number 3 (August 2002): 439-473. Accessed January 10, 2014. Stable URL: http://www.jstor.org/stable/10.1525/phr.2002.71.3.439.

Kennerly, David Hume. *Shooter.* New York: Newsweek Books, 1979.

Kilpatrick, Carroll. "Nixon Tells Editors, 'I'm Not a Crook.'" *Washington Post*, November 18, 1973. From *Washington Post* Politics: The Watergate Story. Accessed September 19, 2014. http://www.washingtonpost.com/politics/nixon-tells-editors-im-not-a-crook/2012/06/04/gJQA1RK6IV_story.html.

Kimball, Jeffrey. "The Nixon Doctrine: A Saga of Misunderstanding." *Presidential Studies Quarterly*, Volume 36, Number 1 (March, 2006): 59-74. Accessed April, 24, 2014. Stable URL: http://www.jstor.org/stable/27552747.

Kinnard, Douglas. "Vietnam Reconsidered: An Attitudinal Survey of U.S. Army General Officers." *The Public Opinion Quarterly* Volume 39, Number 4 (Winter, 1975-1976):445-456. Accessed January 16, 2014. Stable URL: http://www.jstor.org/stable/2748499.

Kissinger, Secretary of State Henry. Telegram. Secretary of State Henry Kissinger to Ambassador Graham Martin. October 26, 1974. Folder Two: VN-SD TG SECSTATE–NODIS (1). Box 21, NSA Presidential Country Files For East Asia and the Pacific: Country File: Vietnam – Department of State Telegrams. Gerald R. Ford Presidential Library, Ann Arbor, Michigan.

----. Telegram. Sectary of State Henry Kissinger to Ambassador Graham Martin. January 28, 1975. Folder two, VN-SD TG SECSTATE-NODIS (1). Box 21, NSA Presidential Country Files for East Asia and the Pacific: Country File: Vietnam - Department of State Telegrams. Gerald R. Ford Presidential Library, Ann Arbor, Michigan.

----. Telegram. Sectary of State Henry Kissinger to Ambassador Graham Martin. January 30, 1975. Folder two, VN-SD TG SECSTATE-NODIS (1). Box 21, NSA Presidential Country Files for East Asia and the Pacific: Country File: Vietnam - Department of State Telegrams. Gerald R. Ford Presidential Library, Ann Arbor, Michigan.

----. Telegram. Sectary of State Henry Kissinger to Ambassador Graham Martin. February 20, 1975. Folder two: VN-SD TG SECSTATE-NODIS (1). Box 21, NSA Presidential Country Files for East Asia and the Pacific: Country File: Vietnam – Department of State Telegrams. Gerald R. Ford Presidential Library, Ann Arbor, Michigan.

----. Telegram. Secretary of State Henry Kissinger to U.S. Ambassador to the Republic of Vietnam Graham Martin. March 30, 1975. Folder one, VN-SD TG to SECSTATE-EXDIS. Box 21, National Security Advisor, Presidential Country Files for East Asia and the Pacific; Country File: Vietnam Department of State Telegrams. Gerald R. Ford Presidential Library, Ann Arbor, Michigan.

----. Telegram. Secretary of State Henry Kissinger to the U.S. Ambassador to the French Republic. April 11, 1975. Folder 3, VW CD – 2, March24, 1975 – December 11, 1975. Box 38, National Security Advisor Kissinger-Scowcroft West Wing Office Files, 1969-1977, General Subject File: Vietnamese War 'Camp David File.' Gerald R. Ford Presidential Library, Ann Arbor, Michigan.

----. Telecon. Secretary of State Henry Kissinger and Soviet Ambassador to the U.S. Anatoly F. Dobrynin. April 19, 1975, 12:10 P.M. Folder 4, TP Con – (2), April 10, 1975 – May 1, 1975. Box 34, National Security Advisor Kissinger – ScowcroftWest Wing Office Files, 1969-1977, General Subject File: USSR – Dobrynin in Kissinger Exchanges. Gerald R. Ford Presidential Library, Ann Arbor, Michigan.

----. Telecon. Secretary of State Henry Kissinger and Soviet Ambassador to the U.S. Anatoly F. Dobrynin, April 22, 1975, 11:52 A.M. Folder 4, TP Con – (2), April 10, 1975 – May 1, 1975. Box 34, National Security Advisor Kissinger – ScowcroftWest Wing Office Files, 1969-1977, General Subject File: USSR – Dobrynin in Kissinger Exchanges. Gerald R. Ford Presidential Library, Ann Arbor, Michigan.

----. *Years of Renewal.* New York: Simon & Schuster, 1999.

----. *Ending the Vietnam War: A History of America's Involvement in and Extrication from the Vietnam War.* New York: Simon and Schuster, 2003.

Lauer, Carolyn. "The Daisy Cutter Bomb: Largest Conventional Bomb in Existence." Last modified by Jim Maher and John Maschmayer of the University of Notre Dame. Accessed July 3, 2015. https://www3.nd.edu/~techrev/Archive/Spring2002/a8.html.

Lewis, Alfred E. "5 Held in Plot to Bug Democrats' Office Here." *Washington Post*, June 18,1972. From *Washington Post* Politics: The Watergate Story. Accessed September 16, 2014. http://www.washingtonpost.com/wp-dyn/content/article/2002/05/31/AR2005111001227.html.

Lunch, William L. and Peter W. Sperlich. "American Public Opinion and the War in Vietnam." *The Western Political Quarterly* Volume 32, Number 1 (March, 1979): 21-44. Accessed September 27, 2014. Stable URL: http://www.jstor.org/stable/447561.

MacKenzie, John P. "Court Orders Nixon to Yield Tapes; President Promises to Comply Fully." *Washington Post*, July 25, 1974. From *Washington Post* Politics: The Watergate Story. Accessed September 19, 2014. http://www.washingtonpost.com/politics/court-orders-nixon-to-yield-tapes-president-promises-to-comply-fully/2012/06/04/gJQAZSw0IV_story.html.

Martin, U.S. Ambassador to the Republic of Vietnam Graham. Telegram. U.S. Ambassador to the Republic of Vietnam Graham Martin to Secretary of State Henry Kissinger. March 27, 1975. Folder six, VN SD TG to SECSTATE EXDIS (3). Box 21, National Security Advisor, Presidential Country Files for East Asia and the Pacific; Country   File: Vietnam Department of State Telegrams. Gerald R. Ford Presidential Library, Ann Arbor, Michigan.

----. Telegram. U.S. Ambassador to the Republic of Vietnam Graham Martin to Secretary of State Henry Kissinger. April 20, 1975. Folder 5, VW–Final Stages, April, 1975. Box 38, National Security Advisor Kissinger-Scowcroft West Wing Office Files, 1969-1977, General Subject File: Vietnamese War 'Camp David File.' Gerald R. Ford Presidential Library, Ann Arbor, Michigan.

----. Telegram. U.S. Ambassador to the Republic of Vietnam Martin to Secretary of State Kissinger. April 21,1975. Folder 2, Saigon to Washington, D.C, April 9, 1975 – April 28, 1975 (2). Box 8, National Security Advisor, Embassy Files Taken by Ambassador Graham Martin (Copies), 1963-1976 (1976). Gerald R. Ford Presidential Library, Ann Arbor, Michigan.

McCarthy, Brigadier General James R. and Lieutenant Colonel George B. Allison. *Linebacker II: A View from the Rock, United States Air Force Monograph Series, Volume VI, Monograph Eight.* Washington, D.C.: Office of Air Force History, United States Air Force, 1985. Accessed October 27, 2014. http://www.afhso.af.mil/shared/media/document/AFD-101013-045.pdf.

McFadden, Robert D. "Anatoly F. Dobrynin, Longtime Soviet Ambassador to the U.S., Dies   at 90." *New York Times*, April 8, 2010. Accessed April 25, 2015. http://www.nytimes.com/2010/04/09/world/europe/09dobrynin.html?_r=0.

McMahon, Robert J. "Rationalizing Defeat: The Vietnam War in American Presidential   Discourse, 1975-1995." *Rhetoric and Public Affairs*, volume 2, number 4 (Winter, 1999): 529-549. Accessed April 7, 2015. doi: 10.1353/rap.2010.0041.

Meeting Minutes. Memorandum of Conversation. President Gerald Ford, Sectary of State Henry Kissinger, and Deputy National Security Advisor General Brent Scowcroft. January 8, 1975. Box 8, National Security Advisor Memoranda of Conversations – Ford Administration. Gerald R. Ford Presidential Library, Ann Arbor, Michigan. Accessed May 25, 2015. http://www.fordlibrarymuseum.gov/library/document/0314/1552907.pdf.

----. Memorandum for the Record with Bipartisan Congressional Leadership. January 28, 1975. Box 8, National Security Advisor's Memoranda of Conversation Collection. Gerald R. Ford Library, Ann Arbor, Michigan. Accessed May 25, 2015. http://www.fordlibrarymuseum.gov/library/document/0314/1552931.pdf.

----. Memorandum of Conversation: Cabinet Meeting. January 29, 1975. National Security Advisor's Memoranda of Conversation Collection. Gerald R. Ford Library, Ann Arbor, Michigan. Accessed May 25, 2015. http://www.fordlibrarymuseum.gov/library/document/0314/1552932.pdf.

----. Memoranda of Conversation: President Gerald R. Ford with General Frederick C. Weyand and U.S. Ambassador to the Republic of Vietnam Graham Martin. March 25, 1975. Central File Code: 036600012. Box 10, Memoranda of Conversations – Ford Administration. PDF. Gerald R. Ford Presidential Library, Ann Arbor, Michigan. Accessed May 25, 2015. http://www.fordlibrarymuseum.gov/library/document/0314/1553000.pdf

----. Memoranda of Conversation: Joint Leadership Meeting. Early April, 1975. Box 10, Memoranda of Conversations – Ford Administration. PDF. Gerald R. Ford Presidential Library, Ann Arbor, Michigan. Accessed May 25, 2015. http://www.fordlibrarymuseum.gov/library/document/0314/1553017.pdf.

----. Memorandum of Conversation. April 3, 1975. Central File Code: 0366001113. Box 10, Memoranda of Conversations – Ford Administration. PDF. Gerald R. Ford Presidential Library, Ann Arbor, Michigan. Accessed May 25, 2015. http://www.fordlibrarymuseum.gov/library/document/0314/1553015.pdf.

----. Memoranda of Conversation. April 8, 1975. Box 10, National Security   Advisor, Memoranda of Conversations – Ford Administration. Gerald R. Ford Presidential Library, Ann Arbor, Michigan. Accessed May 25, 2015. http://www.fordlibrarymuseum.gov/library/document/0314/1553016.pdf.

----. National Security Council Meeting. April 9, 1975. Central File Code: 031200012. Box 1, National Security Advisor, National Security Council Meeting File. Gerald R. Ford Presidential Library, Ann Arbor, Michigan. Accessed May 252015. http://www.fordlibrarymuseum.gov/library/document/0312/1552383.pdf.

----. Memoranda of Conversation. April 18, 1975. Box 11, National Security Advisor's Memoranda of Conversation Collection, Memoranda of Conversations–Ford Administration. Accessed April 27, 2015. Gerald R. Ford Presidential Library, Ann Arbor, Michigan. http://www.fordlibrarymuseum.gov/library/document/0314/1553035.pdf.

----. Conversation between the Secretary General of the French Foreign Office and the Head of the PRG Mission in Paris and Relayed to General Brent Scowcroft by Minister de la Force. April 19, 1975. Folder 5, VW–Final Stages, April, 1975. Box 38, National Security Advisor Kissinger-Scowcroft West Wing Office Files, 1969-1977, General Subject File: Vietnamese War 'Camp David File.' Gerald R. Ford Presidential Library, Ann Arbor, Michigan.

----. National Security Council Meeting. April 28, 1975. NSC Meeting, April 28, 1975. Box 1, National Security Advisor's NSC Meeting File. Gerald R. Ford Presidential Library, Ann Arbor, Michigan. Accessed May 2, 2015. http://www.fordlibrarymuseum.gov/library/document/0312/1552385.pdf.

Merriam-Webster, Incorporated. "Definition of Dove." Last modified 2015. Accessed July 25, 2015. http://www.merriam-webster.com/dictionary/dove.

----. "Definition of Hawk." Last modified 2015. Accessed July 25, 2015. http://www.merriam-webster.com/dictionary/hawk.

Mieczkowski, Yanek. *Gerald Ford and the Challenges of the 1970's.* Lexington, Kentucky: University Press of Kentucky, 2005.

Military History Institute of Vietnam. *Victory in Vietnam: The Official History of the People's Army of Vietnam, 1954-1975,* translated by Merle L. Pribbenow. Lawrence, Kansas: University of Kansas, 2002.

Minnesota Historical Society. "Donald McKay Frasier." Last modified 2015. Accessed July 10, 2015. http://www2.mnhs.org/library/findaids/00290.xml.

Murray, Major General John. RVNAF Quarterly Assessment: Fourth Quarter, Fiscal Year,1973. Defense Attaché, Saigon. Folder One 228-07/ RVNAF Quarterly Assessment/ Fourth Quarter, Fiscal Year 1973. Entry #A1 1727: RVNAF Quarterly Assessment Reports; 1973-1975, 228-07 Fourth Quarter 1973 Through 228-07 Second Quarter 1974. Box 1, DAO, Operations and Plans Division/ Readiness Section. Record Group 472, U.S. Forces in Southeast Asia, 1950-1975. National Archives, College Park, Maryland.

Murray, Major General John. RVNAF Quarterly Assessment: Third Quarter, Fiscal Year, 1974. Defense Attaché, Saigon. Folder One 228-07/ RVNAF Quarterly Assessment/ Third Quarter,

Fiscal Year 1974. Entry #A1 1727: RVNAF Quarterly Assessment Reports: 1973-1975, Third Quarter 1974 through Second Quarter 1975. Box Two, DAO, Ops and Plans Division/ Readiness Section. Record Group 472, U.S. Forces in Southeast Asia, 1950-1975. National Archives, College Park, Maryland.

National Archives and Record Administration. "Statistical Information about Fatal Causalities of the Vietnam War: DCAS Vietnam Conflict Extract Files Record Counts by Incident or Death Date (Year) (As of April 29, 2008)." Last modified August 2013. Accessed July 26, 2015. http://www.archives.gov/research/military/vietnam-war/casualty-statistics.html#date.

New York Times News Service. "Nixon Vows He Will End War." *The Milwaukee Journal*, March 6, 1968. Accessed September 28, 2014. http://news.google.com/newspapers?nid=1499&dat=19680305&id=XlgaAAAAIBAJ&sjid= FygEAAAAIBAJ&pg=5069,2870566.

Nessen, Press Secretary Ron. Statement by Press Secretary. Statement by Press Secretary on the evacuation. April 29, 1975. Gerald R. Ford Administration White House Press Releases: April 18, 1975-May 13, 1975. Box 10, White House Press Releases, 1974-77. Gerald R. Ford Presidential Library, Ann Arbor, Michigan. PDF. https://www.fordlibrarymuseum.gov/library/document/0248/whpr19750429-020.pdf.

----. *It Sure Looks Different from the Inside.* Chicago: Playboy Press, 1978.

Nguyen Cong Luan. *Nationalist in the Viet Nam Wars: Memoirs of a Victim turned Solder.* Bloomington: Indiana University Press, 2012.

Nixon, President Richard. "129 - Address to the Nation o Vietnam, April 26, 1972." From *The American Presidency Project.* Last modified 2014, by Gerhard Peters and John T. Woolley. Access October 12, 2014. http://www.presidency.ucsb.edu/ws/index.php?pid=3384.

----. "276 – The President's News Conference, August 29, 1972." From *The American Presidency Project.* Last modified 2014, by Gerhard Peters and John T. Woolley. Accessed October 20, 2014. http://www.presidency.ucsb.edu/ws/index.php?pid=3548.

----. Letter. President Richard Nixon to President Nguyen Van Thieu. October 16, 1972. Vietnam – Correspondence from Richard Nixon to Nguyen Van Thieu. Box 13, Richard B. Cheney Files. Gerard R. Ford Presidential Library, Ann Arbor, Michigan. Accessed May 24, 2015. http://www.fordlibrarymuseum.gov/library/document/0005/1561601.pdf.

----. "414 – Remarks on Being Reelected to the Presidency, November 7, 1972." From *The American Presidency Project*. Last modified 2014, by Gerhard Peters and John T. Woolly. Accessed October 26, 2014. http://www.presidency.ucsb.edu/ws/index.php?pid=3702&st=&st1=.

----. Letter. President Richard Nixon to President Nguyen Van Thieu. November 18, 1972. Vietnam – Correspondence from Richard Nixon to Nguyen Van Thieu. Box 13, Richard B. Cheney

Files. Gerard R. Ford Presidential Library, Ann Arbor, Michigan. Accessed May 24, 2015. http://www.fordlibrarymuseum.gov/library/document/0005/1561601.pdf.

----. Letter. President Richard Nixon to President Nguyen Van Thieu. December 17, 1972. Vietnam – Correspondence from Richard Nixon to Nguyen Van Thieu. Box 13, Richard B. Cheney Files. Gerard R. Ford Presidential Library, Ann Arbor, Michigan. Accessed May 24, 2015. http://www.fordlibrarymuseum.gov/library/document/0005/1561601.pdf.

----. Letter. President Richard Nixon to President Nguyen Van Thieu. December 18, 1972. Vietnam – Correspondence from Richard Nixon to Nguyen Van Thieu. Box 13, Richard B. Cheney Files. Gerard R. Ford Presidential Library, Ann Arbor, Michigan. Accessed May 24, 2015. http://www.fordlibrarymuseum.gov/library/document/0005/1561601.pdf.

----. "12 – Address to the Nation Announcing Conclusion of an Agreement on Ending the War and Restoring Peace in Vietnam, January 23, 1973." From *The American Presidency Project*. Last modified 2014, by Gerhard Peters and John T. Woolly. Accessed October 27, 2014. http://www.presidency.ucsb.edu/ws/?pid=3808.

Office of the Historian of the United States House of Representatives. "Abzug, Bella Savitzky" From History, Art, and Archives, U.S. House of Representatives. Accessed July 10, 2015. http://history.house.gov/People/Detail/8276.

----. "Congressional Profiles: Ninety-Fourth Congress, 1975-1977." From History, Art, and Archives, U.S. House of Representatives. Accessed July 13, 2015. http://history.house.gov/Congressional-Overview/Profiles/94th/.

----. "Fenwick, Millicent Hammond." From History, Art, and Archives, U.S. House of Representatives. Accessed July 10, 2015. http://history.house.gov/People/Listing/F/FENWICK,-Millicent-Hammond-(F000078)/.

Organization of the Petroleum Exporting Countries. "Organization of the Petroleum Exporting Countries: Brief History." Last modified 2016. Accessed April 23, 2016.http://www.opec.org/opec_web/en/about_us/24.htm.

Parker, F. Charles. "Vietnam and Soviet Asian Strategy." *Asian Affairs*, Volume 4, Number 2 (November – December, 1976): 94-116. Accessed January 30, 2014. Stable URL: http://www.jstor.org/stable/30171458.

"Protocol Concerning the Cease-fire in South Vietnam and the Joint Military Commission." *American Society of International Law* Volume 67, Number 2 (April, 1973): 389-407. Accessed September 26, 2014. Stable URL: http://www.jstor.org/stable/2199475.

Reconstruction and Development Conference Presentations at the Independence Palace, Section G, July 27, 1973. Folder seven, Reconstruction and Development Conference/ Independence Palace (Second Copy), July 27, 1973. Entry # A1 531: General Records; 1969-1975. Box 3, HES Question Elimination Study, 1973 through Reconstruction and Development

Conference/ Independence Place (Second Copy), 27 July, 1973. MACV, Headquarters CORDS/ Special Assistant to U.S. Ambassador for Field Operations (SAAFO). Record Group 0472 U.S. Forces in Southeast Asia, 1950-1975. National Archives, College Park, Maryland.

Reynolds, David. *Summits: Six Meetings that Shaped the Twentieth Century.* New York: Basic Books, 2007.

Schecter, Jerrold L. "The Final Days: The Political Struggle to End the Vietnam War." In *Gerald R. Ford and the Politics of Post-Watergate America*, Volume Two, Edited by Bernard J. Firestone and Alexei Uginsky, 539-551. Westport, Connecticut: Greenwood Press, 1993.

Schwartz, Daniel. "The Fall of Saigon: How CBC, CTV covered the 1975 Events." *CBC News*. April 30, 2015. Accessed July 20, 2015. http://www.cbc.ca/news/world/the-fall-of-saigon-how-cbc-ctv-covered-the-1975-events-1.3055237.

Scowcroft, Deputy National Security Advisor General Brent. Telegram. Deputy National Security Advisor Brent Scowcroft to Ambassador Graham Martin. 14. January 7, 1975. Folder Two VW CD-1, August 9, 1974 – March 3, 1975. Box 38, National Security Advisor, Kissinger – Scowcroft West Wing Office Files, 1969-1977. General Subject File: Vietnamese War – 'Camp David File.' Gerald R. Ford Presidential Library, Ann Arbor, Michigan.

----. Telegram, 25. Deputy Assistant to the President for National Security Affairs Brent Scowcroft to Ambassador Graham Martin. January 27, 1975. Folder nine, Washington to Saigon January 5, – April 1, 1975 (1). Box 7, NSA, Saigon Embassy Files Taken by Ambassador Graham Martin (Copies), 1963-1975 (1976). Gerald R. Ford Presidential Library, Ann Arbor, Michigan.

----. Telegram, 27. Deputy Assistant to the President for National Security Affairs Brent Scowcroft to Deputy Ambassador Wolf Lehmann. Folder nine, Washington to Saigon January 5, – April 1, 1975 (1). Box 7, NSA, Saigon Embassy Files Taken by Ambassador Graham Martin (Copies), 1963-1975 (1976). Gerald R. Ford Presidential Library, Ann Arbor, Michigan.

----. Telegram. Deputy National Security Advisor General Brent Scowcroft to General Frederick C. Weyand. March, 1975. Folder nine, Washington, D.C. to Saigon January 5, 1975 – April 1, 1975 (1). Box 7, National Security Advisor, Saigon Embassy Files Taken by Ambassador Graham Martin (Copies), 1963-1975 (1976). Gerald R. Ford Presidential Library, Ann Arbor, Michigan.

----. Diplomatic Paper #91, 6C. Deputy Assistant to the President for National Security Affairs General Brent Scowcroft to Soviet Ambassador Anatoliy Dobrynin. April 22, 1975. Folder: Ten, Items #86-#91, circa April,1975-April 22, 1975. Box 30, National Security Advisor Kissinger-Scowcroft West Wing Office Files, 1969-1977: General Subject File: USSR- 'D' File (Dobrynin). Gerald R. Ford Presidential Library, Ann Arbor, Michigan.

Simpson, Howard R. *Dien Bien Phu: The Epic Battle America Forgot.* Washington, D.C.: Brassey's, 1994.

Smith, Major General H.D. RVNAF Final Assessment: January through April, Fiscal Year, 1975. Defense Attaché, Saigon. Folder Three 228-07/ RVNAF Final Assessment/ January Through April, Fiscal   Year, 1975. Entry # A1 1727: RVNAF Quarterly Assessment Reports; 1973-1975, Final Assessment January –April, 1975 Through Final Assessment January-April, 1975. Box 3, DAO, Operations and Plans Division/ Readiness Section. Record Group 472, U.S. Forces in Southeast Asia, 1950-1975. National Archives, College Park, Maryland.

Sonnonfeldt, Helmut. Memorandum for the Secretary #91, 6D. Helmut Sonnonfeldt to Secretary of State Henry Kissinger. April 19, 1975. Folder: Ten, Items #86-#91, circa April, 1975- April 22, 1975. Box 30, National Security Advisor Kissinger-Scowcroft West Wing Office Files, 1969-1977: General Subject File: USSR- 'D' File (Dobrynin). Gerald R. Ford Presidential Library, Ann Arbor, Michigan.

Sontag, Sherry and Christopher Drew with Annette Drew. *Blind Man's Bluff: The Untold Story of American Submarine Espionage.* New York: Harper Collins, 1999.

Special Assistant to U.S. Ambassador for Field Operations Studies. Statistical Trends: Security Situation from SAAFO Studies. Research and Analysis (SRA). March, 1975. Folder Four, 228-08/ Stat. Trends (SAAFO Studies) January through March 1975. Entry# A1 531: General Records; 1969-1975. 228-08/ Hamlet by Military Region, January – February 1975 through 228-08/ Villages by RVN, January – February 1975. Box Nine, Record Group 472, U.S. Forces in Southeast Asia, 1950 – 1975. MACV, HQ CORDS/ Special Assistant to U.S. Ambassador for Field Operations (SAAFO). National Archives, College Park, Maryland.

St. John, R. B. "Marxist-Leninist Thoery and Organization in South Vietnam." *Asian Survey* Volume 20, Number 8 (August, 1980): 812-828. August 18, 2014. Stable URL: http://www.jstor.org/stable/2643636.

Thi, Lam Quang. *The Twenty-Five Year Century: A South Vietnamese General Remembers the Indochina War to the Fall of Saigon.* Denton, Texas: University of North Texas,   2001.

Thieu, President Nguyen Van. Telegram. President Nguyen Van Thieu to President Gerald Ford via Deputy Ambassador Wolf Lehmann to Deputy National Security Advisor General Brent Scowcroft. March 26, 1975. Folder Twelve: Saigon to Washington, January 5, 1975–April 1, 1975 (3). Box 7, National Security Advisor, Saigon Embassy Files Taken by Ambassador Graham Martin (Copies), 1963-1975 (1976). Gerald R. Ford Presidential Library, Ann Arbor, Michigan.

Tobin, Tomas G., Arthur E. Laehr, and John F. Hilgenberg. *Last Flight from Saigon.* Washington, D.C.: United States Printing Office. Accessed May 22, 2015. http://www.afhso.af.mil/shared/media/document/AFD-100928-008.pdf.

Tower, John G. "Congress Versus the President: The Formulation and Implementation of American Foreign Policy." *Foreign Affiars*, Volume 60, Number 2 (Winter, 1981): 229-246. Accessed September 9, 2014. Stable URL: http://www.jstor.org/stable/20041078.

Trong, Le Hoang. "Survival and Self-Reliance: A Vietnamese Viewpoint." *Asian Survey* Volume 15, Number 4 (April, 1975): 281-300. Accessed January 12, 2014. Stable URL: http://www.jstor.org/stable/2643234.

Tuan, Nguyen Anh. *South Vietnam Trial and Experience: A Challenge for Development.* Athens, Ohio: Ohio University Center for International Studies, 1988.

United States Air Force, Management Information Division Directorate of Management Analysis Comptroller of the Air Force Headquarters. "United States Air Force Statistical Digest: Fiscal Year 1972, Twenty-Seventh Edition." Published September 15, 1973. Accessed October 14, 2014. http://www.afhso.af.mil/shared/media/document/AFD-110412-052.pdf.

United States Air Force. *The Vietnamese Air Force, 1951-1975: An Analysis of its' Role in Combat and Fourteen Hours at Koh Tang*, edited by Major A.J.C. Lavalle. Washington, D.C.: Office of Air Force History, United States Air Force, 1985. Accessed May 22, 2015. http://www.afhso.af.mil/shared/media/document/AFD-101013-043.pdf.

United States Ambassador to the French Republic. Telegram. U.S. Ambassador to the French Republic to Secretary of State Henry Kissinger. April 11, 1975. Folder 3, VW CD–2, March 24, 1975–December 11, 1975. Box 38, National Security Advisor Kissinger-Scowcroft West Wing Office Files, 1969-1977, General Subject File: Vietnamese War 'Camp David File.' Gerald R. Ford Presidential Library, Ann Arbor, Michigan.

United States Department of State: Bureau of Public Affairs–Office of the Historian. "Biographies of the Sectaries of State: Henry Alfred Kissinger." Accessed August 2, 2015. https://history.state.gov/departmenthistory/people/Kissinger-henry-a.

----. "Decades of Change - 1960-1980: The Rise of Cultural and Ethnic Pluralism." United States Department of State: International Information Programs (Digital). Last modified April 5, 2008. Accessed October 26, 2015. http://iipdigital.usembassy.gov/st/english/publication/2008/04/20080407123655eaifas0.7868769.html#axzz3pe0tea3e.

United States Embassy of Saigon. Telegram. United States Embassy of Saigon to Secretary of State Henry Kissinger. April 29, 1975. Box 21, National Security Advisor, Presidential Country Files: East Asia and the Pacific, Country File: Vietnam – Department of State Telegrams. Gerald R. Ford Presidential Library, Ann Arbor, Michigan. PDF. https://www.fordlibrarymuseum.gov/library/exhibits/vietnam/032400112-001.pdf.

United States Joint Chiefs of Staff. Telegram. U.S. Joint Chiefs of Staff to Ruhohoa/ CINPAC, Honolulu, Hawaii. April 28, 1975. Folder six, VN SD TG to SECSTATE Exdis (3). Box 21, National Security Advisor, Presidential Country Files for East Asia and the Pacific:

Country File: Vietnam – Department of State Telegrams. Gerald R. Ford Presidential Library, Ann Arber, Michigan.

Valdes, Benigno. "An Application of Convergence Theory to Japan's Post-WWII Economic 'Miracle.'" *The Journal of Economic Education* Volume 34, Number 1 (Winter, 2003): 61-81. Accessed January 18, 2015. Stable URL: http://www.jstor.org/stable/30042525.

Veith, George J. and Merle L. Pribbenow II. "Fighting is an Art: The Army of the Republic of Vietnam's Defense of Xuan Loc, 9-21 April 1975." *The Journal of Military History* Volume 68, Number 1 (January, 2004): 163-213. Accessed April 17, 2014. Stable URL: http://www.jstor.org/stable/3397252.

Veith, George J. *Black April: The Fall of South Vietnam, 1973-1975.* New York: Encounter Books, 2012.

Vien, General Cao Van. *The Final Collapse.* Washington, D.C.: Center of Military History, United States Army, 1985. PDF. Accessed April 20, 2015. http://www.history.army.mil/html/books/090/90-26/CMH_Pub_90-26.pdf.

"War Powers Resolution." Yale Law School: Lillian Goldman Law Library's Avalon Project. Last modified 2008. Accessed January 19, 2015. http://avalon.law.yale.edu/20th_century/warpower.asp.

Washington, Lieutenant Colonel James W. "Operation Frequent Wind: South VietnameseRefugee Evacuation Operations: How it Looked in Provisional Marine AircraftGroup 39 (ProMAG 39)." *Marine Corps Gazette* volume 99, issue 5 (May, 2015): Accessed April 24, 2016. https://www.mca-marines.org/gazette/2015/05/operation-frequent-wind.

Watt, Alan. "The Geneva Agreements 1954 in Relation to Vietnam." *The Australian Quarterly*, Volume 39, Number 2, (June, 1967): 7-23. Accessed November 30, 2014. Stable URL: http://www.jstor.org.ezproxy.emich.edu/stable/20634125.

Westing, Arthur H. "Environmental Consequences of the Second Indochina War: A Case Study." *Ambio* Volume 4, Number 5/6, War and Environment: A Special Issue (1975): 216-222. Accessed January 16, 2015. Stable URL: http://www.jstor.org.ezproxy.emich.edu/stable/4312150.

Weyand, General Frederick C. Telegram. General Frederick C. Weyand to Deputy National Security Advisor General Brent Scowcroft. March 28, 1975. Folder twelve, Saigon to Washington, D.C. January 5, 1975 – April 1, 1975 (3). Box 7, National Security Advisor, Saigon Embassy Files Taken by Ambassador Graham Martin (Copies), 1963-1975 (1976). Gerald R. Ford Presidential Library, Ann Arbor, Michigan.

----. Report to the President of the United States on the Situation in South Vietnam. General Frederick C. Weyand to President Gerald R. Ford. April 4, 1975. "Vietnam Assessment Report by General Frederick C. Weyand." From Selected Documents on the Vietnam War.

PDF. Gerald R. Ford Presidential Library, Ann Arbor, Michigan. Accessed May 25, 2015. http://www.fordlibrarymuseum.gov/library/exhibits/vietnam/032400081-001.pdf.

White, John Kenneth. "Seeing Red: The Cold War and American Public Opinion." From *Conference on the Power of Free Inquiry and Cold War International History*. Accessed October 12, 2014. http://www.archives.gov/research/foreign-policy/cold-war/conference/white.html.

Willbanks, James H. *Abandoning Vietnam: How America Left and South Vietnam Lost its War.* Lawrence, Kansas: University Press of Kansas, 2004.

CPSIA information can be obtained
at www.ICGtesting.com
Printed in the USA
LVHW062207140621
690236LV00023B/599